STUCK

STUCK

HOW THE PRIVILEGED AND THE PROPERTIED BROKE
THE ENGINE OF AMERICAN OPPORTUNITY

YONI APPELBAUM

RANDOM HOUSE

NEW YORK

Published in the United States by Random House, an imprint
and division of Penguin Random House LLC, New York.

RANDOM HOUSE and the HOUSE colophon are registered
trademarks of Penguin Random House LLC.

LIBRARY OF CONGRESS CATALOGING-IN-PUBLICATION DATA

Names: Appelbaum, Yoni, author.
Title: Stuck / Yoni Appelbaum.
Description: First edition. | New York: Random House, 2025 |
Includes bibliographical references and index.
Identifiers: LCCN 2024035355 (print) | LCCN 2024035356 (ebook) |
ISBN 9780593449295 (hardcover) | ISBN 9780593449301 (ebook)
Subjects: LCSH: Residential mobility—United States—History. |
Zoning, Exclusionary—United States—History. | Discrimination in housing—
United States—History. | Social mobility—United States—History.
Classification: LCC HD7288.92.U6 A77 2025 (print) | LCC HD7288.92.U6 (ebook) |
DDC 304.8/040973—dc23/eng/20240903
LC record available at https://lccn.loc.gov/2024035355
LC ebook record available at https://lccn.loc.gov/2024035356

Printed in Canada on acid-free paper

randomhousebooks.com

2 4 6 8 9 7 5 3 1

First Edition

Book design by Caroline Cunningham

For Emily

CONTENTS

PART I

CHAPTER ONE: A NATION OF MIGRANTS   3

CHAPTER TWO: THE DEATH OF GREAT AMERICAN CITIES   24

CHAPTER THREE: THE FREEDOM TO MOVE   38

CHAPTER FOUR: A MIGRATORY PEOPLE   58

PART II

CHAPTER FIVE: DIRTY LAUNDRY   87

CHAPTER SIX: TENEMENTOPHOBIA   113

CHAPTER SEVEN: AUTO EMANCIPATION   156

CHAPTER EIGHT: THE HOUSING TRAP   178

CHAPTER NINE: A PLAGUE OF LOCALISTS   202

CHAPTER TEN: BUILDING A WAY OUT   224

ACKNOWLEDGMENTS   257

NOTES   261

INDEX   291

PART I

A NATION OF MIGRANTS

The last thing I ever wanted to do was move. Most of what I needed lay within an easy walk of our Cambridgeport apartment. In the mornings, I took my children to preschool, stopping to run errands at the local shops on the way home. From our back porch, I could see a city park, with a playground and basketball hoops and a broad grassy field. Our neighbors who had been strangers when we moved in had since become our friends; I could pop downstairs for a couple of eggs when I ran short and expect a knock if they needed a cup of sugar. My office at Harvard was just under a mile down the street.

But the apartment had only two bedrooms. Rent was costing us a third of our income each month, and it kept going up. Our daughter and son wouldn't want to share a room forever, and an apartment with a third bedroom in Cambridge was well beyond our reach. Every year, more friends in our position gave up and left. They moved out to the suburbs or to cheaper cities in other parts of the country—not where they wanted to be, but where they could afford to live. One family in our building had come back to the States with their daughter after years of humanitarian work abroad. When I learned they were expecting twins, I offered my congratulations and was met with a despondent sigh. They'd discovered what a larger apartment in the Boston area would cost—much less a freestanding house—and decided that the only rational thing for them to do was return to Africa.

If theirs was an extreme case, it represented a common problem. Every year, fewer Americans can afford to live where they want to. The crisis shows up in lengthening commutes; the average commuter now travels almost thirty minutes each way to their job, and one in ten spends more than an hour. It shows up in soaring home prices, pushed skyward by the desperation of buyers—up by more than 60 percent over the past decade, to an average of about half a million dollars. It shows up in painfully high rents; half of all renters now spend more than 30 percent of their income on housing, the threshold for being "rent burdened," and a quarter spend more than 50 percent. And it shows up in the record number of Americans unable to afford those rents and forced into homelessness.

In fact, it shows up so pervasively that I hardly needed studies and statistics to see it. I thought about it every time I walked past a glitzy new condo for sale across the street from a homeless man sleeping on a sidewalk. I thought about it while sitting in traffic alongside thousands of other drivers who had infinitely better ways to spend their time. I thought about it when I encountered a school in an expensive neighborhood that had been converted to some other use, because so many families had been priced out of the area that Cambridge had lost two-thirds of its children. I thought about it as I watched anti-gentrification protests, led by neighbors concerned that they, too, would have to leave the city they loved. And I thought about it each month as I wrote a check to cover the rent.

Some Americans have become so accustomed to the places with the greatest opportunities being effectively reserved for the rich that it somehow seems natural that they should be. In fact, it represents a recent and profound inversion. For centuries, Americans at the bottom of the economic ladder moved toward such places, not away from them, searching for a foothold on the first rung of that ladder, looking for the chance to climb. Entrepreneurs raced to erect housing to hold them. Cambridge had long been a magnet for such people. The city had hardly run out of space; it hadn't even returned to the postwar peak of its population. And yet instead of drawing people in, Cambridge was now driving them out. And it wasn't alone. Throughout the country, the places where ordinary Americans were likeliest to find better jobs, earn higher incomes, and give their children better lives were increasingly priced beyond their grasp. Families were stressed. Cities were struggling. And the country was growing ever more unequal.

What happened? As a historian, I suspected the answers lay in the past, and I started right at home, with my own apartment. Digging through property records, census manuscripts, insurance maps, municipal directories, and old newspapers to piece together its story, I could tell, at a glance, that it hadn't always been so pricey. My century-old building was a three-decker—one of the iconic flat-roofed wooden structures, with apartments stacked like layer cakes, built to house the workers of New England's industrial cities. When they were constructed, far from being seen as luxurious, they were regarded as a sure sign of a neighborhood's decline. "Foreigners are coming in increasing numbers," the Massachusetts Civic League warned in 1911, bringing with them the three-decker, "which, besides being objectionable on other grounds, is a flimsy fire-trap and a menace to human life."

Built in 1901 by Joseph Doherty, a local real estate man who saw opportunity in Cambridgeport's rapid growth, our menacing building was wider than most, with a central staircase, two units on each floor, and mild delusions of grandeur. If the building showed its age, it also showed a certain pride of craftsmanship. Moldings ran along the ceilings, sliding doors separated the front parlor from the bedroom, and—a delightful absurdity—a butler's pantry with drawers and shelves opened off the dining room. Doherty had bought the lot and the handsome ten-room, single-family home that occupied it. He tore the house down, replacing it with a pair of double three-deckers and making room for twelve families in a space that had previously accommodated only one.

To the west lay Old Cambridge, home to Harvard and stately mansions on sedate tree-lined streets. In the opposite direction lay East Cambridge, a gritty industrial area filled with factories and recent immigrants. Cambridgeport was a neighborhood in between, in every way—neither an industrial slum nor an elegant suburb, but something new in the world. A settlement house worker named Albert Kennedy studied the neighborhood and watched as the children of immigrants moved in and then moved on to greater prosperity. Deciding he needed a novel term to capture its distinctive role, he dubbed it a "zone of emergence."

Doherty had made a clever investment. He had no trouble renting the units in his building, erected opposite a large Catholic church, to other second-generation Irish Americans. The butler's pantries and other small flourishes he'd added to his buildings appealed to his tenants' aspirations. Their parents might have sweated in the factories, but their children were now graduating from high school. Thomas Sweeney, for example, was a self-employed plumber; his daughter Margaret put her education to work as a government stenographer. My building's six apartments also housed a telephone operator, postal letter carrier, car salesman, store clerk, and gym instructor. Half a century later, the building still housed a similar mix of residents, although as Irish Americans ascended the economic ladder, other second-generation immigrants had arrived behind them. Our own apartment was rented by Jessie White, whose father emigrated from Canada, and her two adult daughters. When Jessie's husband, a brass finisher, died in 1940, she took in a shipping clerk as a boarder to help make ends meet. One daughter operated a boxing machine at a factory; the other, who had finished high school, found an office job at an oil company.

And yet, by the time we moved in half a century after that, something had gone wrong. Instead of a new generation of blue-collar families, the building held a very different mix of tenants: graduate students, doctors, architects, engineers. The neighborhood was no longer a zone of emergence; only people who had already emerged could possibly afford to move in. And it wasn't just changing in our building, or on our block. Prices throughout the city had skyrocketed. And in fact, throughout the country, in the areas where the economy was growing fastest and jobs paid the most, demand for housing far outstripped the supply.

Today, the problem I'm describing is generally referred to as our affordable housing crisis. But that's not quite right. If affordability were the underlying problem, then moving to places like Flint,

Michigan—where housing is so cheap it can't be given away—would be the solution. Americans, though, are not beating a path to Flint, a city of few jobs and bleak prospects. What we actually face is a mobility crisis. The distinction matters. Americans used to be able to choose where to live, but moving toward opportunity is now, largely, a privilege of the economic elite.

The notion that people should be able to choose their own communities—instead of being stuck wherever they happen to be born—is America's most profound contribution to the world. Many of the cherished features of our society trace, in one way or another, back to this innovation; many of our country's most glaring injustices result from the ways in which this freedom has been denied to those who needed it most. The fact that it is now endangered is not just a problem for housing markets; it's a lethal threat to the entire American project.

A decade ago in Cambridge, as I began researching this book, I didn't yet understand that. I knew only that the city where I was born no longer had space for my family—that we were going to have to move, whether we wanted to or not. But that, as it happens, is something Americans have been doing from the very beginning.

America is a nation of migrants. No society has ever been remotely so mobile as America at its peak. In the late nineteenth century, the heyday of American mobility, roughly a third of all Americans changed addresses each year. European visitors were astonished, and more than slightly appalled. The American, Michel Chevalier observed in 1835, "is devoured with a passion for locomotion, he cannot stay in one place." On Moving Day, when leases expired in tandem, the greater part of a city's population might relocate to new quarters between sunup and sundown, in a great jumble of furniture and carts and carpetbags. On average, Americans moved far more often, over longer distances, and to greater advantage than did people in the lands from which they had come. They understood this as the key to their national character, the thing that made their country distinctive. "We are a migratory people, and we flourish best when we make an occasional change of base," explained one nineteenth-century newspaper. "We have cut loose from the old style of human vegetation, the former method, of sticking like an oyster to one spot through numberless succeeding generations," wrote another.

Every American has ancestors who decided to stop being oysters. The earliest of them came across Beringia and quickly peopled the land. Millennia later, people arrived from Europe and were just as quick to spread out, dispossessing those who had come before. But they did not simply arrive in one place and put down roots. Having come to this land, they never stopped moving. They loaded the cart, the wagon, the steamer trunk, or the moving van. They left the towns where they grew up to plant settlements, and then their children left those towns in turn to begin anew. In different eras, they headed in different directions: meadowlands and marshes, to graze their cattle; market towns, to ply their crafts; factories, to earn a wage; prairies, to lay claim to the land and till the soil; booming cities, to open a shop of their own. They went in search of economic opportunity, or liberty, or community. They went because they were forced to go, or because they sought freedom and equality. They went because they could not stay where they were, or because they did not want to. But they went.

My own ancestors came to the United States from a wide array of places, at different times and for different reasons. One grandfather was born to Greek immigrants from a village in the mountains above Sparta; the other to Jewish immigrants from what is now Belarus. I have ancestors who fled the persecution of Puritans in England, of Jews in Ukraine, of independence activists in Spanish Cuba. In the lands they left behind, successive generations lived in the same towns, inhabited the same houses, plied the same trades, and farmed the same land. Experience had taught them that admitting new members left a community with less to go around, so they treated outsiders with suspicion and hostility. They learned that rifts and feuds produced lasting bitterness, so they placed a priority on consensus and conformity. Village life placed the communal above the individual, tradition ahead of innovation, insularity before acceptance.

But in America, the ceaseless migrations of the population shaped a new set of expectations. "When the mobility of population was always so great," the historian Carl Becker observed, "the strange face, the odd speech, the curious custom of dress, and the unaccustomed religious faith ceased to be a matter of comment or concern." A mobile population opened the possibilities of pluralism as diverse peoples learned to live alongside each other. The term "stranger," Becker wrote, in other lands synonymous with "enemy," instead became "a common form of friendly salutation." In a nation where people are forever arriving and departing, a newcomer can seem less a threat to the settled order than a welcome addition to a growing community: "Howdy, stranger." Mobility has long been the shaper of American character and the guarantor of its democracy.

Americans turned migration from the last resort of the desperate and the destitute into the exercise of a fundamental right. When my Puritan forebearers arrived on American shores in the seventeenth century, they justified the abandonment of their proper homes and stations with the audacious claim that relocation can sometimes be respectable, or even laudable. They soon codified this right, the right to leave, into law. Their towns, though, were semi-sovereign entities, policing their boundaries, selecting their members, and regulating the behavior of their populations. Anyone could leave, but not just anyone could stay. Two centuries later, as the young United States pushed west, it would add a complementary liberty, if only to some: the right to belong. Together, these ideas constituted a new and transformative freedom. Instead of allowing communities to choose their own members, Americans decided to allow most individuals to choose their communities.

As Americans moved around, they also moved up. The extraordinary geographic mobility of the United States drove its equally distinctive levels of social and economic mobility. Though the process of moving was always wrenching, the pain of relocation real, people who went to new places often found new beginnings, new connections, new communities, and new opportunities. They had the chance to break away from stultifying social hierarchies, depleted farmland, and dead-end jobs. On average, migrants have always grown more prosperous than those who stayed in place, and conferred better futures on their children—a correlation that, remarkably, has remained robust across four centuries, in a society that has changed in countless other ways.

There were no guarantees. However green the grass appeared, many Americans crossed to the other side of the fence, only to find it withering beneath their feet. Boomtowns turned to ghost towns; entire industries became obsolete. And mobility was never uncontested. Waves of immigrants faced discrimination from those who had come only slightly before, turned away from communities they sought to join just because they were Irish, or Italian, or Jewish. Laws excluded the Chinese, and vigilantes hounded them from their homes. Women seldom enjoyed the full privilege of mobility, constrained by social strictures, legal barriers, and physical dangers. And even after the end of slavery, Black Americans had to fight at every turn to exercise their mobility in the face of segregation and racist violence.

But members of all these groups, and others besides, kept moving whenever they were able, because they understood the link between mobility and opportunity. Where racists and nativists sought to keep new arrivals out, they insistently demanded to be let in. And when the first move didn't work out, Americans of different backgrounds could always see some more promising destination beckoning them onward. They could light out for the territory, hit the road, stake their claim, or make a brand-new start of it in a city that never sleeps. Our culture is thick with the clichés of mobility.

The freedom to move opened space for political and religious diversity. People unhappy with the decisions their communities made were not locked into endless feuds, but could, with a minimum of capital, move to a place they found more congenial, voting with their feet. Social identities, too, were transformed from heritable characteristics into self-fashioned choices. The voluntary communities Americans created led to a remarkable flourishing of religious and associational life as new arrivals invested effort in building up relationships, making America a nation of joiners. Freed from the heavy weight of tradition, of the constraints of habit and precedent, the new nation became famed for its entrepreneurship and innovation and for the rapidity of its economic growth. Mobility distinguished the United States from the relative stasis of Europe. American institutions were tuned for the perpetual motion of the population, adapted to individuals relocating again and again in search of greater opportunity. The most distinctive features of the young republic all traced back to this single, foundational fact: Americans were always starting over, always looking ahead to their next beginning, always seeking to move up by moving on. Mobility has been the great engine of American prosperity, the essential mechanism of social equality, and the ballast of our diverse democracy.

But for the last fifty years, the engine of American opportunity has been grinding to a halt, throwing society into crisis. Americans have grown less likely to move from one state to another, or to move within a state, or to switch residences within a city. In the late nineteenth century, the heyday of American mobility, a third of all Americans might have changed addresses each year. In the 1940s and 1950s, about a fifth of Americans moved annually. By 2021, only one-twelfth of Americans moved. The drastic decline in geographic mobility is the single most important social change of the past half century, and perhaps the least remarked.

Fewer kids are watching moving vans pull in to their neighborhoods or loading their own belongings into the back of a truck and setting off for someplace new. Fewer adults are starting over in a new town or taking a better job in a different state. For all its limits and despite all its costs, the geographic mobility of the American population produced an unprecedented degree of social fluidity, allowing many people to transcend the circumstances of their birth, to define their own identities, and to choose their communities. Its decline has left many Americans feeling trapped and hopeless, stripping them of agency and denying them the chance to give their own kids a better life.

What killed American mobility? There is no shortage of suspects. People have always been most mobile while they're relatively young, and the country is aging. The median American was just sixteen years old in 1800 and twenty-eight in 1970, but more than thirty-eight today. The spread of occupational licensing might have made it more costly to find jobs in new places. Or perhaps the answers reflect positive trends. As more women have gained entry into the workforce, two-career households might have found it increasingly difficult to relocate. The prevalence of joint custody makes it harder for members of divorced couples to move. More Americans own their homes, and renters have always been more mobile. Maybe Americans are just growing more successful and better able to locate jobs and communities that meet their needs, reducing their impulse to move someplace else. Maybe they are relying on remote work to stay where they are.

But none of these answers can possibly explain the broad, persistent declines in geographic mobility by itself, or even if you add them all together. The country may be older, but the drop has been particularly steep among younger Americans. The spread of occupational licensing is real, but most jobs aren't licensed, and it accounts for perhaps 5 percent of the total decline. Two-earner households may be less mobile, but their mobility has declined in tandem with that of other groups. Mobility is down not just among homeowners but also among renters, and its decline antedates the rise of remote work. And just look around. Do Americans look happier and more satisfied to you?

But there is one more set of suspects, and the evidence for their guilt is damning: American mobility has been slowly strangled by generations of reformers, seeking to reassert control over their neighborhoods and their neighbors. At the beginning of the twentieth century, reformers sought to apply the fruits of science and reason to manage growth, reimposing order and control on a jumbled and chaotic landscape that mixed shops and apartments in among the houses, and occupants of varied ethnicities and income brackets. Their chosen tools were building codes and restrictive covenants and zoning ordinances, designed to segregate land by use and class and race. New Deal bureaucrats next took up the cause, requiring local jurisdictions to apply these tools to their communities and putting new construction firmly under the purview of government. Then, in the postwar decades, skepticism of big business and big government led a new generation of activists to empower individuals and groups to challenge decisions made by bureaucrats. This varied lot of reformers acted from a wide mix of motives, some laudable and others despicable. Some would probably appreciate what they have wrought, while others would be appalled at the unintended consequences of their work. But taken together, the reforms that they enacted have created a peculiarly dysfunctional system. Almost all new construction in the United States now requires government approval, and anyone with sufficient time and resources and education can effectively veto that approval, or at least impose great expense and delay. The result is that in the very places that need it most desperately, housing has become prohibitively difficult to build. If the freedom to move was originally secured by allowing Americans to choose their own communities, then it has been undone by a series of legal and political changes that restored the sovereignty of local communities and allowed them again to select their own members.

These changes took hold so gradually that most Americans are unaware of how radically they have altered their society. For most of our history, a highly mobile population moved toward opportunity. When a place prospered, it quickly swelled with new arrivals. Builders rushed to meet the demand with housing. Farms gave way to clusters of houses, which turned into town houses, which sprouted into apartment buildings or even high-rises. But in today's burgeoning metropolises and boomtowns, restrictions have effectively frozen the built environment. As a result, housing has grown artificially scarce and prohibitively expensive. A fortunate few can still afford to move where they want. Most people, though, would have to pay so much more for housing in prospering cities that offered better jobs that relocation would leave them worse off overall. Americans aren't moving anymore, because for so many moving threatens to cost more than it delivers.

The costs of our national sclerosis are frightening to contemplate. More Americans have stopped starting new businesses. Between

1985 and 2014, both the total share of entrepreneurs in the population and the share of people newly becoming entrepreneurs fell by half. More Americans have stopped finding new jobs. Switching jobs frequently when you're young correlates with occupational and economic mobility, but the share of people switching industries, occupations, and employers has fallen dramatically, particularly among younger workers; they've grown less likely to work for four or more employers by the time they're thirty and more likely to work for just one or two. And more Americans are ending up worse off than their parents. In 1970, about eight out of every ten children turning twenty could expect to earn more than their parents did; by the turn of the century, that was true of only half, and the proportion is likely still falling.

As grim as the economic indicators might be, the measures of social health are even more alarming. Compared with Americans at the beginning of the 1970s, the average American today belongs to about half as many groups. Church membership is down by about a third, as is the share who socialize with folks around them several times a week. A majority of Americans tell pollsters that their social isolation has left them anxious and depressed. Americans are having fewer children. And while half of Americans used to think most people could be trusted, today only a third think the same.

So Americans aren't starting new businesses, switching to better jobs, or climbing the social ladder the way they used to. They're not joining groups, gathering in prayer, having kids, or hanging out the way they used to. They don't even trust each other anymore. They are, in a word, *stuck*.

Maybe this doesn't worry you. Perhaps you're living in a beautiful community, surrounded by a loving family and caring neighbors, and commuting to a fulfilling job. If so, congratulations! You lie within the privileged slice of the country where things have never been better. But over the past decade, you might have detected signs that not all Americans feel this way about their lives.

The election of Donald Trump in 2016 shocked many Americans, including Donald Trump. But although there were many reasons voters backed his candidacy, at its core his success reflected the anger, frustration, and alienation of his most ardent supporters and was an outgrowth of America's social decay. In 2016, I worked with Robert Jones and his team at the Public Religion Research Institute on a series of polls. As the Republican primary narrowed down to a three-way battle between Senator Ted Cruz, Governor John Kasich, and Trump, we asked respondents how often they participated in a nonreligious activity group, such as a sports team, book club, PTA, or neighborhood association. We found that Trump secured the Republican nomination by winning over voters who were disengaged from their communities. Among those who were highly engaged in their communities, participating at least once a week, Trump and Cruz were effectively tied. Among those who seldom or never participated, Trump led 47 to 25. The same was true of church attendance, where Cruz had a narrow lead among the regulars but Trump opened a dominating lead among those who stay home on Sunday.

How had so many Americans found themselves cut off from their neighbors and isolated from any regular social structures, in a nation once renowned for its civic vitality? The short answer is that as Americans moved from place to place, leaving behind all they knew, they built their churches and bowling leagues and book clubs to create new communities. And as they've stopped moving, those structures have atrophied, leaving many Americans feeling alienated and alone. Trump spoke to the anger and resentment of these Americans, stuck in declining towns and regions within a prospering country, cut off from the organizations that give many of their compatriots a sense of worth and meaning.

Once Trump had the nomination in hand, these numbers shifted; prosperous, civically engaged, and churchgoing Republicans rallied to their party's standard-bearer. But Trump won the general election by adding to the Republican base a new tranche of typically disengaged voters. A month before the election, we found that among white voters who had moved more than two hours from their hometown, Hillary Clinton enjoyed a solid six-point lead. Those living within a two-hour drive, though, backed Trump by nine points. And those who had never left their hometown supported him by a remarkable twenty-six points. We also surveyed white working-class voters, testing a wide array of potential explanations for their votes. After adjusting for other factors, we found just three views that were independently predictive of support for Trump: his voters were much likelier to regard college as a gamble than as an investment, to be hostile to immigration, and to report feeling like strangers in their own country. If Trump won the primary by appealing to alienated Republicans, he won the general election by appealing to white working-class voters who had lost their geographic mobility. Trump supporters didn't believe they could use education to get ahead, they stayed where they were born, and they resented the intrusion of new arrivals, a resentment that often curdled into overt racism.

And Trump won in 2016, and again in 2024, because by making the nation's most prosperous places prohibitively expensive, Democrats have undercut their own political power. Red states are gaining electoral votes while blue states are losing them, as Americans migrate toward places that are still willing to build. The rapidly escalating cost of housing in Democratic strongholds has squeezed younger and lower-income voters particularly hard, eroding the party's traditional base of support. And these divides are increasingly present even within individual states, where prosperous urban enclaves have walled themselves off, becoming islands of deep blue. Exurban and rural areas, meanwhile, are tinged in ever brighter shades of red. Partisan sorting within states has never been this high, going back to the first election between Democrats and Republicans in 1856, and the differences between states have been increasing for the past fifty years. Democratic voters are now tightly concentrated in the densest places, facilitating Republican gerrymandering and undercutting Democratic political power even in its absence. And as they have retreated into these enclaves, Democrats have walled themselves off from new arrivals. A study of California found that as the share of liberal votes in a city increased by ten points, the housing permits it issued declined by 30 percent.

The journalist Bill Bishop famously dubbed this rising geographic concentration the "big sort" and blamed it on mobility. "We have built a country where everyone can choose the neighborhood . . . most compatible with his or her lifestyle and beliefs," he wrote. "And we are living with the consequences of this segregation by way of life: pockets of like-minded citizens that have become so ideologically inbred that we don't know, can't understand, and can barely conceive of 'those people' who live just a few miles away." But that explanation gets the problem precisely backward. Over the past fifty years, as Americans have moved less, spatial polarization has risen sharply. We're less able to choose our neighborhoods freely and less likely to move anywhere new. At the same time, we're more divided than ever.

The problem isn't that we're sorting ourselves out; it's that we've ceased to mix ourselves together. Zoning has made our neighborhoods far less economically diverse, reducing the odds we will come into sustained contact with people of different backgrounds or with those who hold different perspectives. And regulations have separated areas with rental housing from areas with single-family homes. When one in five Americans moved each year, neighborhoods were regularly infused with new arrivals, often bearing the views they'd adopted in their previous communities. Now, with only one in twelve Americans moving, that happens much less often. A more sedentary community will homogenize itself over time as social forces press longtime residents toward conformity and the flow of new neighbors bearing novel ideas and customs and beliefs slows to a trickle. The result is deepening polarization.

Geographic mobility long served as a counterweight within American politics against the more virulent strains of racism, nativism, and populism. When people can move toward opportunity, confident that they can improve their own prospects and give their children a better life, they are likely to feel hopeful and empowered. Arriving in new communities, they might invest in relationships and join organizations. They might find new jobs, switching from declining sectors to thriving industries, or even starting new businesses of their own. And in prospering places, people are less likely to resent other new arrivals, or to believe that the success of others comes at their own expense. Take away that mobility, though, and the world looks very different. Americans who feel locked into place lack the chance to fashion their own identities through the choices they make, making them more likely to gravitate toward the identities they inherit. Those who live in communities where economies are shrinking see new arrivals as threats who diminish their own prospects. Those who are unable to leave home tend to settle into habits, without the impetus to forge new relationships that moving to new places imparts, so their connections, even to the surrounding community, atrophy over time. American society was shaped by our extraordinarily high rates of mobility, and as these have declined, it has become sclerotic.

Most Americans live in freestanding houses set along quiet streets. If you ask them, nine out of ten will tell you that they prefer these sorts of single-family homes. Americans say they would rather live on larger lots, some miles from the nearest stores, than packed closer together, but with shopping close at hand. And they prefer to own their houses, not to rent them. Drive around the periphery of any American city, and you can see these preferences translated into the comfortably familiar landscape of suburbia.

But there are other things that Americans say they want, too—things they expected to have and worry may be slipping from their grasp. They would like more affordable homes and shorter commutes. They want young families to be able to move in down the block, and they want economic opportunities to be widely shared. They want lively communities with an active civic life and a rich array of locally owned businesses. They want good jobs so they can provide for their families. They want to do better than their parents did and for their children's success to outstrip their own. They want to live in a diverse, tolerant, democratic society where people of all backgrounds and faiths can thrive. And they want to be in control of their own destinies.

Fifty years ago, these desires seemed broadly compatible. The nation had suburbanized, even as it grew more prosperous and diverse. But there was, it turned out, a catch. A nation built around the idea that people should be able to choose their communities functions properly only so long as those communities are prepared to let them in. As America's most prosperous communities developed a new set of legal tools that enabled them to bar the doors to most new arrivals, however, they drove the price of new housing too high for almost anyone to afford, or barred new development entirely.

The good news is that addressing this crisis of mobility doesn't depend on your moving anywhere, if you'd rather stay where you are. It doesn't depend on your surrendering your single-family home, if you're lucky enough to have one. You can keep your freshly mowed green lawn and your white picket fence, your driveway and your garden. Solving crises often requires tremendous sacrifice. The simplest solution to this one, by contrast, promises to leave everyone better off. All you have to do is make room for some new friends and neighbors to join you, by allowing them to build new housing on their own property. If you put it this way to Americans—if you ask them whether they'd be prepared to allow construction in their neighborhoods, if it meant making room for young families—they suddenly become overwhelmingly supportive of the idea.

When Americans seized the right to choose their communities, they gained a strong sense of personal agency. Instead of leading the lives to which they were born and wearing the identities they had inherited, they began to believe that they could decide where to live, what to do, who to be—that they were the agents of their own destiny. The curtailment of mobility has eroded that belief. When people can choose where to move, they can also choose not to move. But either way, it is their choice. Today, too many Americans no longer feel as if they can make that choice for themselves. They live where they are able, not where they want; they experience their lives less as the result of their own decisions than as the consequence of vast and impersonal forces. And with that decline in agency has come a deep embitterment.

I wrote this book in our new home, in the Washington, D.C., neighborhood of Shepherd Park. As I typed, a mixed-use development rose outside my window, and the shuddering rumbles of earth being dumped, the metronomic chirps of heavy machinery moving in reverse, and the insistent chattering of jackhammers have provided my soundtrack. Soon, I will have thousands of new neighbors, moving in search of better lives for themselves and for their children— just as my own ancestors came to this country and then moved ceaselessly around it, seeking to build better lives for themselves and for me. In that sense, this book is unavoidably a personal narrative as well as a national one.

The house in which I am typing these words was built in 1923 by a high school mechanical arts teacher named Joseph Wilson who came here in pursuit of his own dreams. Like most Americans of his era, Wilson spent his life on the move. Born to a shoe merchant in a western Pennsylvania boomtown, he left home for college and then landed a job as an instructor at the Thaddeus Stevens Industrial School in Lancaster. From there, he moved to Washington, D.C., into a dismal four-room rental in a large apartment building. Smoke-damaged wallpaper was tacked to the wall. On the front lawn, where rowdy kids threw fruit skins at each other, there was not a blade of grass to be seen. It wasn't much, but there was a wartime housing crunch, and at least it was affordable. When World War I ended, though, and rent control eased, his monthly payments jumped by a third, up to $40. The notion that a prospering city might not be able to provide affordable places for workers to live was then sufficiently novel that it sparked a congressional investigation, and Wilson testified about his struggles.

When he had a daughter in 1922, he sought a home of his own in which to raise his family. He found one in a Sears catalog for $1,947. The model he chose, the Puritan, fit six rooms into a two-story square, twenty-four feet to a side, topped with a peaked roof. It arrived by rail in thousands of pieces with instructions for assembly, like a life-sized Lego kit. Wilson bought a lot on which to build it, in a recently subdivided neighborhood near the top of the District of Columbia. His mortgage from Sears, for the land and the house together, worked out to $30 a month—just what his rent had been before the landlord jacked it up. Instead of a run-down apartment, though, it bought him a house with a green lawn and a one-car garage on a tree-lined street of single-family homes. Here was the American dream of homeownership made manifest.

At least for some. Because then, and now, the neighborhood where Wilson landed was not for everyone. In the words of one developer, the land had been "legally safeguarded by covenants from every element that might endanger its value," housing, as a resident later put it, a "solid Anglo-Saxon yeomanry." Most of my neighbors would not have been welcome here in 1923. The deeds stipulated that the land could not be "rented, leased, sold, demised, transferred, or conveyed unto or in trust for any negro or colored person or persons of negro blood or extraction." I would not have been welcome, either; Jews were barred by convention, not generally by legally enforceable covenants, but the rule was equally rigid. Other restrictions in parts of the neighborhood set street frontages, minimum dollar values for homes, and setbacks from the street. Only detached and semidetached houses were allowed. The developers aimed to create a bucolic refuge from the bustle of city life—and from the diversity of its people—and sell it to prosperous white families. In 1920, Washington layered onto these covenants the force of law, adopting a zoning ordinance that set maximum heights in the neighborhood and restricted it to residential use.

At one level, exclusion failed. Jews arrived in the 1940s, setting off a massive wave of white flight. By the 1960s, according to one estimate, 80 percent of the neighborhood was Jewish—complete with synagogues, butchers, and delicatessens. That same decade, Black families began to arrive, following Supreme Court rulings striking down racial covenants and desegregating the schools. Realtors used blockbusting tactics in nearby neighborhoods to precipitate racial panic, but local civil rights activists were determined to show that integration could work. They banded together into a group dubbed Neighbors Inc. "You shouldn't have to tell a Jew what is wrong with ghettos," Marvin Caplan, the driving force behind the group, wrote in The Atlantic. Soon, Neighbors Inc. was advertising for new residents to come "live your convictions." Today the neighborhood is 55 percent Black, and as integrated as any in America. One local resident, a leading expert on housing, inequality, and racial discrimination, recently praised it as a "diverse Eden."

But there is trouble in paradise. The rules intended to enforce economic segregation proved more effective, and more lasting, than those aimed more explicitly at racial and ethnic segregation. High school teachers like Wilson cannot afford to build homes here anymore, nor can anyone build a house like mine on so narrow a lot. Although Neighbors Inc. pushed for racial integration, it achieved that by standing fast against economic diversity, agitating, for example, against the conversion of basements into rental apartments. Its goal was less ensuring affordability than preserving affluence. "Stabilization has been achieved . . . in terms of property values," its executive director boasted in 1969. He was right. The median value of a house in the neighborhood jumped from $25,000 in 1960 to $132,000 in 1980, nearly doubling in inflation-adjusted terms, even as integration proceeded. In previous decades in other parts of the city, rising demand had led developers to build town houses or apartment buildings, providing affordable places for new arrivals to live. But while the courts might have invalidated racial restrictions, they upheld the legality of single-family zoning. Rising demand for a fixed supply of houses kept prices climbing. As professional-class families had fewer kids and eschewed intergenerational households, and as the rising affluence of the residents led them to renovate apartment conversions back into single-family homes, the community actually began to shrink. The population has declined by a quarter since 1970, and the number of children by more than a third.

I love my neighbors, and my neighborhood. I think more people should have the chance to live here, and in Cambridge, and in places like them around the country—where jobs are abundant and incomes are climbing and services are robust. I want them to be able to raise their kids in a place that will expand their horizons and let them go further than their parents. But instead, American mobility is in sharp decline. The places that today offer the greatest opportunities have grown exclusionary, turning away the next generation of Joseph Wilsons. And there is a bitter irony at work here. Progressive communities like Cambridge and Shepherd Park, which pride themselves on their openness and tolerance and diversity and commitment to social justice, are the worst offenders. That mixed-use development out my window? It's just on the other side of an invisible line. The children who live there won't be able to attend our schools. When a developer tried to build a similar mixed-use project in my own neighborhood a few years ago, adding nearly two hundred new apartments atop a grocery store, residents rallied to kill the proposal. The objections they lodged offered a survey course in NIMBYism—the impulse to say, "Not in my backyard."

Not far to the south, two lawn signs sit side by side on a neatly manicured lawn. One proclaims, NO MATTER WHERE YOU ARE FROM, WE'RE GLAD YOU'RE OUR NEIGHBOR, in Spanish, English, and Arabic. Beside it, another reads, SAY NO, urging residents to oppose the construction of an apartment building that would house the new neighbors the other sign welcomes. Ironic, yes. But also instructive. In theory, the drives toward inclusion and exclusion should exist in tension. In practice, though, progressivism has produced a potent strain of NIMBYism, a defense of communities in their current form against those who might wish to join them. Mobility is what made this country prosperous and pluralistic, diverse and dynamic. Now progressives are destroying the very force that produced the values they claim to cherish. How could that happen?

This book is my effort to answer the question that I first encountered in Cambridge and that has been repeated insistently by what I see around me each day. The story that unfolds in these pages, though, is not quite the one I set out to write. I thought I knew the basic contours of the tale. But as I dug into archives, scrolled through microfilm, talked to people around the country, and read through the brilliant work of historians and sociologists and economists, I found a richer and more complicated narrative than I expected, filled with colorful characters, questionable motives, and unintended consequences. I also encountered unlikely heroes—people like Hang Kie and Fred Edwards—whose stories we've largely forgotten, but who fought to secure the freedom to move at great personal risk. And I learned that while this country has always been imperfect, it was also once remarkably fluid, allowing its people to pursue their dreams and make it more perfect. And that gives me great hope that it can do so once more.

CHAPTER TWO

THE DEATH OF
GREAT AMERICAN CITIES

All his life, Rudolph Hechler moved toward opportunity. Born into a Jewish family in Austrian Galicia around 1886, he was perhaps thirteen when he boarded a steamship for New York. Within a decade, he was living in the East Village—married, with a young son and twin daughters—and working in a sweatshop, making ladies' clothes. Soon, he'd saved enough to rent an apartment in the Bronx. And after decades of working as a tailor, he made his biggest move of all. Hechler left his occupation, and then, by 1940, he left the Bronx for the West Village—moving downtown but moving up.

His new neighborhood was lined with warehouses and town houses and small apartment buildings and generously sprinkled with storefronts. It was filled with immigrants—from Spain and Latvia, Holland and Cuba, Italy and Ireland—and the families they were raising. On his own block of Hudson Street stood a row of three handsome redbrick town houses, built a century before by a local mason. The first housed a Welsh housepainter and his family. The second was rented by Samuel Halpert, a Russian immigrant, for $40 a month. With the help of his two adult sons, Halpert operated the Palace Laundry on the ground floor—"A service to suit every need"—and lived with his family on the top two floors.

Hechler rented the last town house in the row, capped with a handsome cornice, its top two stories adorned with pairs of sash

windows. Below the windows, he put up a large sign that read, FOUN-
TAIN SERVICE—SODA—CANDY, and a cheerful awning adding cigars,
sodas, and toys to the list of promised delights. Smaller signs adver-
tised Coca-Cola and 7-Up, along with Horton's MelOrol ice cream—
three-inch cylinders of frozen ecstasy served atop a cone to any child
with a nickel. To adults, the Hechlers sold loose cigarettes for a penny
apiece. A rack by the door held newspapers, their headlines inviting
passersby into the store.

Rudolph Hechler's store at 555 Hudson Street, shown in a photo taken by
New York City tax survey, between 1939 and 1941.
DOF MANHATTAN 1940S TAX PHOTOS, NEW YORK CITY DEPARTMENT OF RECORDS & INFORMATION
SERVICES.

You could find Hechler working behind the counter with his
thirty-five-year-old son, Louis, sixty hours each week. Like Halpert,
and many of the other shopkeepers in the neighborhood, Hechler
lived above his store, along with his wife, Bertha, and one of his adult
daughters. He pulled in just $1,200 a year to support his family, and
rent for the building claimed a quarter of what he earned. But if it
wasn't much, it was his.

In the middle of the twentieth century, the United States was filled with Hechlers—people on the move. They were doing what Americans had done for generations, changing where they lived in order to change their fortunes. But although Hechler could not possibly have suspected it, within a few decades few working-class Americans would have the chance to do the same. Something fundamental was about to change in the United States. In fact, it would change right there where Hechler lived. He moved into the redbrick apartment at a time when America was still defined by its remarkable geographic mobility, and the social and economic mobility it produced. But the next resident of 555 Hudson Street would do as much as anyone to change that, celebrating American dynamism even as she helped bring it to a crashing halt. Hechler died in 1945, and his landlord died the following year. The building was sold "well below market values to quick buyer," who promptly flipped it to an eager pair of purchasers. And Jane Jacobs moved in.

In 1947, when Jacobs and her husband moved to the West Village, it was still a zone of emergence, filled with immigrants and their children, people constantly moving in and moving out. Robert and Jane were different. The young, urban professionals both held full-time jobs, Robert working as an architect and Jane writing for a State Department magazine. And they came to stay. With dual incomes, and no kids, they were able to pay more for their house than the Hechlers earned in five years, putting down $7,000 in cash. Their purchase placed them among the scarcely 1 percent of families in all of Greenwich Village who owned their homes at the time.

Instead of finding a new tenant who could turn the candy store back into a social center, the Jacobses set about adapting the building to meet their needs. They cleared the bricks from the lot behind the house, turning it into a fenced-in garden. On the first floor, they ripped out the counters and the shelves, installing a modern kitchen, dining room, and living room, with French doors opening on to the backyard. "The front of No. 555," a city report later noted, "was rebuilt in 1950 at considerable expense, using metal sash and two-colored brick to complete the horizontality of the wide windows. It retains no vestige of its original appearance." (The "unsatisfactory alterations" of the "badly remodeled" facade, the report concluded, rendered it "completely out of character" with the neighborhood.) In 1956, in front of her house, Jacobs planted "the only tree on Hudson Street for many blocks."

555 Hudson Street in 1969 after the Jacobses' renovation replaced the facade with two-tone brick and metal sash, leaving "no vestige of its original appearance."
NEW YORK CITY LANDMARKS PRESERVATION COMMISSION.

Jacobs arrived in the West Village just as many Americans were abandoning dense, urban neighborhoods for the attractions of suburbia. For decades, city officials and reformers had worried about the spread of urban blight. They looked at the crowding, chaos, and confusion of immigrant neighborhoods like the West Village with horror. They wanted to sweep away neighborhoods that grew and decayed organically and replace them with carefully planned blocks, bringing stability to urban life. Urban planners sought to provide families with affordable homes, consolidate the jumble of corner stores into supermarkets, and keep offices at a remove. Everything would be rational, everything modern. They wanted to plate the rich stew of urban life and separate out its components like a toddler's dinner—the peas to one quadrant, the carrots to another, the chicken to a third—safely removed from direct contact.

In 1916, the year Jacobs was born, New York City ushered in an ambitious effort to achieve this sort of separation, the first comprehensive zoning code in the United States. By the time she moved to New York almost two decades later, the once-radical scheme of zoning, with sections of the city separated out for different uses, seemed less a startling change than a natural feature of the city's environment. The reformers who introduced zoning had hailed it as a cure for poverty, slums, and urban blight; it was supposed to ensure a better future for the city. Measured by that standard, it failed. In the years after World War II, the flight of middle-class families from the city to suburban single-family housing accelerated the economic segregation of the neighborhoods of town houses and apartment buildings they left behind and produced a sense of acute crisis. Government officials soon embraced a more radical scheme of urban renewal, bulldozing old, dense neighborhoods in the name of slum clearance. And Jacobs, to her great and lasting credit, had the courage to stand up and demand that it stop.

From her home on Hudson Street, Jacobs fell in love with the city as it was—not the city as urban planners dreamed it might be. Sitting in her room, looking out at the streetscape below, she saw the shopkeepers greeting customers and the schoolchildren buying candy. She watched Samuel Halpert wheeling his laundry handcart, in what she later described as the "intricate ballet of the sidewalk." She realized that the things professional planners hated about cities were often precisely what most benefited their residents.

At a Harvard conference on urban planning in 1956, she told the assembled mandarins that they were thinking about cities all wrong. The small stores peppering residential streets, she said, were not dangerous intrusions, but instead the "glue that makes an urban neighborhood a community instead of a dormitory." The storefronts were hubs of activity, the storekeepers anchors of their neighborhood. They were social centers, Jacobs said, especially the bars, the diners, and the candy stores. Where many of her contemporaries saw chaos and tumult and noise, it was the genius of Jacobs to discern order and vitality and the hum of human interaction. Storekeepers who kept their eyes on the street, allowing people to walk about in safety. Countermen who doubled as concierges for the working classes, holding their keys or their packages. Shop owners who dwelled amid their customers and cared for their communities.

Returning home to Hudson Street, Jacobs pounded out *The Death and Life of Great American Cities* on her Remington. Her book, published in 1961, took aim at urban renewal and painted a vivid picture of all that it destroyed in the name of progress. When, that same year, Jacobs learned that the city intended to designate her own neighborhood for renewal, she rallied the inhabitants to its defense. And it worked. Jacobs and her collaborators were the first residents of a city neighborhood to successfully block an urban renewal scheme. Jacobs's book—its brilliantly observed account of urban life, its adages and conjectures—paired with her success as an activist to catapult her to fame. She became the apostle of urbanism, and eager disciples sought her out to learn how they might defend their own neighborhoods or persuade their communities to see cities as resources and not as problems to be solved.

In 1969, Greenwich Village was landmarked, safeguarding it from redevelopment in perpetuity. The city's official report ratifying its landmark designation credited the neighborhood's "united effort to preserve the distinctive character of their community." But that character was frozen at a very particular moment in time. For centuries, the built form of the West Village had continually evolved. Old buildings were torn down and larger structures erected in their place. The three-story houses adjacent to Jacobs's at 553 and 551 Hudson, which had once held small businesses of their own, had been bought up by a developer in 1901 and replaced with a six-story apartment building. By the time Jacobs moved in next door, though, that building had acquired the patina of legitimacy conferred by the passage of time. Instead of decrying a long-ago redevelopment, she gave the tenement pride of place in her account of her neighborhood.

But Jacobs's activism put a halt to efforts to add any more buildings like it. Other three-story houses could no longer be consolidated into six-story apartment blocks; the existing six-story walk-ups couldn't be turned into twelve-story elevator buildings. Any effort to replace an existing building with one that might accommodate more residents, after all, might risk displacement, and that was where Jacobs and her allies drew their line. "Nothing that was done in connection with the community association could displace any person or business in the area," she later explained. "That was like a rule against murder." Always before, the neighborhood had grown to accommodate demand, to make room for new arrivals. Old buildings had come down, and new ones had gone up in their place. Now it froze.

Simply preserving the historic buildings that constitute a neighborhood, though, cannot preserve its character. At an intellectual level, Jacobs understood this, warning that zoning should not seek "to freeze conditions and uses as they stand. That would be death." A neighborhood is defined by its residents and their interactions, as Jacobs herself so eloquently argued, and it continually evolves. It bears the same relation to its buildings as does a lobster to its shell, periodically molting and then constructing a new, larger shell to accommodate its growth. But Jacobs, charmed by this particular lobster she'd discovered, insisted that it keep its current shell forever.

Jacobs, in short, had moved into a vibrant immigrant neighborhood, bought a historic mixed-use rental property, and transformed it into a modern, single-family home. Then she pushed to change the rules so that no one else could easily do the same. Nor was Jacobs alone. A newspaper columnist visiting shortly after the publication of *Death and Life* praised her affection for the "spontaneous hubbub of her neighborhood," citing her neighbor working on a sculpture in the yard behind his house "while not laboring for his pay-check at Macy's." But what sounded bohemian was actually bourgeois. Her neighbor Abe Greiss wasn't sweating in the loading dock at the department store; he was an art director. When his work was exhibited at MoMA, it was not the sculpture he pursued in his free time but an advertisement promoting savings bonds. Like Jacobs, he had purchased the house in which he lived, taking it off the rental market. And as the president of the West Village Committee, he would become one of Jacobs's key allies in her fight to freeze the physical form of her neighborhood. Instead of new apartment towers, the West Village Committee pressed for development on vacant lots, with the new buildings carefully scaled to match the old and with no one forced to move. "Not a single person—not a single sparrow—shall be displaced," they vowed.

Jacobs's book crystallized a shift in American attitudes. Where civic boosters once sketched fantastical visions of future development, competing to lure migrants their way, by the 1960s they had begun to hunker down and focus on preserving what they had against the threat of what the architectural critic Lewis Mumford called the "disease of growth." They pressed for decentralization and local control, for what the writer Calvin Trillin called "neighborhoodism." What began as a well-intentioned effort to curb the excesses of urban renewal would ultimately have consequences neither Jacobs nor anyone else anticipated. As America turned toward local sovereignty, it would lose its distinctive mobility and all the opportunities and benefits it had conferred.

What saved the West Village from being bulldozed like other working-class areas in Manhattan was not the vibrancy of its street fronts and its ethnic communities and its small shops. Instead, it was that the displacement of working-class immigrants by college-educated professionals was already further along than the urban planners appreciated when they decided to designate it a slum. The night after the first public meeting of the Committee to Save the West Village, the activists reconvened in the apartment of a recent arrival who conducted market research for a living. He showed them how to survey residents in order to compile a demographic profile of the area. Jane's husband, Bob, an architect, began looking at the

condition of the existing buildings. Carey Vennema, who'd graduated from NYU Law School a few years before, began researching
tax records. A sound engineer compared recordings he took in the
West Village with those in affluent neighborhoods. They leveraged
their training and expertise to mount a challenge to the planning
process—a form of bureaucratic warfare unavailable to the majority
of Americans. The fight against urban renewal was righteous. It was
successful. But it was by no means democratic.

Like many reformers of her generation, Jacobs herself had largely
lost faith in electoral democracy. Relatively few voters turned out for
municipal elections, she argued, and politicians frequently betrayed
their promises after securing office. "Responsiveness is what makes
a government democratic, not the fact of election in itself," she said.
She looked at local government and saw unaccountable bureaucrats
making decisions of tremendous consequence. She worried about
the corrupting influence of money. "The art of negating the power of
votes with the power of money," she wrote in *Death and Life,* "can be
practiced just as effectively by honest public administrators as by
dishonest representatives of purely private interests." She had in
mind the machinations of the developer Robert Moses, who used his
control of public funds to keep politicians in line and supportive of
his large-scale projects. And, as usual, her critique was spot-on; it
was her remedy that proved problematic.

When the citizens of a democracy are unhappy with what government officials are doing in their name, they possess a remarkable
privilege: they can vote them out of office. If Jacobs honestly believed that low turnout was the problem, she might have urged her
readers to register voters and knock on doors and get voters to the
polls. If she thought politicians were corrupt, she might have encouraged her acolytes to run for office or to perform the arduous
labor of engagement and persuasion, persuading their neighbors to
vote incumbents out of office. And if she thought bureaucrats were
using their sway over public funds to control elected officials, she
could have campaigned to reform the administrative structures that
gave them that discretion. But because she was deeply distrustful of
large institutions and bureaucratic processes, she held up her West
Village activism as a model.

The solution, Jacobs explained, was to organize small groups of dedicated activists whose energy and activity could create the false impression of broad-based public support for their agenda. Once, when the West Village Committee decided to hold a rally, she related, it sent children out to plaster flyers all over the neighborhood, using a small number of volunteers to create an illusion of broad public support to impress public officials. When Jacobs wrote that the true measure of democracy is responsiveness, this is what she had in mind. A government catering to the policy preferences of a few dozen privileged denizens of the West Village, allowing them an effective veto over any plan, was responsive; a government in which a majority of the voters selected officials on the basis of their record and views was not. Jacobs saw clearly the threat of unrestrained government bureaucracy and correctly believed that she could block urban renewal by empowering local communities. The collaborative planning that she championed, in which well-organized groups pressure officials into implementing their vision for their neighborhoods, has now become the norm.

What Jacobs failed to anticipate was that arming small groups of activists with the power to halt all construction would imperil the very things she intended to save: the diversity of uses within a neighborhood, the vibrancy of its street life, an openness to change. Her critique of electoral democracy's shortcomings was not wrong, but she replaced it with a system that was even less representative and far less able to defend the public interest.

The failure to build in the West Village hasn't just kept the neighborhood from expanding; it's helped to empty it out. The neighborhood that Jacobs fought to preserve in the 1960s was, in many ways, already just a shell of its former self. Jacobs celebrated the fact that her neighborhood's population, which peaked at sixty-five hundred in 1910, had dropped to just twenty-five hundred by 1950. This represented, she argued, "unslumming"—otherwise known as gentrification. Despite her strident insistence that not a sparrow be displaced from the Village of the 1960s, she cast as a triumph the displacement of a dynamic community of immigrant renters in the 1950s—its denizens constantly striving to get ahead—by a stable, gentrified population of homeowners. "The key link in a perpetual slum is that too many people move out of it too fast—and in the meantime dream of getting out," she wrote. Like so many other reformers before her, she regarded that dream of mobility as deeply threatening to stability and public order.

Ironically, though, all the things that Jacobs treasured about her neighborhood were already being threatened by the way she had chosen to preserve it. If the same row houses and apartment buildings now housed scarcely a third as many residents as they had at their peak, then there were also scarcely a third as many customers to patronize the local shop fronts, a third as many neighbors to chat with on the stoop, a third as many dancers in the ballet of the sidewalk, a third as many eyes on the street. Jacobs was right to celebrate the fact that New Yorkers could afford to live in more spacious quarters, but if each person was going to have three times the floor space, then the buildings to house them would need to reach three times as high, or else the neighborhoods would empty out. And that's where she and her allies drew the line.

The Hechlers, with their rented storefront and reasonably priced apartment above it, had found the West Village to be a wide rung on the ladder of opportunity. But their children needed to look elsewhere to live. Lou Hechler, who had worked in the candy store on Hudson Street with his father, moved with his wife to New Orleans. Abe, another of Rudolph's sons, raised his family in an apartment on Miriam Street, off the Grand Concourse in the Bronx. His son David recalls his childhood there, roller-skating in the street and playing stickball with the neighborhood kids, with great fondness. "We never had *everything* that we wanted, but it was never a problem," he told me.

Opportunity was drifting out of the center of cities and pushing toward their periphery, where people could still afford to build. Abe operated a dry-cleaning business in the Bronx and then went in with a partner on a new store in Jackson Heights during the postwar boom. In Queens, he found a ticket to the middle class. After commuting for years, Abe moved into Jackson Heights himself. In 1966, David joined his father at Briar Cleaners, working alongside him for thirteen years. David's life, too, was marked by mobility. He sold the

Jackson Heights store in the face of rising crime; when a young man walked in, picked up the entire cash register, and walked out, he knew he'd had enough. Like so many other New Yorkers of his generation, he looked to the suburbs for the sorts of opportunities the city had once provided. He found a partner, and they opened a new dry-cleaning store out on the newest American frontier, in a shopping plaza in Nassau County. When that partnership dissolved, he operated a store in Rockland County, and then after that another in Woodbury.

In the suburbs, though, he found it harder to form face-to-face relationships with customers. Instead of walking over on their way to or from work, they drove, or asked to have their clothes delivered. His grandfather had lived above his store in the Village; he and his father had lived near their store in Jackson Heights. But the new spatial geography of American life, defined by restrictive zoning, had separated these aspects of his life. David still lived in Queens, and the commutes were grinding. He suffered a heart attack and got out of the business.

On a summer evening, as I walk down Hudson Street, I see a gray-haired woman juggling three bags and her dry cleaning as she tries to open a door. "Do you live here?" I ask. She does. I hold the bags while she turns her key in a stubborn lock. When Susan Spehar was a girl in St. Louis, her father—who chaired the fashion giant Associated Merchandising—would take her on business trips to New York. She dreamed of living in the West Village one day. Fifteen years ago, after her husband died, she decided it was time. She landed in a rental; in one of those "only in New York" stories, her landlord was Calvin Trillin, coiner of "neighborhoodism." When a town house came on the market, she jumped at the chance to buy it. She'd been living in the house for less than a year when she opened the door onto the street to find a crowd of forty people staring at her. "I don't think that's Jane Jacobs," said a voice from the back of the crowd. That's how Spehar learned whose house she had bought.

In its first circular in 1961, the Committee to Save the West Village had inveighed against redevelopment, warning ominously that "even when some buildings are saved and rehabilitated, their rents are usually doubled or tripled." Preservation, in this respect, proved far more lethal to the texture of the community than redevelopment would have been. Jacobs bought her home for $7,000, saved and rehabilitated it, and sold it twenty-four years later for $45,000. "Whenever I'm here," Jacobs told *The New Yorker* in 2004, "I go back to look at our house, 555 Hudson Street, and I know that I could never afford it now."

Property records say Spehar paid $3.35 million in 2009; today, the city assesses it for $6.4 million. If you could scrape together the down payment at that price, your monthly bill would be—even adjusted for inflation—about ninety times what the Hechlers paid each month to live in the same building. The West Village is no longer a zone of emergence, welcoming successive waves of new arrivals. The buildings lining the block present a lifelike appearance, like a row of exquisitely taxidermied beasts, forever frozen at a moment of high activity. But by preserving the built forms of the neighborhood in the name of diversity, Jacobs and her allies left it insufficient room to continue growing. As units turned over, only the affluent could afford to move in. Today, in the storefront where the Hechlers once sold candy to working-class immigrant kids, you can find Next Step Realty, specialists in finding homes for "professionals entering the workforce and recent college graduates." And a few blocks away, there's another Jacobs town house, but this one is linked to Marc, not Jane; the fashion designer recently sold his home for $10.5 million.

Jacobs and her allies beat back the efforts of unaccountable bureaucrats to level a vibrant community, but their triumph came at a steep price. To defend the West Village, they asserted a proprietary right to control their neighborhood. It belonged, they argued, to those who were already there, and it should be up to them to decide who would get to join them. Over the decades that followed, that idea would take hold throughout the United States. A nation that had grown diverse and prosperous by allowing people to choose their communities would instead empower communities to choose their people.

I had seen the fruits of this logic in Cambridge, where my once-diverse neighborhood had priced out all but a wealthy few, and I saw it again in the West Village. But Jane Jacobs didn't invent the logic of the village so much as revive it. For most of human history, communities have been exclusionary, carefully policing their boundaries and selecting their members. Your birth generally determined your fate. But for much of its existence, the United States was truly exceptional, at least in this respect. It was a place where people like Rudolph Hechler could come from nothing and make something of themselves, by moving toward opportunity.

Understanding why America is no longer the sort of place where stories like Hechler's are common requires understanding how it ever allowed such a radical degree of individual freedom in the first place. It was not by design. When Europeans first settled in North America, they brought with them the logic of the village, with all its exclusionary implications. The men in charge intended to re-create a society that was just as rigid and hierarchical as the one they had left behind. But instead, they created something genuinely new in the world, a society with an unprecedented degree of fluidity. And to tell that story, we need to travel back in time, from the West Village to the Puritan village.

CHAPTER THREE

THE FREEDOM TO MOVE

On a sandy stretch of land along Massachusetts Bay, people pretending to be my ancestors dress in antiquated clothing and welcome visitors into their rude wooden huts. They call this tourist trap "Plimoth," misspelling it for added authenticity. None of the structures are original; the buildings are miles distant from the historic site they imaginatively re-create. As a child, I was impressed with the smoke and the sparks of the blacksmith's forge, the weathered grays of the thatched and shingled roofs, and the reenactors gamely sticking to their seventeenth-century parts.

As clever as the reenactors were, though, the most important truth about Plimoth wasn't something you could learn on the tour. The English village at Plymouth was reconstructed to mark the first spot in New England where Europeans placed a permanent settlement, a monument to a fixed population. But what the reenactors cosplaying Pilgrims don't tell you is that of the millions of Americans who can trace their ancestry back to the *Mayflower*, almost none of them live anywhere nearby. The real significance of Plymouth is captured not by the name of the town but by the name applied to the separatists who landed there. They were called Pilgrims because they had chosen to set out on a journey, a remarkable act for their day and age.

The Pilgrims first left their homes in Nottinghamshire, crossing the English Channel to Leiden, in Holland, and then, in 1620, moved again, this time crossing an entire ocean and settling in Plymouth. Over the next two decades, tens of thousands of other Puritans would follow them, in a movement known to historians as the Great Migration. But at the time they left their homes, there was nothing great about migration. In fact, moving from one place to another was downright suspicious. In early-modern England, every person had a proper place, tied to their land, their employment, and their family. Families were responsible for the care of their members, and if they were unable to provide for them, communities assumed the burden. To move away from home was to abandon your responsibilities and, worse yet, to challenge the proper order of society. But by the sixteenth century, the burgeoning population had produced a glut of labor in rural areas, forcing landless workers to search for seasonal work elsewhere or to find some other means of sustenance. Most migration in England had been local; now growing numbers of destitute laborers journeyed far from home, many landing in towns and cities.

These masterless men, unmoored from patriarchy and place, didn't fit into the carefully ordered hierarchies of English society. Settled populations saw them as a direct threat to public order. Migration was disreputable, a course pursued only in desperation. "Vagrants, begone!" enjoined a London schoolboy in a 1675 oration, lamenting "that such a verminous brood should swarm and poyson our streets." A new and sinister word entered the English language to describe this *mobile vulgus,* or moving crowd—this dangerously rootless mass of ordinary people, with its quicksilver moods, which had dared to leave its proper place. They were known as the "mobile," and then the slang of fashionable Londoners contracted that into the "mob." The authorities responded to the tide of vagrancy with harsh laws, to push migrants back into their proper spots in the social order. Men caught far from their homes could be put to work, or else jailed, impressed into the navy, or transported to the colonies. Women and children were to be returned to their husbands and fathers, or to the places of their birth.

So, as the seventeenth century dawned, and some Puritans contemplated leaving their homes and their communities for a new world, they were uneasy. English Protestants took a dim view of itinerancy, associating it with Catholic pilgrimages and urging instead a spiritual (and literal) stillness. Puritans were already regarded as slightly suspect for their habit of gadding about to nearby towns to listen to prominent preachers and mix with like-minded reformers. Now they were planning to migrate not just across a county for a Sunday afternoon but across an ocean for good. How could they pursue their project of creating godly communities, forged with unity and cohesion and love, by abandoning the places to which they belonged? How could they claim to be a holy congregation, when they behaved like a mob of shiftless vagabonds? What was godly about leaving home? To answer those questions, Puritans created, as the historian Scott McDermott has argued, a new ideology of mobility.

In 1630, a fleet of eleven ships set sail for Massachusetts Bay, led by John Winthrop. The sermon he famously delivered on the voyage is best known today for likening the Puritan enterprise to a city upon a hill, subject to the scrutiny of the world. But while that phrase is often invoked, the core message of the sermon has largely been lost. "Wee must be knit together, in this worke, as one man," Winthrop told the colonists, or else all would witness their failure. For Winthrop, as for many other Puritans, being "as one man" was more than a figure of speech. If communities were corporate bodies, they reasoned, then they should obey the same principles as actual, nonmetaphorical bodies. Galenic medicine taught that a human body needed to be properly proportioned, its humors held in balance. Communities, it followed, likewise required careful tending. "There is noe body but consists of partes and that which knitts these partes together, giues the body its perfection," Winthrop explained. Love had knit Christ and his church into one body, and now it would knit the colonists together in their new project.

Here was an answer to the critics who took the Puritans leaving their proper place as a confession of error and inadequacy. They were not fleeing England but choosing to depart, because England had grown disordered and distempered. In their new colony, they could produce a properly balanced body politic, to serve as a model for restoring England's health. Migrating across the Atlantic did not mean abandoning their responsibilities like impecunious vagrants; in Winthrop's telling, migration was a fulfillment of their duty as Christians, an act of love and caring. They were not a mob, after all, but a cohesive congregation. Leaving their established homes behind and moving someplace new was not just a respectable behavior but a desirable one. Mobility was good. Or, at least, this particular act of mobility.

Winthrop intended to justify his own departure from England—and the broader Great Migration of Puritans to Massachusetts Bay that brought twenty thousand people across the ocean between 1620 and 1640—as an exceptional circumstance. He had no desire to license people to pick up and leave whenever they pleased; the whole point of the migration was to create a healthy, cohesive body and to preserve its integrity. He imagined a new England, just as sedentary and stable as the old. But revolutionary ideas have a habit of twisting back upon their authors in ways they least expect. Just a few years later, when the prominent minister Thomas Hooker requested permission to relocate with his congregation from Massachusetts to what would become Connecticut, Winthrop was distinctly unamused. "They ought not to departe from vs," he complained, "beinge knitt to vs in one bodye." Here was the same objection raised against Winthrop leaving England, now employed by Winthrop to object to Hooker leaving Massachusetts.

But Hooker turned Winthrop's logic against him. Leaving a community, he later explained, needn't be treated as an extraordinary act, an attack on social cohesion. All sorts of people left their communities. "Solomon sent ships to Ophir, which returned not by the space of some years," he wrote. "All states may be compelled to send some men to Sea for trafick; sometimes by way of just war, and yet no prejudice done to any rule of Christ, or Church-order in that case."

Hooker, of course, wasn't proposing to take a little cruise down to Ophir. He was moving away for good. But, he insisted, the basic logic held. If people could depart on a voyage because it served the greater good, then "upon the same ground the Church may send out some . . . to begin plantations, in case the body require it." And, as McDermott argues, there were many reasons for Hooker to believe that the body required it. His community felt squeezed for resources, without enough land to farm or to graze its cattle. Hooker himself chafed under Winthrop's autocratic approach to governance, doubting whether the reign of a single magistrate was compatible with the rule of law. The body politic was again distempered; setting out for Connecticut was a means of bringing it back into balance.

Entirely against his will, Winthrop had conferred upon the people of Massachusetts a profound right: the freedom to leave. If moving from England to Boston could be godly, then so could moving from Boston to Ipswich, or to Hartford. The colonists he'd settled refused to stay put. In 1641, the Massachusetts Body of Liberties codified this understanding into law, promising that every man "shall have free liberty . . . to remove both himself and his family at their pleasure" from the colony. That might not sound like much: *If you don't like it, you can leave.* But it was likely the first time anywhere in the world that this individual freedom was put into writing and defined as a fundamental right.

The Puritans were hardly the first to conceive of the freedom of movement as a central human liberty. In classical times, Epictetus imagined a slave envisioning his freedom with the declaration "I go where I will." But a philosophical right was not the same as a legal one. While the laws of some nations acknowledged a right to depart, it was at best a qualified right—usually recognized only negatively, as in England, by the designation of large categories of individuals who required affirmative permission to leave the state. As the European powers sent forth their colonial tendrils, trading and settling wherever they desired, though, their theorists also rushed to discover a moral right to migration, a liberty for European empires to intrude wherever they liked, grounded in natural law. Francisco de Vitoria declared that his fellow Spaniards had "a right to travel into the lands in question and to sojourn there." Hugo Grotius announced that the Dutch "have the right to sail to the East Indies, as they are now doing." These, however, were rights that served the interests of the state. In Massachusetts, the Body of Liberties translated the idea of a national right to intrude into a personal, individual liberty—not a right asserted by the power of the state, but a right asserted *against* the power of the state. A resident of Massachusetts could just pick up and go whenever he pleased, and no one could stop him.

No longer would people belong to a place simply because they had been born to it. And if people could leave whenever they chose, then the decision to remain became an equally active choice. Though, in many ways, the freedom to leave would prove to be the foundational American liberty, in early colonial Massachusetts it had more immediate effects. During the seventeenth century, as England was torn apart by bouts of civil war, the Bay Colony remained remarkably cohesive. Massachusetts had more than its share of struggles over politics, ideology, theology, and scarce resources, but it also had a means of resolving them. The freedom to leave provided a safety valve, bleeding off the pressure of open conflict. If people were discontented with their own community, they could either relocate or decide that, on the whole, they'd prefer to stay put despite their dissatisfactions. Either way, putting the decision into the hands of an individual transformed them from passive victims of fate into active agents of their own destinies.

Mobility also opened the door of economic opportunity. In new towns, there were fortunes to be made by the rich and well connected, but even those who arrived as indentured servants often succeeded in carving out farms of their own. As families of settlers came off the boats during the Great Migration, they paused in the port towns and then set out to join in the division of Massachusetts's abundant land, there for the taking just as swiftly as its Native inhabitants could be dispossessed. They seized on their freedom to move toward opportunity. But the right to leave, they soon discovered, is not the same as the right to belong.

In colonial Massachusetts, the town was sovereign. Not technically, of course: in any English colony, the sovereign was sovereign. And not even legally: on paper, towns were corporations formed by the colonial government, subject to its authority. But in practical terms, towns were the seat of power. They wielded a degree of control over the lives of their inhabitants that is today difficult to comprehend, regulating behavior, land, and labor. The secret to success in Massachusetts was to be a full member of a town, to share in its prosperity, to revel in its liberties. But if there was a single principle that governed the towns of the commonwealth, it was exclusion.

As the colonists discovered the virtues of mobility, they applied to the General Court for new town charters. When the General Court granted their petitions, they collectively became the proprietors of a large chunk of land. Sometimes, these proprietors gave each of their number an equal plot of land, but more commonly they doled the land out in proportion to the stature and contributions of the proprietors. And they held back large amounts of land for common use, or for future allocations.

Towns were responsible for the welfare of their inhabitants—caring for the indigent and disabled was usually their greatest expense—and so took pains to ensure that no one would be able to establish residency who might later become a public charge. They continued the English system of "warning out" any new arrivals who might not be able to support themselves or might threaten public order. Overseers of the poor exercised a high degree of surveillance and control over their communities. Walking the streets of their towns, they could stop and interrogate newcomers. Those who were warned out could be loaded into a cart by the town sergeant and driven back to the town to which they belonged and whipped if they dared return. By law, no one could remain in the Bay Colony for more than three weeks without formal license, but the rules were even stricter in most towns. In general, Black people, the disabled, and the impoverished were particularly likely to be warned out. Residents had to report anyone they took into their homes, so that their presence might be reviewed, and post a bond against future expenses incurred by the town.

Between 1690 and 1795, for example, townsfolk in Dedham reported 573 new arrivals; the majority were then warned out. But unlike in England, most of those whose cases were reviewed weren't itinerant laborers or vagrants. They were largely tenants and hired help invited by townsmen to earn a wage or pay rent but turned away by the town. Dedham operated as a members-only club, and it was hard to gain admission.

As much as Dedham's politics of exclusion were intended to protect access to land and public order, they were also intended to protect the value of labor. Land itself remained fairly abundant in the commonwealth, but the soil was thin and rocky. Many families made much, or most, of their income from commercial activities other than farming. Tenants and hired laborers from outside the community were prospective rivals, depressing the wages that the town-born could earn or the prices they could command for their crafts. Towns like Dedham regulated their labor markets carefully. From 1650 to 1683, an annual meeting assigned every young bachelor to a yearlong term of labor, generally with families other than their own, in exchange for a wage. Younger children could be removed from their families and placed in households where they could be properly disciplined and productively employed. Servants and children were punished harshly for infractions. But those fortunate enough to be born within or admitted to the town and who abided by the communal rules could, in exchange, expect stability and prosperity. They would be surrounded by a like-minded community, protected from competition, and cared for in hard times.

As the first generation of settlers gave way to the second and third, the many children of the town's large, flourishing families pressed for farms of their own. The original landholdings close to the cluster of houses could be subdivided only so far, but mobility offered a solution. They moved away from the original cluster of dwellings, planting new villages on other parts of the original grant that offered land and independence. With no small degree of contention, Dedham slowly allowed these villages to be separated into new towns. In the seventeenth century, chunks of its original grant would be carved off to form Medfield and Wrentham; in the eighteenth century, Bellingham, Needham, Dover, Westwood, Norwood, and Walpole would follow. Dedham itself, though, remained stable, even stagnant. By the early eighteenth century, a hundred years after it was founded, eight of every ten men born in the town would live there for their entire lives. Some residents of Massachusetts moved serially, participating in the planting of multiple towns. For the most part, though, they moved just once, leaving their birthplaces to join or create a covenanted community that safeguarded the interests of its own members at the expense of those it excluded.

The word "town," ironically, does not even appear in the charter that Charles I granted to Massachusetts Bay in 1629. Instead, the document established the investors in a joint-stock company as a sort of governing council and, in a novel clause, permitted them to add "freemen" to the company who would meet on a quarterly basis. As in other colonial ventures, the investors were expected to stay in England, where they would remain in control of the new colony. But the most important words of the charter proved to be those it omitted. Other royal charters of the era stipulated where the officers of the corporation had to reside, or where their meetings would be held; the charter for Massachusetts Bay was silent on these points. When Charles I disbanded Parliament, the Puritan backers of the Bay Colony met in Cambridge, England, and decided to take the charter with them to Massachusetts. The joint-stock corporation swiftly evolved into something very like a freestanding republic, arrogating to itself a set of powers never contemplated by the Crown.

The colonial government soon chartered towns, usurping a royal prerogative. But when the king tried to reassert his authority by installing a royal governor, and the people revolted in 1689, it was the towns that reinstated the colonial government. In the years that followed, many towns would not even bother with the expense of sending delegates to the General Court. They were left largely free to run their own affairs. The sovereign town—a self-governing community, prioritizing the interests of its own members at the expense of others—became the basic element of New England life.

As the eighteenth century began, Massachusetts had evolved into a society embracing the mutually contradictory principles of mobility and exclusivity. Its residents believed that they had the right to leave home to create or join a community that could offer them land, economic opportunity, or a more congenial theological or political community. They likewise believed in the sovereignty of their covenanted communities, each of which had the right to select its members and tightly regulate their behavior but owed them in return a high degree of care. What allowed these ideas to coexist was the abundance of American land, taken from its original inhabitants. Those excluded from or denied opportunity in one community could help start another.

"Noe dwelling howse shalbe builte above halfe a myle from the meeting howse," declared the Massachusetts General Court in 1635, in legislation as remarkable for its spelling as for its content. A few towns dutifully passed echoing ordinances and then ignored them. The mandate was extended to all towns the following year, and then, when someone actually tried to enforce it against a resident of Charlestown in 1640, promptly repealed. A handful of early settlements actually clustered their houses together around the church, to make them easier to defend, or to share resources during the initial clearance of the land. Some, like Cambridge, even passed ordinances trying to arrange housing in an orderly fashion, set back a common distance from the street. But settlers insisted on moving toward opportunity, planting their farms and their farmhouses to best advantage. They wanted to site their homes for easy access to the various resources their system of mixed agriculture required, including meadows for grazing and fields for planting. They found it easier to walk some distance to church on Sundays than out to their fields on the other six days of the week. Within a generation of settlement, New England was composed of self-governing communities filled with single-family homesteads scattered across the countryside.

The distribution of the farms reflected the third tenet of the Puritan way of land use: productivity. One early essayist quoted Genesis—"Replenish the earth and subdue it"—to assert that for people to have a theological right to the land, they must do all they can to make it maximally productive. In colonial Massachusetts—indeed, throughout the British colonies—local governments extensively regulated land. The rules, though, are a photo negative of the zoning codes of the contemporary United States. In place of the dense web of regulations intended to preserve the status quo against the dangers of untrammeled growth, colonial governments had a simpler set of rules, written to ensure that the land was developed to its maximum potential.

The colonial experiment was, after all, precarious. The success or failure of each new town rested on the industriousness of the inhabitants and the speed with which they built out their communities. Towns aimed to advance the collective interest, and as the Massachusetts Bay Colony saw it, the collective interest lay in continuous economic growth. In each case, the logic was the same: the land had been granted by the colony to facilitate economic development, and if landowners were failing to advance that goal, the land should be entrusted to someone who would.

To the extent that towns restrained property owners from developing their land, it was usually out of concern that the activity on one lot might somehow discourage the development of others. So, for example, in 1692, Massachusetts asked officials in its most populated cities and towns to designate sites for tanneries, distilleries, chandleries, and slaughterhouses—all notably messy, smelly industries that fit the classic definition of public nuisance. Some laws insisted that buildings be hardened against the threat of fire—imposing maximum heights, to ensure fires could be fought, or mandating burn-resistant materials like bricks or shingles—but these, too, were intended to promote development by safeguarding built-up areas against conflagrations. Prosperous homes of the era were generally surrounded by a sprawl of other structures, either attached to the main building or freestanding. Cities made some effort to control the locations of those, like privies or hog pens, that might pose a public nuisance, but others, like kitchens or sheds, were accepted as a matter of course.

Mobility, exclusivity, and productivity. Guided by these principles, the initial settlers arriving in New England produced a new sort of society. At its heart remained a set of unresolved tensions—a mobile society that aimed to produce stable communities, a voluntary society not everyone could join, a godly society focused on material gain. And yet, if it remained somewhat hierarchical, it had no hereditary aristocracy. If a few grew wealthy and others poor, it fostered a remarkably broad middle class. Traveling by horse from Connecticut and into the farmland of Massachusetts in 1789, George Washington, a Virginian, was struck by what he found. "There is a great equality in the People of this State," he wrote. "Few or no opulent men—and no poor—great similitude in their buildings." He came from a state that had embraced a very different set of choices and produced a very different set of outcomes. And so it is to the Old Dominion that we now must turn to understand how a second slice of American colonial heritage shaped the country's relationship to mobility and opportunity.

On the surface, there was little to distinguish the Virginia Company from the Massachusetts Bay Company: two corporations, both created by royal charter, both controlled by a small group of wealthy investors, both intended to plant colonies in North America. Each company financed shiploads of settlers, who crossed the Atlantic seeking better lives for themselves and their descendants. But despite these superficialities, the two were deeply unalike. Massachusetts filled with Puritans, mostly arriving in family units and sometimes journeying together as complete congregations, aiming for self-sufficiency. Early Virginia was settled mainly by men, without families in tow, driven less by a sense of divine purpose than by their own ambition and by desperation. Above all, they aimed for profit.

By the summer of 1619, the Virginia Company's settlers had survived their first difficult years, received a new charter, and set about turning themselves into something more like a self-governing colony than a mere commercial enterprise. Virginia's new assembly, meeting with the governor and his council, enacted a series of statutes, which in many ways set the pattern that would prevail for centuries. One concern, in particular, stands out to the modern eye. As in Massachusetts, Virginia's ruling class was discovering that bountiful land made laborers difficult to keep in their place. The great mobility of the Native peoples, a key asset in their struggles against the new European arrivals, also proved an alluring model for ordinary laborers—some of whom ran off. In response, the leaders of the colony passed a raft of laws aimed at maintaining social distinctions. Officers of the company, for example, were not subject to the same punishments for their crimes as were their employees, and sumptuary laws aimed to ensure that Virginians dressed according to their social rank. There were also regulations to hold indentured servants to their contracts. If the geography of the New World militated toward equality, the elite men of Virginia were prepared to use whatever level of violence was required to counteract it, ensuring that they remained atop a clearly defined social hierarchy.

Among free Virginians, land was not, initially, difficult to acquire. But the leading colonists were desperate for labor. A man could turn the sweat of laborers into tobacco—using them to girdle trees, clear forestland, plant tobacco seeds, tend the plants, and cure their leaves—and tobacco was money. With little cash in circulation, it functioned as the medium of exchange, with debts and payments denoted not in pounds sterling but in pounds of tobacco. But mortality was high, and maintaining the labor supply required the continual importation of new laborers—and a regime strict enough to keep them working for their bosses rather than for themselves. Indentured servants were the primary source of labor in the early years but not the only one. When the Virginia assembly met for the first time in 1619, a shipment of young urchins, rounded up on the streets of London, had just arrived, to be bound out to colonists. Within a month, more than twenty Africans would be sold to the governor by an English privateer, the event for which 1619 is now best known.

In the 1620s, Virginia surrendered its independence and became a royal colony, but its leading men soon discovered that in practical terms they remained largely autonomous. The Crown could exercise little control over their lives from across an ocean. And they set about amassing land. Unlike Massachusetts, Virginia, from the beginning, assumed that land belonged to the individual rather than the community. Virginia granted headrights—the right to lay claim to a tract of land—to each new arrival, at the rate of fifty acres per person. Indentured or enslaved laborers didn't receive their own headrights; instead, their portion went to the person who had paid to import them. But these rights could be bought and sold, allowing impoverished Virginians to trade their theoretical claim to a tract of uncleared forest somewhere beyond the edge of settlement for cash to tend to their more immediate needs. The wealthy snapped up these headrights and set about claiming enormous swaths of land. Between 1650 and 1675, they patented 2.35 million acres, reaching far beyond the edge of settlement and pushing the Native inhabitants ever farther west.

As in New England, power shifted toward the local level as the colony grew. In Virginia, that meant a steady expansion of the authority of the county courts, which were filled by men appointed as justices of the peace. Parishes, governed by their vestries, handled purely local matters. In practice, the three separate levels of government—colony, county, and parish—were dominated by the same elite landholding families. The justices of the peace and the vestrymen generally selected their own successors. Even the small degree of social fluidity that characterized the Virginia Company's early years declined over time as the largest property holders of each county coalesced into a governing class. This group regulated the lives of their social lessers, enforced a harsh regime of slavery, and, above all, protected their own freedom and autonomy to do as they pleased with their property.

The planter class of Virginia aspired to re-create the English nobility, but it ended up forging a novel social order, which, like New England, was filled with unresolved tensions. They lauded liberty and fought for its defense, even as they built their fortunes on land they had violently expropriated and on the labor of the enslaved people they brutally exploited. They erected an elaborate social hierarchy, but also offered a fictive solidarity to the adult white men of the colony, extending social recognition in exchange for their aid in policing their enslaved laborers. And in a colony without a formal aristocracy, they worshipped hereditary privilege as an aspirational ideal. In Virginia, as in England, to succeed was to own enough land to free yourself from arduous labor, to become the master of your own domain, and to establish dynastic wealth. Even, or perhaps especially, many of the small planters and tenant farmers and servants who could not enjoy these privileges aspired to them.

Virginia's pseudo-aristocracy, with its exaltation of individual liberty and hierarchy and dynasty, contrasted sharply with New England's veneration of mobility and exclusivity and productivity. As settlers from both regions moved west, they brought these two competing sets of ideals along with them, shaping the political culture of the new territories that they settled. Though these contrasting cultures would eventually lead to civil war, as settlers marched westward, they also intermingled, blending the two systems. They produced a country with distinctively regional attitudes to mobility and opportunity, but these differed more in the degree to which they emphasized certain ideals than in the nature of those ideals themselves. Today, Americans are a nation of individual landholders who expect to be able to do as they please with their own property, just as if they were Virginia gentlemen—even as they also expect to be able to tell their neighbors what they may do with theirs, just as if they lived in New England's covenanted communities. Those beliefs may seem wildly inconsistent, but then, they always have been.

———

The American Revolution secured the independence of thirteen colonies in North America, but it took a second revolution—the Mobility Revolution—to forge them into a cohesive nation. The new states had distinct political cultures and widely varied economies. Promoters of the new union could take little comfort in their common Christianity; different strains of the faith predominated in different states, separated by the doctrinal and theological disputes that had produced centuries of bloodshed in Europe. With the war behind them, how much did the people of the Union share? They identified as Virginians, as Pennsylvanians, as citizens of the several states, as members of their local communities. It was not obvious that their common interests would overwhelm their differences.

The federal Constitution aimed to construct of these pieces a coherent nation, but while it provided a framework for integrating the states, it had little to say about the primary concerns of daily life. After its ratification, a shoemaker in Savannah became a citizen of the same nation as a shoemaker in Lynn. But what if he wanted to move from Georgia to Massachusetts? States could decide on their own whom they would recognize as citizens, whom they would give the right to vote, and whom they would bar from admission. Most often, they delegated these decisions to individual communities. Local governments were the basic building blocks of the new nation, but concerning them the Constitution was entirely silent.

There was a second founding document, though, also unveiled in 1787, and it had quite a bit to say about the topic. The Northwest Ordinance was itself a sort of constitution, intended to govern a third of the nation's new territory—what would later become Ohio, Indiana, Illinois, Michigan, Wisconsin, and northeastern Minnesota. At the time, it was home to Native peoples and traversed by trappers and traders. Congress intended to claim the land and then open it for settlement. Here, for the first time, the citizens of different states could mingle on land that belonged to none of them. In carefully delineated stages, the new territories could establish their own governments and eventually apply for admission to the Union as coequal states. Congress would provide raw materials to the established states, markets for their goods, and an outlet for their people. But before any of that could happen, Congress first had to decide how to allocate the land it would seize from its Native peoples.

The Northwest Ordinance of 1787 settled on a hybrid system. Townships would be the basic unit of settlement, as in New England, laid out on a grid of squares measuring six miles to a side—thirty-six square miles each. As in the South, though, they would be grouped together in counties with substantial powers of governance. And while entire townships could be purchased at once and their lands allocated by the group that acquired them, they could also be sold off piecemeal, in mile-square lots or 160-acre quarter sections, to individual buyers. The titles would be as solid and specific as in New England, but individuals could choose the land they wished to claim, as in Virginia.

That, at least, was the theory. But experience soon showed some gaps in the design. Settlers flooded into the territory, and in 1803, Ohio was admitted to the Union. First, it had to grapple with the rush of migrants eager to own farms of their own. Then, as they moved about within the state—seeking better farms, moving to market towns, migrating along the bustling canals, settling at railroad crossings, gravitating toward cities—the state had to cope with their serial mobility. And, by 1850, it faced a new challenge as its rural precincts emptied out, losing residents who sought more fertile farmland to the west or who were ready to try their chances in the towns and cities. These would become defining characteristics of American mobility, with its boom-and-bust cycles and its ever-shifting population. To navigate these peaks and troughs, Ohio had to redefine what it meant to belong.

As the Northwest Territory opened for settlement, migrants poured in. "Taking their fortune in their hands, and their destiny in their hearts, they burned the bridges behind them, and came to a new country to plant the seeds of civilization," as a singularly self-congratulatory history of Shelby County, Ohio, later put it. Ohioans modeled their townships on the towns of New England, where many of their early settlers started their westward journeys, and preserved the system of "warning out." In New England, that system had evolved over the course of the eighteenth century. The enforcement of conformity had declined, and physical removal had become rare. Instead, towns focused on their exclusion of the indigent. Newcomers might be forced to post bond against the possibility of becoming a public charge, or they might be formally warned or cautioned, without being forcibly expelled. That enabled them to remain in the town, but not as equal citizens; instead, they were forced into a sort of probationary existence. They could remain as long as they could support themselves, but if they fell on hard times or were incapacitated, they would be forced to return to the town from which they had come to receive public assistance.

In Ohio, as in New England, people couldn't simply move into a town where they had purchased land and declare themselves residents. New arrivals needed to be accepted by the established residents of the township. If the existing residents suspected someone might eventually need their aid, they could warn them out. After 1816, a new Ohio resident was considered settled if a year passed without a warning, but that simply formalized the existing arrangement. The key—and it is so alien to our contemporary understanding of American citizenship that it bears repeating—was that living someplace was not enough to establish legal residency. If you wanted to join the members-only clubs that were Ohio townships, the existing residents had to agree to let you in.

The historian Kenneth Winkle offers a vivid illustration of what this meant in practice, at least for the poor. In 1826, a teenager named Edmund Jackson fell ill while working in Jefferson Township, Ohio. Jefferson paid for his care for four months, until he recovered, then sued Letart, a township a hundred miles away where the boy had previously worked and resided, to recover the money it had spent. But Letart had never recognized his residence, and neither had any of the other towns he'd wandered through on his way to Jefferson. The Ohio Supreme Court instead charged his care to Lebanon, the township where his parents had last established residence, although his father was dead and his mother had moved to Virginia.

This case reveals a system in flux. The old assumption was that all people were from some particular place and belong to it and that they remained attached to it until some new place accepted them. Communities were members-only clubs, and you couldn't join unless accepted as a member. By the time the court ruled in Jackson's case, though, the voluntary community was already in ascendance. Dedham and other towns in colonial New England had warned out most of their new arrivals, turning away aspiring residents for a wide variety of reasons. By the nineteenth century, only the 1 percent of Ohioans on poor relief needed to worry about warning out; the process now focused more on poverty than incompatibility or theological purity or competition for jobs. So long as new arrivals had the means to support themselves, they could stay.

Staying, though, was not the same as belonging. For most of Ohio's settlers, the question of legal residence revolved around voting; would they be permitted to help govern the communities where they settled? Even before the Revolution, the franchise was extraordinarily widespread in the American colonies; between half and three-quarters of adult white men could vote, while in England only one in seven could do the same. And over the next two decades, enfranchisement expanded further, with perhaps 80 percent of adult white men—90 percent in some states—gaining the right to vote. In Ohio, elections were at first communal affairs, with all the voters in a township gathering in a single space; the vote of any man could be challenged by any other, with the local election judge deciding whether he qualified as a resident. This was the old model of the corporate community, policing the boundaries of its membership. But in 1841, as new residents poured into the state, the legislature created a nine-part test for assessing whether someone was a resident, centered on individual intent. Instead of the members of a township deciding whether a new arrival could join their number, what mattered was whether the new arrival himself *intended* to join.

Crucially, it was the state legislature and the state courts that took these steps. Local communities strongly favored the interests of the comparative handful of settlers who stayed put, at the expense of those who had recently arrived. Left to their own devices, many communities would have remained exclusionary. But it was in Ohio's interest to encourage settlement and protect the rights of individuals as they made their serial moves through the state. And so the state legislature of Ohio intervened. First, it gave fixed criteria establishing the right to vote, centered on the choices made by voters. Then, in 1854, a revised statute eliminated the right of communities to warn out new arrivals. And while Ohio retained its vagrancy laws and continued to use them to restrict the mobility of its poorest residents, they came to seem less bulwarks of the natural order than anachronisms. After the panic of 1873, the use of these laws to confine those left destitute by the economic collapse brought a fierce backlash. "A poor American citizen is no longer to be allowed to travel. Is this the land of the pilgrims, the land of Independence? Are the poor wanderers to be denied the blessed privilege of breathing the heaven-born air of freedom?" asked Ohio's *Portsmouth Daily Times*. At the beginning of the nineteenth century, Americans had assumed communities could select their own members. By its end, they assumed individuals could select their own communities.

Like other freedoms, the benefits of the freedom to move were unequally enjoyed and its costs unequally borne. Ohio passed a series of racist laws that limited the mobility of Black Americans. The state's 1802 constitution barred slavery, but the same convention, by a single vote, denied free Black residents the franchise and excluded them from enumeration for the purpose of representation. Legislators piled on other restrictions, requiring new arrivals who were Black to file certificates with the county clerk proving they were not fugitives from slavery, and to post a $500 bond guaranteed by two or more white citizens against the possibility they would become public charges. The bonds and certificates were not always required in practice, but the message of exclusion they sent was unmistakable. Even so, these measures failed to stop Black Americans from migrating to Ohio and pursuing opportunity there.

To the Puritan recognition of the right to leave, midwesterners added the right to belong—the right to choose your own community, to move where you want, to declare a place your home. Americans embraced their new freedom to move with wild abandon, inaugurating a revolutionary age of mobility. By the middle of the nineteenth century, millions of Americans moved from state to state, fusing traditions and identities. Even at the height of this age of mobility, though, these freedoms were enjoyed unequally and respected imperfectly. As Americans came into closer contact with each other, they confronted their differences, and some reverted to erecting walls around their communities, to exclude those they disdained.

CHAPTER FOUR

A MIGRATORY PEOPLE

In 1809, a boy named Abraham was born on a farm in Kentucky. His father, Thomas, was from Virginia but traced his family back to the early Puritan settlers of Hingham, Massachusetts, by way of Pennsylvania and New Jersey. His mother, Nancy, was born out of wedlock, also in Virginia. Both came to Kentucky as children and had already relocated several times before they met. Thomas inherited no land but by working a variety of jobs amassed enough to buy a farm. When he married Nancy, they moved to Elizabethtown and then, two years later, to the one-room cabin on a farm near Hodgenville where Abraham was born. But although the 348-acre farm was large enough to support a family, the soil was poor, and it was afflicted with the typical Kentucky complaint: the title was in dispute. So when he was two, Abraham moved with his family to Knob Creek, twelve miles to the northeast. Here, his father found better soil and, together with his skill as a carpenter, became one of the most prosperous men in the area.

But when he was seven, Abe moved again, this time all the way to Indiana. The move, he later remembered, was partially due to a distaste for slavery, but "chiefly on account of the difficulty in land titles," the old Kentucky complaint striking again. In Indiana, where the Northwest Ordinance made titles secure, Thomas squatted on a quarter section of land, then purchased it from the federal government on the installment plan, ultimately amassing a hundred acres. When Abe was twenty-one, the whole extended family relocated again, this time to Illinois, lured by the promise of better land and proximity to relatives. Having attained his majority, Abe soon moved to the nearby village of New Salem, pursuing a variety of trades. He was elected to the state legislature and, after half a dozen years, moved once more, this time to the new capital of Springfield. He took up the law and rode circuit twice a year, following the court from town to town over an area more than twice the size of Connecticut. Then, in 1844, he bought a home in Springfield. Two years later, Abe Lincoln was elected to Congress and set off for a term in Washington.

The life of the best-known American of his era is worth retelling in this fashion because although Lincoln was himself extraordinary, much of his story is not. His father was born without land but managed to secure farms of his own—not just once, but repeatedly. When his Kentucky investments were twice wiped out by title disputes, he started over by moving on and ultimately prospered in Indiana. Although his final move, to Illinois, set him back financially, it also placed his son in a state with expanding possibilities. Abe, brought up on a series of farms, moved first to a small village, then to the state capital, and ultimately to Washington. Those moves traced the shifting geography of opportunity as America's agricultural society began to urbanize.

Back in England, the Lincolns had lived in Norfolk for generations, on land passing through the family. For better or worse, they were tied to the place, until three sons decided to cross the Atlantic, to a land where opportunities could be created and not just inherited. Had Thomas stayed in Washington County as a landless younger son; had he remained in Kentucky, wiped out by bad titles; had he lingered in Indiana, instead of gambling on new prospects, his son might never have come to Illinois. And had Abe stayed on the farm, where he was desperately needed; had he remained in New Salem, as his friends there urged; had he not gone to Washington, the states might not now still be united. Both men sought to improve their finances, their prospects, and their social relationships through their serial relocations. And although they both hit a variety of set-backs, mobility provided them with the chance to start again. In this respect, at least, the Lincolns were entirely typical of their time and place.

But not of ours. The lives of kids growing up in the United States today are much more tightly correlated with the incomes and occupations of their parents. In large part, that's because they're less likely to move. About two-thirds of children born today near the Lincoln homesteads in Kentucky and Indiana and Illinois still live in the same general areas as adults. Somewhere in Springfield right now there is surely a child every bit as bright and ambitious as Abraham Lincoln, but she is much less likely to ever leave the city and, as a consequence, unlikely to land a better job or earn a larger income than her parents.

Nineteenth-century Americans would be shocked by our stagnation. Contemporary observers agreed that the inclination to keep moving was a defining feature of the American character, though whether it was a virtue or a flaw was the subject of considerable debate. Those who came from Europe to see the experiment in democracy for themselves were particularly flummoxed. The American, Michel Chevalier discovered as he traveled about in the 1830s, "is always disposed to emigrate, always ready to start in the first steamer that comes along, from the place where he had but just now landed."

Chevalier was not the only Frenchman to be disconcerted by American mobility. "In the United States," Alexis de Tocqueville complained, "a man builds a house to spend his latter years in it, and he sells it before the roof is on: he plants a garden, and lets it just as the trees are coming into bearing: he brings a field into tillage, and leaves other men to gather the crops: he embraces a profession, and gives it up: he settles in a place, which he soon afterwards leaves, to carry his changeable longings elsewhere." He might well have been describing the life of Thomas Lincoln. Tocqueville found "something surprising in this strange unrest of so many happy men, restless in the midst of abundance," and diagnosed it as a sort of discontent organic to meritocracy, where no one is assigned a fixed station in life, and so each man imagines he can rise to the top.

"A Yankee will start off with his household gods, and seek a new home in the wilderness, with less fuss than a Cockney would make about packing up a basket of grub to go and pic-nic in Richmond Park," wrote the Englishman Henry Anthony Murray admiringly in 1857, even as he lamented the "total absence it exhibits of those ties of home" that he felt this betrayed. "Perhaps there is nothing more remarkable in the character of the Americans than the indifference with which they leave their old habitations, friends, and relations," Simon Ansley Ferrall concurred. That was a charge that stung, and one that some Americans also leveled against their countrymen. But most American accounts of the migratory urge differed from those of Europeans in one important respect. While visitors from abroad tended to focus on the constant movement, and on what migrants were leaving behind, Americans instead stressed what the migrants hoped to find.

"Migration has become almost a habit in the west," John Peck wrote in 1836. But it wasn't simply rootlessness to which he was pointing, but a determination to seek out a better life. "Any sober, industrious mechanic can place himself in affluent circumstances, and can place his children on an equality with the children of the merchant and professional community, by migrating to any of our new and rising western towns," he wrote. (He, like these other observers, had in mind white men, although such aspirations were by no means confined to them.)

American accounts of migration also stressed that it wasn't just their own condition that people sought to improve. "All was motion and change. A restlessness was universal," one historian, looking back on the country of his youth, later wrote. "Men moved, in their single life, from Vermont to New York, from New York to Ohio, from Ohio to Wisconsin, from Wisconsin to California, and longed for the Hawaiian Islands. When the bark started from their fence rails, they felt the call to change. They were conscious of the mobility of their society and gloried in it. They broke with the Past and thought to create something finer, more fitting for humanity, more beneficial for the average man than the world had ever seen." The language was grandiose, but then, so were the ambitions. Throughout the nineteenth century, and well into the twentieth, Americans remained remarkably mobile, and as a result their society remained fluid, their economy strong, and their communities vibrant.

"Westward the course of empire takes its way," the Anglican bishop George Berkeley wrote. The iconic image of American migration took its caption from Berkeley, a monumental mural displayed in the stairwell of the U.S. Capitol, showing a Pilgrim on a rock gesturing toward the Golden Gate, with pioneers streaming in to fill the vast wilderness. And although it concealed the brutality of the conquest, the boom-and-bust cycles of speculation, and the disease and deprivation, it also captured the essential flow of the population over the first half century of independence.

Expansion was, in fact, one goal of independence. Before the Revolution, most of the colonies had become fairly stable, even stagnant. Their clearest path to economic growth lay in the expansion of trade and the development of domestic manufactures. A careful study of nine New England families at the end of the eighteenth century showed the highest rates of geographic mobility among the middling classes. The rich were often content to stay where they were, and the poor lacked the resources to start over. But in the wake of the Revolution, with the opening of new land to the west, mobility increased—most sharply among those in the middle, but also among those toward the bottom. The newly available land in Kentucky, and then in the Northwest Territory, drew adventurers and younger sons, new arrivals and scions of established families, young men looking for a place to start and older ones looking for a fresh start.

The Northwest Ordinance, the Homestead Act, the Pacific Railroad Acts, the Mining Act—the legislation that opened the land for settlement and exploitation forms a familiar litany, drilled into high school students as if memorizing the titles and dates of bills might somehow produce an understanding of their significance. These bills accelerated the westward movement of the population, but they didn't level the playing fields on the prairie. It still took resources to buy land, to stake a claim to free land, even to fail and start over. Even so, ordinary laborers from the largest urban places were over-represented among those who moved out to the frontier in the mid-nineteenth century, and they made greater relative gains in wealth than most other migrants. And those who moved west improved the lives of those unable to follow. They expanded the American economy, bringing more food and raw materials east and opening new markets where they lived. Crucially, the new farms kept labor markets tight, although perhaps less by luring factory workers away from eastern cities than by hiring agricultural laborers, who saved up and then claimed farms of their own. In Europe, as agriculture mechanized, displaced workers drained from the countryside toward the cities, creating a glut of labor. In America, the ready availability of farmland meant that instead of moving toward urban centers in response to mechanization, farmworkers could acquire land of their own and boost overall productivity. Farmworkers' mobility also kept labor scarce and spurred higher wages across the board. It wasn't just the migrants themselves who benefited from migration; by moving, they enriched their whole society.

The results were dramatic. Imagine two sets of unskilled laborers, one in Britain and one in the United States, in 1850 as both societies navigated the Industrial Revolution. Thirty years later, only half the sons born to those in Britain would have managed to climb the social ladder to more skilled occupations. In the United States, more than four out of five would have done the same. But this was not the primary difference in their lives. In nineteenth-century Britain, a quarter of men over the age of thirty had relocated from one county to another, moving, on average, twenty-four miles. In the United States, nearly two-thirds of such men had moved between counties, and they had journeyed, on average, more than two hundred miles from home. The children of those who moved between American counties—think of Abraham Lincoln—were substantially more likely to also jump occupational brackets. Simply put, migration in America was more common, took place over longer distances, and produced better outcomes than it did in England, even at the height of its Industrial Revolution.

This is the familiar story of American migration, with new arrivals pushing back the frontier and settling in the plains. "There is land enough in America for the inhabitants of all Europe," Edward Everett said in 1852. And then, quite suddenly, it seemed as if there weren't.

———

By the time Frederick Jackson Turner stood up to deliver the conference paper that changed the world, his audience was half-asleep. The mercury outside had neared ninety degrees on that mid-July day in 1893, and though it had cooled a little by 8:00 p.m. when the historians began their presentations in Hall 3 of the Columbian Exposition, the air inside was stifling. Scholars had spent the day wandering the fairgrounds; some accepted Buffalo Bill's invitation to a special performance of his Wild West Show. Not all had bothered coming back that evening. And Turner was fifth to present, forced to follow a weighty paper on lead mining in Illinois and Wisconsin. Although he was thirty-one, the slender, youthful professor appeared little older than his students, a problem the addition of a brown mustache had not entirely corrected. Years later, a colleague searching his memory for impressions of the momentous event could recall only that the presentation had been met with bored indifference.

Turner looked out at his listless audience and began:

In a recent bulletin of the Superintendent of the Census for 1890 appear these significant words: "Up to and including 1880 the country had a frontier of settlement, but at present the unsettled area has been so broken into by isolated bodies of settlement that there can hardly be said to be a frontier line. In the discussion of its extent, its westward movement, etc., it can not, therefore, any longer have a place in the census reports." This brief official statement marks the closing of a great historic movement. Up to our own day American history has been in a large degree the history of the colonization of the Great West. The existence of an area of free land, its continuous recession, and the advance of American settlement westward, explain American development. . . . And now, four centuries from the discovery of America, at the end of a hundred years of life under the Constitution, the frontier has gone, and with its going has closed the first period of American history.

He told them that the world as they knew it was over, and hardly anyone noticed. For Turner, the closing of the frontier was more than a curiosity. He argued that "the forces dominating American character" had come from the "fluidity of American life" brought on by the "expansion westward with its new opportunities." The individualism, confidence, strength, and inventiveness of Americans, even their penchant for democracy, Turner attributed to the frontier. What he called its free land—almost entirely absent from his account of the frontier were the Native peoples whose land these European settlers were stealing—had secured the relative equality of the American condition. To declare the frontier closed, then, was to call into question whether the United States could continue to transform newly arrived immigrants into Americans and whether it would remain a viable democracy.

Turner was hardly the first to warn that the frontier was closing; others had worried about that prospect for decades. "The exhaustion of the public domain has removed one of the best openings for the foreigner who has no capital," one American journalist warned in 1887, adding that immigrants now "congregate in our cities, and, unable to obtain a living or to move westward, fill our charitable and penal institutions." But Turner wasn't offering a warning that the frontier was closing; he was presenting census evidence that it had, in fact, already closed. It was the empirical basis of the claim that had seized the public imagination. But Turner was wrong. His claim that the frontier had closed in 1890 was based on bad data and a misleading map, and there's good reason to believe Turner had fallen victim to an audacious act of fraud.

The frontier loomed large in the American imagination. For decades, the census had drawn it as a line on a map, marking the boundary between the settled land in the eastern part of the country and—at least as Americans saw it—the western wilderness. That line was clearly visible on the 1880 map and the 1900 map. But on the map that appeared in 1890, it was missing. And its absence was likely intentional.

The superintendent of the 1890 census, Robert Porter, suffered from an acute case of tenementophobia. The process of western settlement had "made better citizens and truer patriots than it is possible to produce amid the vice and wretchedness of the slums of our great cities," he wrote in 1891, shortly after the map was released. America, he noted, had once attracted the cream of the European crop, who had conquered the soil, built homes in the countryside, and didn't "flock together in the low tenement quarters of cities." He offered a dark warning against "the unrestricted admission of the diseased, half-fed swarms of helpless humanity from the purlieus of Southern European cities." America, Porter explained, had once welcomed immigrants to its "unlimited acres unsettled," but now, with "its unsettled area greatly reduced altogether," the tide of immigration had become a "curse and blight." Henry Gannett, who crafted the map itself, wrote in 1895 that the overrepresentation of Italians and Jews in American cities showed that "the most objectionable elements of the foreign-born population have flocked in the greatest proportion to our large cities, where they are in a position to do the most harm by corruption and violence," and that immigration had lowered the average "intelligence and morality" of Americans.

The best evidence suggests that the map on which Turner based his thesis was carefully rigged by Gannett to give the impression that America had run out of room for new arrivals. The 1890 map used a new coloring scheme, to blur the difference between settled and unsettled land, and it shaded in broad swaths of land to connect isolated blocs of settlement, even though they were too sparsely populated to count. As a result, the frontier line disappeared. In 1900, under a new superintendent of the census, a clearly visible frontier line magically returned on a map showing "the steady westward movement of the frontier line of settlement." But it was too late. Turner's proclamation that the frontier was closed had already seized the popular imagination.

The country, many Americans had once believed, offered almost endless opportunity, if only it could grow swiftly enough to take advantage of its rich abundance. But when Turner amplified the census's fraudulent claim that the available land had now been taken, it convinced many Americans that they had entered an age of scarcity. Turner himself soon fell into the pessimism his declaration helped bring about. In a series of essays, he worried aloud that newer waves of immigrants were a net "loss to the social organism of the United States" and that Jews, in particular, were so evolutionarily adapted to the "squalor and indecent conditions of a dangerously crowded population" that they would not thrive. While "the immigrant of the preceding period was assimilated with comparative ease . . . the free lands that made the process of absorption easy have gone."

But Porter, Gannett, and Turner were wrong. Recent scholarship has put the actual closure of the American frontier closer to 1910, but more crucially they were wrong about the sources of America's distinctive character. It wasn't the harsh conditions of the frontier that forged Americans but the habit of migration, the passion for locomotion. America would retain its capacity to absorb and acculturate new arrivals as long as its population continued to move toward new opportunities.

And most of all, they were mistaken about where to find the American frontier in 1890. They placed it somewhere out by the 100th meridian, but they were looking in the wrong place entirely.

In the early 1960s, a young doctoral student named Stephan Thernstrom, a leader of the New Left Club at Harvard, was hoping to solve a simple question that on its surface, at least, had nothing to do with migration: Why was there no socialism in America? The answer, he suspected, was that even the nineteenth-century Americans who began their lives as laborers or unskilled workers had a reasonable chance of advancing economically, becoming farmers or craftsmen or the proprietors of small shops. To prove that point, you'd have to identify hundreds of such young men and then spend years hunting them down in the records to see how they'd fared. So that's just what Thernstrom did.

He looked at Newburyport, a coastal town in Massachusetts, and found that its residents were indeed likely to move up economically. But the truly stunning revelation of his work, which he published as *Poverty and Progress* in 1964, was that people in Newburyport were astonishingly likely to move, period. Scholars, like other Americans, had largely assumed that American mobility was concentrated in the West, with a transitory zone along the frontier giving way to increasingly settled and sedentary lives farther east. But although Newburyport had been settled for two centuries, Thernstrom found that four out of five families departed over the course of thirty years. And Newburyport, if anything, might have been relatively sedentary.

When Thernstrom looked at Boston, zooming in on the decade between 1880 and 1890, the math was staggering. Over the course of a single decade, Boston gained an impressive 65,000 residents, growing to a city of 448,000. But add in the annual turnover, and the figure grows to an almost unimaginable 800,000 people arriving in Boston in just ten years and then, for the most part, departing. Those who feared and loathed cities in the nineteenth century often wrote about them as if they were diagnosing cardiovascular disease: streets choked with traffic, clogged waterways, unhealthy buildup of population, festering slums. Looking to the countryside, they saw vigor and vitality. But in the most crucial respects, they got it precisely backward. Cities were the beating heart of the young republic, driving the healthy circulation of the population. Young people and immigrants coursed into urban centers, moved around, and were pumped back out.

When Thernstrom saw this pattern, he assumed he was looking at evidence of failure, of a "floating proletariat" composed of men "ever on the move spatially but rarely winning economic gains as a result of spatial mobility." America, in other words, was split between a small number of successful migrants and a great, shifting mass of the dispossessed.

Those conclusions were necessarily speculative. Thernstrom could trace the lives of those who stayed in a particular city, but not of most of those who departed. Not until census records were digitized was it possible to tell what had happened to the members of the floating proletariat. In 1996, when the economist Steven Herscovici used these new digital tools to trace the lives of the workingmen who had left Newburyport, he found that almost all stayed in New England and most moved only short distances. Even so, they were substantially more likely than those who had stayed put to move up occupationally, to acquire land of their own to farm, and to accrue wealth. The proletariat wasn't floating; it was moving toward greater opportunity.

In the West, movement was visible at a glance. One English visitor to Cincinnati in the 1830s was struck by how quickly new towns appeared. "A log-house is still standing," he marveled, "which is shewn as the first habitation built by the backwoodsman, who squatted in the forest where now stands a handsome and flourishing city." In more settled areas, it was easier to miss the extent of the constant change. A visitor to Boston in 1880 who returned after a decade's absence would have seen a somewhat enlarged city, without any obvious signs that more than 700,000 souls had arrived, lived, labored, and left in his absence. But all the available evidence suggests that as great as geographic mobility might have been in the West, Americans in the East were relocating at far greater rates and achieving even greater success than their western counterparts.

In the colonial era, settlers planted new communities, but tended to remain on the land once they had claimed it. In the first half of the nineteenth century, the predominant flow was westward, because owning farmland or selling services to farmers was the surest path to success in a preponderantly agricultural nation. Migration began to proceed serially, with families relocating not once but several times in search of greater opportunity. Even as that westward flow crested, though, a new stream of migration was already swelling as people drained off the farmland in settled areas toward market towns and county seats. And in the second half of the century, from the farms and the towns and the small cities they moved to the great industrial metropolises. Estimates of migration in the nineteenth century are necessarily imprecise, but the best data suggest that the number of people moving to different states peaked in the decades before the Civil War. As the century wore on, instead of moving out to a new state along the frontier to claim a farm, more Americans moved from rural counties to nearby urban ones to find jobs. Add in the rising percentage of Americans growing up in urbanized places, who pursued opportunity by moving to new neighborhoods within their cities, and people were moving more often even as mobility between states was on the wane.

To see how this played out in practice, I want to introduce you to one of my ancestors. Josiah Bishop Andrews was born in Southington, Connecticut, in 1775, on his father's farm, in a town his grandfather had helped settle. But the young republic offered broader possibilities to an ambitious young man. Josiah attended Yale, in New Haven, then studied for the ministry in Hartford. He married a young woman from a distinguished local family. He was then sent as a missionary along the expanding frontier, preaching in western New York and Pennsylvania, before returning to take the pulpit of a church in Killingworth, Connecticut. He arrived on the cusp of the Second Great Awakening, and within two years the revival he led brought ninety new members into the church.

From that promising start, things went badly wrong for Josiah. His wife took seriously ill, with symptoms that sound—to a modern ear—like clinical depression. His congregation brought him up on charges before an ecclesiastical court over some sort of personal misconduct, and while he was acquitted, he was also dismissed from the pulpit. His thirty-fifth birthday found him disgraced and unemployed, with a disabled wife and four young children to feed. In the world into which he was born, he might well have sunk into poverty.

But by 1810, the chance to move from one place to another had begun to allow for second acts in American life. He moved to New York City and opened a school, somewhat grandly dubbing it the Scientific Institution and promising to educate his pupils not only in Greek, Latin, and French but also in drawing, navigation, and astronomy. The success of that venture helped put him through the College of Physicians and Surgeons, where he earned a medical degree in 1816. Next, he hopped across Staten Island Sound to Perth Amboy, New Jersey, to practice medicine and work as a health officer. He even returned to the pulpit in a Presbyterian church. But for all his resilience, Josiah seems to have been a difficult man. Within a few years, he was again brought up on charges by his congregants, and again left the ministry. When his father died, leaving him the farm, he went back to his native Southington. Ultimately, he returned to New York City and the practice of medicine, dying there in 1853. Josiah's story is hardly inspirational, but that's precisely why it's instructive. There was only one Abraham Lincoln in the young republic, but there were many men like Josiah Andrews who used their freedom to move to find new beginnings.

Forest, village, town, city—each was a new frontier, beckoning settlers onward into the unknown with the chance to raise themselves up. The frontier did not close in 1890; it just moved. When Turner lamented the closing frontier, he was remembering the country of his youth. But by the time he spoke, it was not farmland on the semi-arid plains that promised opportunity, but rather towns and cities, hubs of commerce and industry. He was right to trace the individualism, confidence, strength, and inventiveness of Americans—as well as their penchant for democracy—to the fluidity of American life. But that fluidity was a function of mobility, and even as farmland lost its allure, geographic mobility was actually increasing. During the westward expansion, Americans moved from state to state. Now they moved from rural counties to urban ones, and within cities the population churned without ceasing.

The great holiday of the mobile society was Moving Day, observed by renters and landlords with a giant game of musical houses. Moving Day was a festival of new hopes and new beginnings, of shattered dreams and shattered crockery—"quite as recognized a day as Christmas or the Fourth of July," as a Chicago paper put it. It was primarily an urban holiday, although many rural communities where leased farms predominated held their own observances. And nothing quite so astonished visitors from abroad as the spectacle of so many people picking up and swapping homes in a single day.

For months before Moving Day, Americans prepared for the occasion. Tenants gave notice to their landlords, or received word of the new rent. Then followed a frenzied period of house hunting, as people, generally women, scouted for a new place to live that would, in some respect, improve upon the old. "They want more room, or they want as much room for less rent, or they want a better location, or they want some convenience not heretofore enjoyed," *The Topeka Daily Capital* summarized. These were months of general anticipation; cities and towns were alive with excitement. Early in the morning on the day itself, people commenced moving everything they owned down to the street corners in great piles of barrels and crates and carpetbags, vacating houses and apartments before the new renters arrived. "Be out at 12 you must, for another family are on your heels, and Thermopylae was a very tame pass compared with the excitement which rises when two families meet in the same hall," warned a Brooklyn minister. The carmen, driving their wagons and drays through the narrow roads, charged extortionate rates, lashing mattresses and furnishings atop heaps of other goods and careening through the streets to complete as many runs as they could before nightfall. Rowdy youths burned the old straw used for bedding in the streets, and liquor lubricated the proceedings. Treasure hunters picked through the detritus in the gutters. Utility companies arrived on the scene and scrambled to register all the changes. Dusk found families settling into their new homes, unpacking belongings, and meeting the neighbors.

In St. Louis, the publisher of a city directory complained that a third of the families moved each year, and estimated that over a five-year span only one in ten remained at the same address. "Many private families make it a point to move every year," the *Daily Republican* of Wilmington, Delaware, reported. In some places, in fact, it was staying put from one year to the next that was seen as unusual. One story, perhaps apocryphal, told of a woman so ashamed not to be moving that she shuttered her windows so her neighbors would assume she had left. Moving Day, the humorist Mortimer Thomson quipped in 1857, had become "a religious observance not [to] be neglected by any man on pain of being considered an infidel and a heathen. The individual who does not move on the first of May 1 is looked upon . . . as a heretic and a dangerous man."

In southern New Jersey and Delaware, they observed the holiday on March 25, three months after landlords gave notice on Christmas Day—and in rural areas, early enough for farmers to move before the planting season. In Pittsburgh, Pennsylvania, it seemed only natural to hold it on April 1, in time for merchants to set up shop with spring wares. In Nashville and New Orleans, both in states blessed with mild weather, moving took place on October 1. Although Moving Day never gained quite the same popularity on the West Coast, other states observed it on a wide array of dates, but May 1 seems to have been the most popular. Few tenants had written contracts; by custom, and occasionally by statute, all unwritten leases expired on the same day. Moving Day was, *The Times-Democrat* of New Orleans attested, "an essentially American institution." Europeans might move "in a sober, quiet, old-world way, once in a decade or thereabout," the paper explained, but not annually, in the "excessively energetic manner of the nomadic, roving Americans." European visitors made a point of witnessing the peculiar ritual and included accounts of carts flying up and down the streets in their travelogues.

For some, Moving Day meant trauma and dislocation. In tightening markets, landlords seized the opportunity to jack up rents, and the courts were jammed with tenants pleading for some sort of relief, mostly to no avail. Families found themselves desperately scrambling for housing, forced to accept less, pay more, or both. The day sometimes brought racist violence as white ethnic communities sought to police their boundaries. Even those who moved volitionally had to pay the carmen, risk treasured belongings getting scraped or stolen, leave behind friends and neighbors, and start over. The costs were real.

But if the math of Moving Day worked out cruelly in constrained markets and for families in financial straits, it worked out very differently in most places and for most people throughout the nineteenth and early twentieth centuries as the housing stock rapidly expanded. You could spot the approach of Moving Day, a Milwaukee paper explained, by the sight of new buildings being rushed to completion and old houses being renovated, repaired, and restored. As wealthier renters snapped up the newest properties to come to market, less affluent renters grabbed the units they had vacated in a chain of moves that left almost all tenants better off. By concentrating their moves on a single day, tenants maximized the number of options that would be available to them. When rental markets softened, landlords faced the ruinous prospect of extended vacancies if they couldn't fill their units on Moving Day. Tenants used their leverage to demand repairs and upgrades to their houses or apartments or to bargain for lower rent.

The habit of annual moves was not confined to the poor or the working classes, and even among them many could have forgone the expense and hassle of relocation. So, if Americans didn't move year after year out of necessity, why did they do it? They were driven by hope. In London, complained the tenement reformer Blanche Geary, moving was properly regarded as a calamity, whereas in New York "the tenant lays down the law to the landlord, and if the landlord doesn't follow it, he picks up and gets out." Moving Day generally gave renters the upper hand. More than that, it allowed them to imagine a better and more prosperous life. A paper in West Virginia warned that Moving Day was a "delusion and a snare" and urged the man tempted "to spend his substance in the fleeting gratifications of the flesh" to regard Moving Day as "little better than Satan." The fleeting gratifications of the flesh, however, sounded pretty good to most Americans. "That people should move so *often* in this city, is generally a matter of their own volition," Lydia Maria Child wrote of New York. "Aspirations after the infinite, lead them to perpetual change, in the restless hope of finding something better and better still." Remove the sneer, and it's not a bad summary of the American dream.

The same force that drove Americans westward, that drove them to leave one farm behind to try their luck with a new one, that drove them off the farms and into county seats, that drove them into industrializing cities, and then drove them out to the suburbs that ringed them, also drove them to trade the house or apartment in which they lived for another on a regular basis. "We are a moving people," the *Chicago Tribune* offered as an explanation of Moving Day, "and therefore a lively, powerful one—it is motion that gives momentum." Americans understood their mobility as an exercise of choice, an act of autonomy, an expression of optimism. So long as speculators erected new buildings, so long as aging houses were turned over to the rental market or split up into flats, so long as immigrant entrepreneurs built new tenements, renters in every segment of the market could reasonably expect to find a new home each year that in some respect exceeded their old. And through the nineteenth century and into the early decades of the twentieth, as towns and cities grew at phenomenal rates, annexing adjoining communities and developing new tracts, the supply of homes steadily expanded.

With Moving Day, Americans made a habit out of change. The annual ritual of relocation, for all its inconveniences, provided the impetus to overcome inertia. Instead of accepting the cards they had been dealt, Americans kept drawing new ones. Moving was a defiant assertion of agency, an insistence that around the next corner or over the next hill lay something better, for anyone who had the nerve to seize it. It wasn't just a larger farmhouse or a newer apartment; they were choosing their own communities and authoring their own destinies. Settling for what they had carried with it a degree of social stigma and smacked of complacence or lethargy. Americans expected that they could find something better than what they presently enjoyed, if only they moved to take it.

In 1890, the census asked Americans for the first time about their housing and reported that the United States was a nation of renters. More than half the households in the United States were tenants, including a third of the farmers, two-thirds of the townsfolk, and three-quarters of the residents of the larger cities, and those proportions were rising. In some places, the number reached even higher. In Brooklyn, which billed itself as the City of Homes, it topped 81 percent; in Manhattan, it neared 94 percent. Moralists reacted with horror; one warned that those who did not own their homes would be easy recruits for anarchists and revolutionaries. But to a surprising extent, tenancy was a matter of choice, not a function of desperation. Land in much of the country remained cheap; homes could be constructed relatively affordably. "The ownership of a home hinders migration, and civilization has not yet proceeded far enough to do away with migration as a means of bettering one's condition," the pioneering (and aptly named) statistician George Kirby Holmes explained.

Americans of the late nineteenth century tended to look at houses the way Americans today look at cars or iPhones, useful contrivances that nevertheless lose their value quickly and are prone to rapid technological obsolescence. Just as a quarter of Americans today prefer to lease their vehicles, turning them in every year or two for the latest and most fashionable models, packed with cutting-edge features, most Americans then chose to lease their homes. Every year, newly constructed and freshly renovated homes offered wonders and marvels: water that ran out of taps, cold, and then hot; indoor plumbing and flush toilets and connections to sewer lines; gas lighting, and then electric; showers and bathtubs; ranges and stoves; steam heating. Factories created new materials and cranked out hinges, doorknobs, hooks, wooden trim, and railings in a dizzying array of styles. Colorful options for paints and wallpapers exploded. One decade's prohibitive luxury was the next's affordable convenience and the third's absolute necessity. A home was less an investment than a consumer good, to be enjoyed until the next model came within reach.

In New York City, the extraordinary institution of Moving Day began to erode in the early twentieth century. During World War I, New York faced an acute housing shortage, brought on by surging demand from people who had moved there to work on the docks and in the factories, churning out arms and munitions and supplies. Zoning, tenement reform laws, and wartime shortages of construction material had increased the cost of new housing. Landlords took advantage of constrained supply by imposing rent hikes and mass evictions, and tenants fought back with rent strikes and political campaigns. Renters, faced with the prospect of paying more and obtaining less, began to treat housing as a scarce resource that needed to be safeguarded, pushing for regulatory reforms—limits on rent hikes, requirements for maintenance, and tenure in their units—that would allow them to retain the housing they already had. But even as tenant organizing efforts began to shift the regulatory regime, they proved difficult to sustain; most tenants continued to believe that the best way to deal with unpleasant circumstances was to move someplace new. As wartime constraints eased, the tenants' movement sputtered out. As late as World War II, a million New Yorkers found new addresses each May 1.

Today, politicians piously intone that homeownership is the cornerstone of the American dream. But until recently, what kept Americans dreaming was the promise that their next home would be better than the one they already had. Moving Day embodied the very American expectation that change would be the constant of their lives and that it would bring expansive opportunities. The iconoclastic composer Charles Ives, told by his father that it was customary to start and finish in the same key, replied that it seemed as silly as having to die in the same house you were born in.

Some Americans worried that their constantly shifting population would produce an atomized society, leaving them unable to develop strong ties, invest in local institutions, maintain democratic government, or build warm communities. Mobility seemed rooted in individualism; people and families relocated to improve their own circumstances, severing their connections to home. In fact, that got the relationship between mobility and community precisely backward. Over the course of the nineteenth century and well into the twentieth, Americans formed and participated in a remarkable array of groups, clubs, and associations. Religious life thrived. Local businesses prospered. Democracy expanded. Communities flourished.

The same European observers who were so disconcerted by the American mania for mobility deeply admired this American ardor for association. "In the United States, associations are established to promote the public safety, commerce, industry, morality, and religion," Tocqueville marveled in 1840. "There is no end which the human will despairs of attaining through the combined power of individuals united into a society." Retracing Tocqueville's steps half a century later, James Bryce, the future British ambassador to the United States, found that organizations had become even more prevalent in the intervening years. "Associations are created, extended, and worked in the United States more quickly and effectively than in any other country," he wrote.

The key to vibrant communities, it turns out, is the exercise of choice. By the early nineteenth century, as associational life blossomed, American communities were transitioning from closed, corporate entities in which position and status were largely inherited into fluid, voluntary groupings. American individualism didn't mean people were disconnected from each other; it meant that they constructed their own individual identities by actively choosing the communities to which they would belong, instead of passively inheriting their identities.

Take, for example, religious faith. "In the United States," as the historian of American religion Lincoln Mullen has observed, "people not only *may* pick their religion, they *must*." As Englishmen sat in their pews, they could look through the slit windows at the stones marking the graves of generations of their ancestors who had lived in the same parish, and expect that their grandchildren would one day sit in the same pews and look at their graves in turn. Americans, though, disestablished their state churches—making religion, like residence, a matter of choice and not inheritance. As some Americans began to convert to new denominations and faiths, all Americans began to understand religion as a form of affiliation that had to be justified to oneself and explicable to others. Disestablishment opened up the possibility of choosing not to belong to any church, but for the great majority of Americans it intensified their religious commitments. Active membership in a church also delivered a transferable credential, providing entry into new communities. Think, again, of Thomas Lincoln. In Kentucky, he chose to join the wonderfully named Baptized Licking-Locust Association of Regular Baptists, an antislavery grouping of churches. When he moved his family to Indiana, he obtained a letter of fellowship from his old church, which allowed him to be received into a new church founded shortly after his arrival in Pigeon Creek.

To town and church, Americans added a host of other communal commitments—all of them actively chosen rather than passively inherited. At the beginning of the nineteenth century, many of these groups were purely local, but as mobility increased, the largest groups federated themselves, operating as local chapters of bigger organizations. Fraternal orders like the Masons and the Odd Fellows were the most successful of these groups, enrolling millions—or, perhaps more to the point, spawning thousands of local lodges that formed tight-knit communities, bound together in fictive brotherhood. Like churches, they provided instant community for new arrivals; most lodge rituals included a pause to welcome visitors from out of town and gave cards to members departing in good standing that they could use to join a lodge wherever their next home might be. "A man may be in a crowd and have no society," the Reverend L. V. Price told an assembly of one popular fraternal group, the Knights of Pythias, in 1885. But, he continued, "a Knight or his children, going as strangers into a strange place where there are brother Knights, can, if they choose to do so, find at once loyal friends."

Voluntary communities also brought considerable pain. Moving to a new town meant leaving friends and family behind. Americans agonized as they chose between religious denominations; making a decision meant selecting one community over another and alienating loved ones in the process. And not everyone could simply choose the voluntary associations they wished to join; many groups discriminated explicitly on the basis of race and gender and implicitly on the basis of ethnicity and class. Even belonging brought its own pains as groups routinely squabbled and split apart. If inheriting identities and affiliations could be stifling, it also brought the reassuring comfort of predictability; if consciously selecting them could be liberating, it also required painful choices.

The surge in voluntary associations in the nineteenth century presents a riddle; most empirical studies suggest that the longer people live in a particular place, the more groups to which they belong. When people intend to stay permanently, they also become more likely to join. Those findings have led researchers to think of mobility as an acid that dissolves social ties. If that were the case, however, we might expect to find the greatest social activity in relatively stagnant communities and the least in relatively mobile ones. Instead, the opposite appears to be true. Early in the nineteenth century, New England was a hotbed of associational activity, but as the century progressed, the densest concentrations of voluntary associations could be found in the small and midsized cities of the midwestern states, where many groups had their largest state-level chapters, and in the West, where there were even more groups per capita. And throughout the United States, rates of membership far surpassed those of Europe.

What if we flip the question around? Instead of asking when and where people belonged to the greatest number of groups, let's ask when they were likeliest to join them. The new members of most voluntary associations signed up in their early adulthood, often shortly after marriage or the arrival of their first child. In Massachusetts, the typical new member of the Knights of Pythias in the late nineteenth century was in his mid-thirties. Some Pythians quickly lost interest, or moved away, and a third were gone within five years. For others, it was a lifelong affiliation. Viewed this way, the apparent contradiction dissolves. Americans, at times and places of high mobility, tended to seek out groups and organizations early after arriving someplace new in the hope that they had found a permanent community. Most voluntary associations posted a steady rate of annual attrition; the difference between thriving, active chapters and those that withered away lay in how many new members joined each year, not in how many departed. Groups located in growing communities with a steady flow of new arrivals prospered, because the migrants invested the effort necessary to build social ties. In stagnant communities, the steady rate of attrition whittled away the membership, and no new neighbors arrived to compensate.

America's distinctively vibrant civil society, in other words, is a by-product of the unusual frequency with which Americans move to new places. Change is uncomfortable. Left to their own devices, most people will stick to ingrained habits, to familiar circles of friends, to accustomed places. When people move, though, they leave behind their old jobs, connections, identities, and seek out new ones. They force themselves to show up at a new church on Sunday, or to try out a voluntary association, despite the awkwardness. It's people who remain where they are who tend to end up bowling alone.

Americans who moved to new states formed voluntary associations to hang on to their sense of identity, just as immigrants formed their *Landsmanschaften* and other groups for people who shared a hometown. Seattle had its New England Club, and Minneapolis its Pennsylvania Club; New Orleans had its Boston Club, and Boston its Southern Club. People moved out of Plymouth in Massachusetts, and people moved into new Plymouths in Vermont, North Carolina, Indiana, and Wisconsin. The older agricultural states along the Eastern Seaboard watched their young people drain away. By the end of the nineteenth century, four out of every ten people born in Vermont were living somewhere else—an exodus equaled only by Ireland, the European nation with the greatest rate of emigration. In 1899, the governor of the neighboring state of New Hampshire, Frank Rollins, invited "all its native-born sons and daughters living in other states" to return for Old Home Week. "They come not only from points in New England, but from the far distant south and west," *The Boston Globe* reported, as the children of the Granite State flooded back by the thousands. The idea swiftly spread through other states. The annual pilgrimages were marked with picnics, parades, grandiloquent speeches, and endless quantities of execrable verse. Homecomings soon spread to colleges, which welcomed their alumni back to campus for a weekend of football, and then to high schools, which held dances and crowned their kings and queens. Only in this remarkably mobile nation could an institution so thoroughly local as a high school assume that enough of its graduates would have drifted elsewhere to make their return to town on a particular weekend an annual event. But after the celebrations were done, and the last choruses of "Auld Lang Syne" drifted off into the wind, the migrants returned to their adopted states, places that had become home.

Mobility helped integrate the various regional cultures of the United States into a coherent national identity. But it also made America remarkably capable of absorbing immigrants, rendering it a particularly attractive destination for waves of people seeking to improve their lives. The playwright Israel Zangwill called America a melting pot in which the base metals of the Old World would fuse into a superior American alloy. The metaphor implied the continuous mixing of the separate elements as its essential mechanism; it took spatial mobility to be the means by which a common American identity might be created. Looking out on "the harbour where a thousand mammoth feeders come from the ends of the world to pour in their human freight," the main character of *The Melting-Pot* exclaims, "Ah, what a stirring and a seething!" President Theodore Roosevelt was deeply affected by the play, telling Zangwill that it numbered "among the very strong and real influences upon my thought and my life." This was one ideal, in which mobility would homogenize a culturally and ethnically diverse population around a vaguely Anglo-Saxon standard.

The philosopher Horace Kallen, though, saw in the nation's diversity not a weakness to be corrected but a potential strength. Kallen came to the States as a small child, with his German Jewish family, and trained at Harvard and Oxford. He suggested America embrace what he termed "cultural pluralism." He was keenly aware of America's geographic mobility: "Hardly anyone seems to have been born where he lives, or to live where he has been born." But Kallen insisted that it was both naive and misguided to expect this mixing of peoples to erase all differences. Instead, he argued, a healthy democracy should be built around voluntary communities. "The family, the tribe, the caste, the nationality, the church, the guild, the state, were all . . . hereditary associations, into every one of which, it was supposed, men were born; within which all had predestined stations," Kallen wrote. "The history of freedom, of the expansion of democracy, has been largely and broadly the tale of how this rigid, involuntary, predestined status has been getting replaced by voluntary contract, and free association has superseded involuntary." Ethnicity and nationality were best regarded in this context, he argued, not as immutable and dangerous distinctions, but as "simply another among the modes of association with his fellows in which the individual lives and moves and has his being."

In the voluntary society constructed by American mobility, some immigrants turned their hereditary identities like ethnicity and nationality into matters of active choice. They could pursue Zangwill's vision, discarding their inherited traditions, or Kallen's, rooting their identity in a community of their fellow immigrants. They could stay in the old neighborhood, surrounded by the familiar shops and smells and voices of immigrant life, or leave it behind. The transformation of nationality into a chosen identity led some to assimilate and others to embrace the nationalism of their native lands with a fervor that outstripped most of those back home. Often, this expressed itself in the form of still more voluntary associations, like the Fenian Brotherhood. But the great majority of immigrants trod a middle path, joining some groups rooted in their ethnic communities alongside others that were not; observing their traditional holidays but adding a Thanksgiving feast.

Different groups, of course, were able to exercise these choices to widely varying degrees, depending on where they sat along the shifting and contested gradient of whiteness. For Black Americans, there was scarcely any choice at all. The United States has been defined, in many ways, by its racism and xenophobia. Communities policed their boundaries with lethal violence, and nativism surged in waves of bigotry. Protestants burned down the Ursuline Convent in Charlestown, Massachusetts, in 1834; in Philadelphia, a decade later, some five thousand militia were needed to restore order during a nativist riot; in 1891, nativists lynched eleven Italian Americans. And these are just a few entries in a long, sad list. But even groups that faced extreme hostility generally managed to gain greater degrees of acceptance over time. The exclusion, discrimination, and even violence that many Americans faced were, unfortunately, all too common in the world. What made the United States distinctive was that, alongside these ills, American culture offered an unparalleled measure of opportunity, and its shortcomings were made all the more painful because it held out the possibility of a better alternative.

The anthropologist Natalia Khanenko-Friesen has written about a corner of the Ukrainian village of Hrytsevolia, near Lviv, that is still known as Madiary—*Hungarian*—a hundred years after a villager and

World War I veteran brought home a bride from Hungary. Her descendants still live there, marked as outsiders. Such stories could be told about the villages in every land from which immigrants came to America. But within the United States, mobility produced a different set of social expectations. The land where the Lincolns settled in Illinois is not known today as Hoosierville, and the descendants of Indianans are not still branded as outsiders. Instead, Illinois itself is known as the Land of Lincoln, named for a man born in Kentucky to Virginia parents. American communities were too new, their populations too mobile, their boosters too ambitious, to make the barrier between the insiders and the outsiders impermeable. American Indians could claim indigeneity; the settlers who drove them off their land could not. As time went on, of course, the older inhabitants of many communities did try to lay claim to the places in which they lived, often as a means of excluding newer arrivals. From the First Families of Virginia to the Mayflower Society to the Early Settlers Association of Cuyahoga County, they formed their own voluntary associations, devoted to the preservation of their primacy. But such efforts to create a hereditary American aristocracy ultimately failed, doomed by the mobility of the population.

President John Quincy Adams, a popular anecdote relates, once asked an Irishman how he liked the United States. "Indeed, sir," said the Irishman, "I like it very much. I like it so much, that I intend soon, *to become* a native!" The joke was told at the immigrant's expense, but it also illuminated a broader truth. If in the villages from which so many Americans had come, a family might live for generations and remain branded as foreigners, here was a land in which membership was mainly a matter of choice. You had to be born an Irishman, but an American was something you could become.

But just as this migratory world was reaching its zenith, it faced a fierce challenge. Some Americans were unhappy with the mixing of peoples it entailed. If mobility had enabled pluralism, it also exacerbated racism and xenophobia. America was growing more prosperous, more tolerant, and more democratic by letting people move to the communities they chose. Not everyone thought that was a good idea.

PART II

CHAPTER FIVE

DIRTY LAUNDRY

In World War I, my great-grandfather won the Croix de Guerre driving ambulances in France. He commanded thirteen thousand troops in the next war, and Prince Umberto hung the Order of the Crown of Italy around his neck. When his time in uniform was done, he retired to Connecticut on his colonel's pension, having survived the bullets, bombs, and shells with nary a scratch. It was zoning that killed him. One evening in the winter of 1961, he went before his town's Zoning Board of Appeals to secure permission to park a trailer on his property. I can't tell you exactly how the hearing proceeded, except that by the end of the night he was dead of a heart attack. A close encounter with land-use law can do that to you.

He had been born at a time when Americans could largely do as they wished with the land they owned, provided they didn't harm their neighbors. By the time he passed on, parking his own trailer on his own residential property required a special dispensation from an appointed government commission, even if no one objected and no one was harmed. Zoning—the system of segregating land by its uses—had transformed the country within a single life span. But it didn't start in Connecticut, and it didn't start with trailers. It began on the other side of the country, with a seemingly innocuous law.

On July 2, 1885, Modesto, California, declared that it would be illegal to operate a laundry "except within that part of the city which lies west of the railroad track and south of G Street." Unlike earlier rules, which regulated *how* businesses were built and operated, the Modesto ordinance aimed to limit *where* they could operate. A way of using land that was perfectly acceptable in one neighborhood would be unacceptable in others. "We can see nothing unreasonable in the ordinance," the California Supreme Court decided, and upheld the law.

Neither the city nor the court announced that in sustaining the nation's first zoning law, they were overturning centuries of legal precedent. But the justices were well aware the law was not what it seemed. Modesto's ordinance was a vicious attack on the city's Chinese residents, an attempt to deny them the chance to pursue economic opportunity through geographic mobility. The white citizens of Modesto and other California cities had been trying for years to purge their streets of Chinese immigrants. Where arson, murder, and mob violence had failed, zoning would succeed. By affirming the law, the court was effectively upholding a city's right to segregate its population, as long as it maintained a veneer of plausible deniability. And over the years that followed, this new tool would be used to direct, limit, and, ultimately, choke off American mobility.

The story starts with the discovery of gold in California, in 1848. The electrifying news sent Americans racing across the country and around Cape Horn, moving toward opportunity. Once again, they treated the Native population as little more than a hindrance to their own ambitions, using lethal violence to shove aside the tens of thousands of American Indians in the newly acquired territory. In addition to the Native peoples, there were perhaps eight thousand residents in California at the time; by 1880, that population had increased more than a hundredfold. People arrived from all over the United States, bringing with them varied legal traditions and sharply differing expectations, but they shared the basic tenets of the American tradition of mobility. They expected to move freely in pursuit of opportunity themselves, but as soon as they arrived in their new communities, they also expected to be able to exclude those they found undesirable. And the two impulses remained unreconciled.

The towns they planted in the West weren't the young orchards of covenanted communities, carefully tended by a cohort of like-minded settlers. They were thickets grown from a medley of wind-borne seeds, springing up wherever conditions proved inviting. The elaborate system of warning out was scarcely practiced any longer in the states from which they departed, and scarcely taken up where they landed. The rush for gold, moreover, sped California through its stages of development, isolated farmsteads turning rapidly into villages, growing into towns, and maturing into cities within a few years. San Francisco went to bed in 1848 a sleepy little port town of perhaps a thousand, and woke up the next year a full-fledged city, twenty-five times that size. No American territory had ever been settled so swiftly. Everything was up for grabs—the gold, the opportunities, the land, the customers—and everyone wanted their share.

The fierce competition, coupled to the bitter reality that most would never strike it rich, led to equally fierce discrimination against the Chinese prospectors. They were slowly forced away from the mines and then squeezed out of most other employment. But they found one opportunity still available to them; they could wash clothes. Men flooded into California from all over the world, but women were slower to arrive. Though labor of all kinds was scarce, and therefore expensive, for tasks that women usually performed—and which most men preferred not to perform themselves—the cost was prohibitive. Prospectors had resorted to sending their clothes to Hawaii to be laundered; now the Chinese stepped in to meet the demand. Within a decade, they dominated the laundry trade.

At first, the arrangement seemed to suit everyone. In urban areas, Chinese immigrants clustered together in ethnic enclaves, where small shops offered goods and services to workers coming back from the goldfields and the railroads. But as laundries proliferated, and other opportunities dried up, entrepreneurial launderers left the Chinatowns to set up shop in central business districts. They found plenty of patrons. The wealthy could count on hired help to clean their clothes at home, but for everyone else cheap and reliable laundry services were a tremendous convenience. The closer the stores were to their homes, in fact, the greater the convenience. So, much as coffee shops do today, laundries followed their customers out of saturated business districts and into residential districts. The trouble was that their Chinese proprietors usually lived inside the shops. And as they moved into predominantly white areas, the Golden State seethed with anti-Chinese bigotry.

In 1879, the Workingmen's Party swept to statewide power, with the slogan "The Chinese must go!" The agitation boiled over into arson, murder, and riots. Washhouses, where the launderers worked, were a particular target, as both the largest employers of Chinese residents and their most visible presence in the lives of white Californians. Pandering to racist passions, Congress effectively barred immigration by Chinese women in 1875 and, with the Chinese Exclusion Act of 1882, blocked Chinese immigrants from obtaining citizenship, halting most immigration by Chinese men.

White citizens of Modesto, a city surrounded by the rich farmland of California's Central Valley, first tried vigilante violence to force out Chinese residents. In 1879, upset at the "encroachment of Chinatown" on residential districts, a mob set off "with the firing of pistols and the shouting of many masculine voices" pulling down suspected opium houses and piling faro tables and pipes into a bonfire in a public square. The violence failed to drive out the city's Chinese residents. In 1884, more than a hundred men in "most ghostly attire" wearing black masks and calling themselves the San Joaquin Valley Regulators, rampaged through Chinatown. They raided opium houses, knocked down one Chinese man who attempted to flee, and even assaulted a white police officer who tried to stop them. In June 1885, a washhouse and a store in Chinatown burned down, in an apparent arson attack. Despite the unrelenting assaults, Modesto's Chinese residents held fast. And following the familiar pattern, they began to set up their laundries in residential neighborhoods.

A week after the washhouse fire, the *Modesto Bee* complained that laundries have "stolen almost into the heart of our city," asking why the authorities wouldn't move them. Railroad tracks cut through the center of Modesto in those years, serving as an unofficial boundary. An 1885 map located Chinatown in the area west of the tracks and south of G Street. It also showed two Chinese washhouses operating east of the tracks and a block to the north. It was the residents of that block, and the one next to it, who petitioned the city council, a day after the *Bee* published its complaint, for the removal of "certain Chinese laundries" to the other side of the tracks, "to what is known as Chinatown." Two weeks later, the city council obliged, passing its zoning ordinance. The Chinese were not mentioned in the legislation. Instead, it simply designated a district for laundries, one whose boundaries happened to be precisely the same as those of Chinatown. The ghetto that Modesto had failed to impose with violence, it would now attempt to enforce with land-use law.

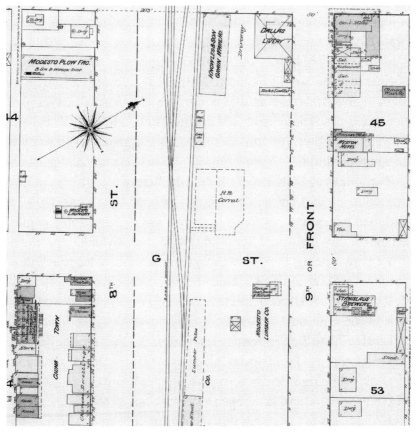

This Sanborn map of Modesto from 1885 shows both Chinatown on the lower left and, in Block 45 on the upper right, two Chinese laundries that had moved north of G Street and east of the tracks, drawing the ire of Modesto's white citizens and producing the nation's first zoning ordinance.

The ordinance went into effect at the beginning of August. Landlords encouraged laundries to stay, promising to stand by their tenants and to challenge the law. Customers continued to patronize the stores. On August 5, police arrested four laundry operators along with fourteen of their assistants. Modesto suffered from an acute shortage of white shirts that week. The town marshal opened one of the shuttered stores on Sunday so that churchgoers could reclaim their Sunday finest. A week later, colored shirts were in style, the better to hide the dirt.

Hang Kie was the first to be tried, convicted by an all-white jury of operating a laundry outside the proper zone, then fined $100 and sentenced to twenty days in jail. The rest of the launderers posted bond, moved their laundries west of the tracks, and waited to see how his case would play out. Kie's attorneys filed a writ of habeas corpus to argue for his freedom. Kie paid a steep price, though, for allowing his trial to be used as a test case in defense of civil rights. Before his case could be heard, another inmate in the jail, arrested for vagrancy, committed an "infamous assault" that left Kie "in a precarious condition."

The following March, Kie's case came before the Supreme Court of California. Kie's lawyers argued that the statute was unreasonable and that, because its regulatory scheme was not uniformly applied across the city, it violated Kie's rights to his person and his property. They were arguing, in other words, that the most basic principle of zoning—that certain uses of land are fine in some areas of a city and, though they do no harm, not fine in others—violated the state and federal constitutions.

Legally, Kie was on extremely solid ground. The common-law tradition offered two great principles for a well-regulated society: *sic utere tuo,* or the right to use your own property only so long as it did not injure others; and *salus populi,* or the welfare of the people. These were the bases for what lawyers termed the police powers of local government—not the powers of the police department, but rather, the government's authority to regulate people and property so as to advance the public good. But police powers were general rules, applied uniformly, and the actions taken under their authority had to be reasonable means of advancing their ends. If laundries were a public nuisance, as their critics alleged—posing fire hazards with their boiling kettles, filling drains with their malodorous soaps, raising the threat of cholera—then cities could inspect them, regulate their operation, and impose building standards. Modesto, though, wasn't proposing to make laundries any safer, or to keep them away from residential areas; it just wanted to relocate the Chinese operators of the laundries to Chinatown, which was even more densely populated than the rest of the city.

In 1880, a member of the San Francisco Board of Supervisors had asked the city attorney to determine "whether or not this Board has the legal right to restrict and confine the keeping and carrying on of laundries and wash-houses by the Chinese to a certain designated portion of this city," and if so, to prepare the order with the locations left blank for the board to complete. The city attorney replied that San Francisco had the power to pass rules protecting against fire, safeguarding public health, and limiting public nuisances—the familiar litany of police powers. If the board determined it was necessary on those bases, it could confine laundries and washhouses to a designated district, as it had already done for slaughterhouses, where the waste posed a threat of disease and the stench a clear nuisance. The city attorney didn't, however, bother drafting such an order, presumably because it was unclear how confining laundries to a specific district—say, Chinatown—might be necessary on those grounds. There is no record to indicate that Modesto consulted an attorney before it passed its ordinance, or it might well have abandoned that effort, too.

The California Supreme Court had a wealth of precedent to consult as it considered the Modesto ordinance. Cities had grown inventive in their cruelty as they tried to regulate Chinese laundries out of existence, and not just on the West Coast. In 1880, Brooklyn passed an ordinance requiring all laundries to be licensed to those with American citizenship, which Chinese immigrants were uniquely barred from obtaining. "I am opposed to Chinese, and to giving them any encouragement," the alderman who proposed the measure explained. Left unchecked, he continued, Chinese immigrants would "sweep over our country in such multitudes that they might become, not the masters of any party, color, or nationality, but masters of all white men."

Other cities tried their own measures, but San Francisco outdid them all. In 1873 and again in 1876, the city tried taxation, imposing a quarterly fee of $2 on laundries with a single horse-drawn cart for deliveries, $4 for two, but a hefty $15 for those without any, like the Chinese laundries that made their deliveries on foot. In 1880, the Board of Supervisors passed a pair of rules banning laundries housed in wooden buildings, unless licensed at its discretion, and barring the sort of rooftop scaffolding used solely by Chinese laundries. It carefully struck the word "Chinese" from the ordinance so that it wouldn't violate the Fourteenth Amendment's guarantee of equal protection. In May 1880, it tried stipulating that any laundry operating east of a certain line—effectively, in the built-up area of the city, including Chinatown—required the consent of at least twelve citizens and taxpayers who lived on the block. And in October of that year, the city took a different approach, mandating that laundries be closed between 10:00 p.m. and 6:00 a.m., ostensibly because of the fire hazards inherent in overnight operation. In fact, the law targeted Chinese launderers, who often leased shared facilities to reduce overhead, running in two shifts around the clock.

The courts were generally skeptical of efforts to eliminate Chinese laundries. Both versions of the laundry-cart tax were struck down; a county court judge found that the first version "discriminates unjustly against the poor" and "substantially prohibits them from the pursuit of a useful and worthy calling," and a district judge found the second did much the same. The law requiring consent from twelve citizens drew a harsh rebuke from a federal judge. Operating a laundry, he wrote, "is not of itself against good morals, or contrary to public order or decency. It is not offensive to the senses, or disturbing to the neighborhood where conducted, nor is it dangerous to the public safety or health. It would be absurd to affirm that it is." A city could impose inspections or safety restrictions on a laundry, but it had no basis for telling people they could not operate one on land they leased or owned. If he were to allow this ordinance to stand, the judge continued, a city might similarly restrict its citizens from the pursuit of any other lawful occupation, even on their own land—something he doubted could be authorized "under our form of government." Moreover, the city couldn't delegate its authority to citizens in that way. But the maximum-hours ordinance was affirmed by the California Supreme Court in 1884, and in January 1885, having wound its way to the U.S. Supreme Court, it was upheld in *Barbier v. Connolly* as a reasonable exercise of police powers to safeguard against the threat of fire.

That thin reed was enough for the California Supreme Court to uphold Hang Kie's conviction. The justices pointed to the decisions in the maximum-hours case and said that Modesto's law was also a "police or sanitary regulation" and, as such, within the city's power to enforce. The decision was conspicuously silent on the aspect of Kie's case that most distinguished it from those precedents. Modesto had restricted a particular use of land to a specific district, and it had done so without even the fig leaf of public necessity. There was nothing in the ordinance to suggest that confining laundries to Chinatown was necessary to prevent fires, protect public health, or abate a public nuisance. If the laundries were dangerous, then forcing them into Chinatown—an even more densely packed residential neighborhood than the rest of the city—would only increase the danger they posed. But of course, as the court certainly understood, the actual purpose of the ordinance was to keep Chinese immigrants out of white neighborhoods. If the popularly elected justices did not share that goal themselves, they knew their voters did. So, they waved their hands, mumbled the magic words "police or sanitary regulation," and affirmed Kie's conviction.

Not that it was immediately clear how much their decision had changed. For one thing, federal courts began mounting a more aggressive attack on anti-Chinese discrimination. Emboldened by its victory in *Barbier*, San Francisco tried enforcing its licensing ordinance for wooden structures. The California Supreme Court affirmed it, but it was no longer the last word. In the crucible of the Civil War and Reconstruction, the nation had forged a stronger federal government and then tasked it to ensure that it lived up to its founding creed of equality. The Reconstruction Amendments to the Constitution took what had once been local matters and subjected them to federal review. A federal court expressed skepticism over the wooden structures ordinance, and the matter wound up back before the U.S. Supreme Court. The decision came down just a month after Kie's conviction was affirmed. The justices learned that 310 of the 320 laundries in the city were housed in wooden buildings and that only 1 of 80 such white-owned laundries had been denied a permit, while permits had been denied to Chinese applicants, even if their facilities fully complied with health and fire codes. "No reason whatever, except the will of the supervisors, is assigned why they should not be permitted to carry on, in the accustomed manner, their harmless and useful occupation, on which they depend for a livelihood," the court found. The justices ordered the laundry workers released, declaring for the first time that the unequal administration of a law could render it unconstitutional.

But even a law equally administered could draw the ire of a federal judge. Two other California municipalities—Stockton and Napa—followed Modesto's lead, passing ordinances entirely excluding laundries from a defined district encompassing most of their cities. The Stockton measure, dressed up as a land-use law, was another effort to purge the community of its Chinese residents. Its prime sponsor told his fellow city councillors that the measure was the best way he knew "for getting rid of the Chinese." A local newspaper reporter conducting man-on-the-street interviews found strong support for the measure in Stockton, from residents saying things like "Yes, I want to see the Chinese go out of town" or "The objection to the Chinese is not on account of the laundries specifically. Everybody knows that that was only a pretense." Stockton's ordinance, as the federal district judge Lorenzo Sawyer pointed out, restricted laundries to still-unsettled marshland southwest of the city. The ordinance harmed laundry operators by limiting "their use of their property" and so violated the Fourteenth Amendment's due process clause and, by banning commercial laundries in the same places where people could still wash their own clothes or conduct other business, violated the equal protection clause. Moreover, he found, the city could regulate public nuisances, but it could not arbitrarily declare things to be a nuisance if they were not, and laundry shops were not.

Citing his ruling in the Stockton case, Sawyer also struck down the Napa ordinance, which had confined laundries to Chinatown, on a narrow finger of land between the Napa River and Napa Creek. Taken together, this pair of rulings was understood to render the California Supreme Court's decision in the Modesto case something of a dead letter. In 1897, a federal judge considering a San Mateo law that mimicked Modesto's cited a subsequent ruling of the California Supreme Court in striking it down, noting that *In re Hang Kie* "has been virtually, although not expressly, overruled." But it turned out that the Modesto precedent was only mostly dead, and mostly dead is still slightly alive.

The Modesto ordinance had flowed from a simple premise: The majority of the city's voters wanted to keep people of Chinese descent out of their neighborhoods. They had tried violence and intimidation. They had tried sponsoring a series of "white labor laundries" to which "no Chinese need apply," all of which quickly folded. They had watched as San Francisco and other cities used a wide array of regulatory tools in a vain attempt to drive Chinese laundries out of business. And they were left to grapple with two certainties. The first was that however they might vote at the polls, most ordinary Californians valued the services and prices of Chinese laundries. Left to their own devices, the people of Modesto would continue to patronize such laundries, and their proprietors would compete for business on the basis of proximity, moving to live among their customers. The second was that any rule that targeted the Chinese explicitly was sure to be struck down by the federal courts.

The genius of the Modesto ordinance was that it provided a facially neutral rule, simply designating a district for the laundries, west of the tracks and south of G Street. There wasn't even a word for this sort of law, yet. Soon, it would be known as districting, and then as zoning. But by any name, it reflected a principle of immense power: control what can be done upon the land, and you control the prospects of the people who inhabit it.

In 1904, Los Angeles commenced designating different districts for different uses in piecemeal fashion. As in Modesto, the process began with the exclusion of laundries from several wards. Five years later, the city designated seven industrial districts and, shortly afterward, declared that the rest of the city comprised residential districts. (In an ironic twist, this pioneering zoning ordinance was touted as a solution to NIMBYism; by removing residences from industrial districts, the ordinance would eliminate the complaints of neighbors about the factories operating in their backyards.) Laundries, naturally, were on the list of businesses confined to the industrial districts. A man named Quong Wo suddenly found that the laundry he had been operating for years was now illegal, despite having two years remaining on his lease. He operated it in a mixed-use neighborhood, close to single-family homes, apartment buildings, and lodging halls, but also churches and a school, a drugstore, carpenter shop, and dance hall. He was selected by his fellow launderers to test the law and was arrested. Seven neighbors testified that his laundry had never caused any problems. The case wound up before the California Supreme Court, which was left to consider whether a city could draw lines on a map and establish certain uses for certain districts. And, facing the question of whether zoning should be allowed, it returned to one of its own neglected precedents.

"It has been held in this state, that an ordinance prohibiting the carrying on of the business within a prescribed portion of a town is a lawful exercise of the police power," the court wrote, citing *In re Hang Kie.* "The correctness of this decision has never, so far as we can ascertain, been questioned by this court or the United States supreme court." If Modesto could do it, the court said, so could Los Angeles. In fact, any city could limit certain uses to certain districts, so long as it could claim to protect public health, morals, safety, or comfort. The court explained that some businesses might not be a nuisance per se, but still create some measure of discomfort in their neighbors.

The public struggled to make sense of this strange new arena of law. In 1931, the American Academy of Political and Social Science devoted a special issue of its *Annals* to offer "a comprehensive view of the zoning problem," turning to a pioneer of the field, G. Gordon Whitnall, to introduce the topic. Whitnall was a serial enthusiast of reforms. He began his political career as a socialist, then advocated for proportional representation and nonpartisan elections, and finally caught the city planning bug. In 1913, he created the Los Angeles City Planning Association, and starting in 1920, he was the inaugural director of the city's planning department. Zoning wasn't an academic pursuit for Whitnall; it was his life's work. And his contribution to the *Annals,* titled, "History of Zoning," aimed to establish how it had all begun. It was Modesto, he wrote, that had enacted "the first zoning ordinance."

Without the "high feeling of racial prejudice" in California in those years, Whitnall observed, it was unlikely the courts ever would have affirmed the early zoning statutes, with their radical expansion of local authority. Modesto's law, he admitted, was "unquestionably a move toward racial segregation." But he congratulated himself that since the statute had not openly stated its purpose, "now that the racial element is eliminated," the Modesto statute itself "would be thoroughly in keeping with all of the accepted practices of zoning." Indeed, he said, it has a "decidedly modern ring." Whitnall was half-right. If Modesto's law had a thoroughly modern ring, it was precisely because its formula—masking the language of exclusion in the arid prose of land-use law—would prove to be remarkably enduring.

Hang Kie's laundry had indeed created some measure of discomfort in his neighbors, but not because it violated health or fire standards. His only crime had been doing what his persecutors had done, coming to Modesto to improve his lot in life. He had established his laundry close to his customers because that's what they wanted. His landlord had stood by him. He had helped pioneer a strategy that would animate later civil rights movements, going to court to challenge a racist law. And yet like Quong Wo, he lost—not because the law had been against him, but because the courts yielded to overwhelming popular demand to produce a mechanism to segregate cities, excluding vulnerable minorities from the best opportunities.

An undated photo shows China Alley, including the Wa-Chung Laundry. Hang Kie's laundry relocated to this area following the passage of the ordinance.

COURTESY OF THE MCHENRY MANSION & MUSEUM, MODESTO, CALIFORNIA.

Kie moved his laundry to Chinatown, but he didn't stop trying to raise himself up. Within a few years, he had saved $400 to send back to China for a bride. Their traditional Cantonese wedding was a celebration for Modesto's entire Chinese community. The bride was met at the station with a coach festooned with lanterns, then wed in a gown of red silk as strings of firecrackers were set off in celebration. Together, they had six children. And they raised them in the zone to which the city had assigned them—west of the tracks, south of G.

Hang Kie accepted imprisonment to challenge an unjust law. Today, though, there is no bronze statue of Hang Kie with an inscription on its base—IN HONOR OF THE CIVIL RIGHTS PIONEER WHO VOLUNTARILY SURRENDERED HIS OWN FREEDOM SO THAT OTHERS MIGHT MOVE FREELY—no plaque on a building, no historic marker on a signpost. If you visit Modesto, instead of memorials to Kie's bravery, you can see the price of his defeat. "The first zoning was racially inspired to keep the minorities out of various places," Bill Nichols, Modesto's planning director, told a local paper in 1984. "It put the laundries on the west side of the tracks." A century later, that section of West Modesto was 44 percent Black, a fact Nichols attributed to the legacy of zoning and of racial steering by realtors. Modesto won the right to segregate itself, and the city is still grappling with the consequences.

––––––

In 1900, California had a million and a half residents, and it added two million more by 1920. Out of every twenty Californians, four were born abroad, and another five had at least one immigrant parent. The state's civic boosters profited from the boom, but they feared California was following the path of the states from which they had emigrated, filling with industrial cities and immigrant workers crowded into tenement-choked slums. So entangled were the three terms—"immigrants," "tenements," and "slums"—that in 1913 the state formed the Commission of Immigration and Housing to tackle the problems together. And it retained the architect Charles H. Cheney as a consultant.

Cheney had moved to Berkeley in 1901, when his father became the supervisory architect of the University of California, and was among its first graduates in architecture in 1905. When the Great Earthquake of 1906 devastated San Francisco, refugees flooded across the bay, and more than a few discovered that they liked it there. Streetcar lines crisscrossed Berkeley, funneling commuters toward ferries that could bring them to San Francisco in just fifteen minutes. Practically overnight, the small college town became a bedroom community. There were scarcely thirteen thousand residents in 1900 and forty thousand a decade later. Charles's father operated a real estate firm, the Warren Cheney Company, that developed tracts of land and brokered sales, and the new graduate pitched in to help. He earned enough in a year to move to Paris in 1907, studying for three years at the École des Beaux-Arts, interrupted by a spell back at home to build up business. He toured Europe, encountering

Parisian boulevards and German planning and British garden cities—verdant suburbs to house industrial workers. Like many young American visitors to the Continent, then and since, he was enchanted with what he saw and determined to apply European solutions to the problems of the United States. Returning to the Bay Area, he launched an architecture practice and threw himself into the city planning movement.

As Berkeley grew, though, it began to press up against the limits of its developable land. Industrial plants clustered along the waterfront, drawn by rail connections. Working-class residents of the region wanted access to all the same amenities that had drawn their social betters across the bay—beautiful views, parkland, easy commutes, shopping, transit. Students needed housing. "Not only do we find this tide of population suddenly come upon us," wrote Oliver Miles Washburn in 1914, "but it has already reached the hills and is being cast back upon us." Washburn, a professor of classical archaeology, was also dean of the undergraduate division of the university, and in that role served on the committee that was drafting a building code for the city. "There is no relief," he warned ominously, "except by building closer and higher—by crowding more people into already occupied areas." He explained that Berkeley was a city of individual homes, each with a yard and garden. "This is as it should be." But now apartments were coming, which would consume the gardens and lawns and "present the monotonous appearance of a great city." The housing code he drafted would help ensure that apartments were constructed to a high standard, with adequate light and air, but it couldn't keep them out entirely.

Most of Berkeley's subdivisions included language in their deeds restricting sales by race, and many also limited development to single-family homes. These restrictions had their roots in the early nineteenth century, when new developments in some East Coast cities inserted covenants into deeds requiring property owners to care for a shared park or to limit the height of any buildings. Nuisance covenants were particularly popular, banning lists of trades and other noxious uses of the land. As the legal scholar Maureen Brady argues, such covenants were more easily enforced than the common law of nuisance—which banned similar practices from residential areas, but without the same clarity—giving property owners swifter remedies, lowering their burden of proof, and allowing them to block a broader array of uses. By the 1870s, some covenants explicitly banned tenements. But, despite repeated efforts to use covenants to bar their spread, courts seldom found apartments to constitute a noxious use and rarely upheld such restrictions.

And that was not the only limitation of covenants. Neighbors had to bring suit in court to bar a sale, the terms were sometimes deemed unenforceable, and the restrictions ran out after a fixed number of years. What was needed, Cheney insisted, was a set of municipal regulations that could extend the restrictions imposed by covenants. "The artificial and sometimes even make-believe restrictions put on by enterprising real estate men are expiring in many places," Cheney warned Los Angeles's influential Friday Morning Club in May 1914. "Unless the cities step in, people with well established homes in comfortable and quiet districts can see the destruction of all they hold sacred and love best, for the greed of some over-enterprising, jerry-building contractor or citizen."

Cheney had a specific example in mind: Elmwood Park. "This is the cream of Berkeley residence property," the ads for Elmwood Park had promised. "We know of no safer investment and of no more beautiful location for a home." Now the cream was threatening to curdle. Despite the promises of the developer, the restrictions in the deeds had expired after just five years. Cheney knew the neighborhood well; his father's firm had sold houses there. "One or two property holders now threaten to put in apartment houses without regard to the wishes of nine-tenths of the property holders," Cheney told his listeners. Surely, he continued, residents should have the right to petition the city to designate their development a "permanent single house residence district."

Cheney shared that wish with other leading members of Berkeley's City Club. "City planning in Berkeley," Duncan McDuffie would later claim, "actually began with an effort to secure for the city as a whole some of the benefits enjoyed by property owners in its restricted residential districts." McDuffie was a leading developer of such districts, and like Cheney he worried that continued demand for housing in Berkeley would lead to greater density. "Already the tenement and its fashionable cousin, the apartment house, have begun to elbow out the comfortable home and the workman's cottage." The city attorney, Frank Cornish, called apartments "the bane of the owner of the single-family dwelling," warning that they "completely change the character of the neighborhood."

In December 1914, the Commission of Immigration and Housing dispatched Cheney on a tour of eastern cities from which he returned "convinced that this State should take immediate steps to forestall the social disaster of crowded slums." Cheney took particular aim at apartment buildings—or, in the language of the era, tenements. New York had passed a revised building code for tenements in 1901, California had adopted similar provisions in 1909, and reformers around the country were building model tenements, austere structures designed to maximize light and ventilation and sanitation. But Cheney was skeptical. "Undoubtedly, some tenements are better than others," the commission's second report observed, "and it is well to have these good examples if tenements must be, but the whole tenement idea seems wrong." Instead of more carefully regulated apartment buildings to house workers, Cheney wanted to build British-style garden cities for them, filled with single-family homes.

To accomplish that, Cheney was going to have to find a way to ban apartments entirely. The commission noted that decent housing was scarcely affordable for workers. Neighborhoods that used restrictive covenants to ban apartments were affordable only for the affluent. Cheney promised he could change that. He put together an exhibition on city planning, which toured the state, with forty posters summarizing his findings. RESTRICTIONS COST NOTHING, one poster read. GIVE LABORERS THE CHANCE TO LIVE IN A RESTRICTED RESIDENCE DISTRICT. Cheney insisted that California could provide workers with affordable, single-family houses, or at worst, row houses, that offered short commutes. The crowded slums of the East would give way to the spacious garden cities of the West.

In 1915, the indefatigable Cheney got the chance to put his vision into effect. Fresh off organizing the state's first planning conference, he became the driving force behind a new state law authorizing municipalities to create planning commissions. When Berkeley, acting on a report Cheney had played a key role in producing, created the Civic Art Commission, he snagged the role of consultant and secretary. Cheney was easy to overlook. In group portraits with other leading reformers, he showed none of the stylish flair of the leading architects; his suits were respectable rather than fashionable. His brown hair, parted on the left, had a tendency to wander back across his forehead. At five feet eight, he was often the shortest in the gathering. About his only distinguishing feature was a bushy mustache, a mark of conventionality when he acquired it which he transformed into a badge of conservatism by retaining it long after its day had passed. And indeed, in histories of zoning, Cheney most often *has* been overlooked, with the commission's work attributed to McDuffie, its chair. But the report—its ideas, its language, its details—unmistakably echoes Cheney's writings of the previous several years.

The commission recommended the adoption of a complicated zoning ordinance, allowing districts to be designated for residential or industrial uses, if property owners petitioned the city for the designation. That much Cheney borrowed from Minneapolis. But the commission's major innovation was that in place of creating one standard residential district, the ordinance created five. The most permissive, Class V, allowed for apartments and lodging houses and hotels. The most restrictive, Class I, permitted only single-family dwellings.

"The police power," the government's authority to regulate people and property, "is the most elastic of all powers," the *San Francisco Chronicle* observed, "but it is doubtful whether the courts are yet ready to stretch it so far as the Berkeley proposition would require." One problem was that unlike restrictions written into the deed at the time of purchase, a zoning ordinance imposed its limits retroactively. And yet the paper found itself wishing "that the class which clings to the good old-fashioned family home" should have its own place in the city, "where the apartment house and the corner grocery shall not intrude."

The ordinance was passed unanimously and went into effect at the beginning of May 1916. The very first petition arrived scarcely a month later. And, surprising no one, it came from residents of Elmwood Park, requesting to be designated a single-family neighborhood. The very same day it received the petition, the Civic Art Commission hired Cheney to investigate the merits of the case. He found that 209 of the 275 lots in the development were already built out, including four two-family residences, a pair of buildings converted into apartments, and a private school. He not only recommended adoption; he suggested extending the district so that the blocks opposite its boundaries could not be developed, either. The existing structures would be grandfathered in, but couldn't be modified, a provision intended to defuse the sorts of objections that had arisen in Los Angeles. Even so, not everyone was pleased. Some Elmwood Park owners, who understood perfectly well that their own development was the prime target of the single-family homes classification, had tried to block the ordinance from being ratified. They claimed that it was discriminatory, illegal, and "contrary to the natural development of the city." Those who owned lots along College Avenue, a major thoroughfare, were particularly upset. Investors had hoped to use their lots for commercial purposes, or to meet rising demand by erecting apartment buildings, and they now stood to lose substantial sums. But the council swiftly ratified the recommendation, creating the first single-family residence zoning classification in the United States.

"If a dairy, an undertaker's establishment or even an apartment house is built on Piedmont Avenue ... in Elmwood Park," Cheney had warned in 1915, "the surrounding property is unquestionably depreciated, further good residences will cease to go in there, the district will deteriorate, and there is bound to be loss." Cheney had wished aloud that the residents of Elmwood Park be able to fend off such a threat by restricting the neighborhood to single-family homes forever, and—having changed state law, pushed through a local commission, and written a pioneering ordinance—he had made his wish come true.

For all his public speaking and prolific writing on the subject, however, there was one thing Cheney never mentioned aloud. He wanted single-family zoning because he hated the immigrant-filled tenements of the major cities. He wanted it because he thought it could provide a better life for working families. He wanted it because he thought Berkeley should be a model garden city. But most of all, he wanted it to keep development out of his own backyard. When he conjured the horrors of apartment buildings on Piedmont Avenue in Elmwood, he neglected to mention that he was living at 2904 Piedmont Avenue in Elmwood. When he recommended extending the boundaries of the new residential zone to encompass the street fronts that faced the neighborhood, he failed to say that from the front porch of his beautiful Arts and Crafts–style home, he looked out on the houses lining the northern side of Russell Street to which he was extending protection. To put it plainly, single-family zoning was invented by a particularly determined and talented NIMBY, to prevent anyone from building apartments nearby.

Cheney had enjoyed all the advantages of American mobility. His mother was born in Iowa, his father in New York. They'd come west and thrived in Berkeley. Cheney himself had gone to Paris, then to New York, in search of professional opportunities. He had become a nationally recognized leader of progressive city planning. But that forward-looking movement was also driven by a search for order, a desire to impose expertise, and a deep suspicion of the chaos of democracy. These were the elements of progressivism that attracted Cheney, who was, as his brother later recalled, "a born conservative." And as he saw others flooding into the community where he himself had found so much success, he reacted like a New England villager, warning out the interlopers.

Single-family zoning was not only essential, Cheney said, but "in demand and ready to be fought for by the people themselves." Or, at least, by some of the people, in order to exclude others. Because however rarely he explicitly acknowledged it, Cheney's objections were less about the forms that buildings took than about the people they housed. He held no principled objection to height. His architectural office was in an eleven-story building in San Francisco, one of the city's first steel-framed skyscrapers. But when he commuted back across the bay, he wanted to return to a city of respectable homeowners, not one filled with upwardly mobile migrants trying to replicate the success Cheney and his present neighbors had achieved. "Evidently the job of the city planning commission was to protect these great numbers of blocks of home owners from the invasion of flats and apartments, with their renter and floater population," he wrote. It needed to defend the "most important social unit," which was the single family, "living and developing by itself. Only single-family zoning, he said, could "firmly establish this great principle of protecting the home against the intrusion of the less desirable and floating renter class."

Cheney's fear of an *invasion* was absurd. While he was reviewing the horrors of tenement-choked slums in eastern cities, the members of the Commission of Immigration and Housing were focused on understanding conditions in California. They came away with a very different set of concerns. "The broad, general housing problem in the state," their report concluded, "with a few exceptions, may be summed up as a single and two family dwellings problem." The report cited "overcrowding, or congestion, poorly constructed and dilapidated shacks, and a lack of sanitary conveniences"—in short, all the evils of tenements, repackaged in districts of single-family homes. In Fresno, inspectors looked at 110 single-family houses and classified most as filthy and in bad repair. Thirty-one of them were single-room shacks housing an entire family. Their floorboards were cracked, windows broken, cracked walls alive with cockroaches, yards filled with waste and sewage. The families who lived in these conditions would have found the new-law tenements on the Lower East Side that Cheney so feared almost inconceivably luxurious. Slums, it turned out, were a product not of density but of poverty. They were just as much a danger in single-family residence districts as in neighborhoods of apartment buildings. The commission recommended extending the state's 1909 Tenement Housing Act to cover all housing so that minimum standards could be enforced.

But the report did nothing to slow the momentum behind the cause of zoning. What began with the persecution of the Chinese did not end there. Discrimination had legitimized zoning, and now zoning would legitimize discrimination. In Berkeley, it became a tool not only of racial exclusion but also of ethnic and economic segregation. And everywhere it spread, it was quickly embraced by residents who wanted to turn their communities back into members-only clubs, just as they had been in the days of the Puritans.

———

Cheney's zoning scheme succeeded beyond his wildest imaginings. Construction of multifamily dwellings in Berkeley reached its high point for the decade in 1914, with twenty-three new buildings, and fell to just thirteen by 1920. Rising enrollment at the university increased demand, but growing numbers of students and other renters were forced to commute from Oakland or Alameda. Over the following decades, development resumed, but demand was channeled away from Berkeley's verdant neighborhoods of single-family homes. By 1950, the population neared 114,000, and there it effectively stagnated, restrained by law from further growth despite mounting demand. In 2021, the census estimated the population at 117,000.

In recent years, though, Cheney's innovation has come under attack as Californians awoke to the racist origins of zoning and the inequalities it has reinforced. The men who were central to the effort to pass Berkeley's zoning ordinance, after all, openly boasted of its racist roots. "The fight against the Chinese wash-house laid the basis for districting laws in this state," one wrote. "We are ahead of most states in our court decisions, thanks to the persistent proclivity of the 'heathen Chinese' to clean garments in our midst," said another. Zoning, argued a third, was a permanent solution to the scourge of laundries. The city had allowed one laundry to operate in a residential area, and, he alleged, it "deteriorated that neighborhood until only negroes and Orientals would rent the nearby buildings." And Berkeley's first zoning ordinance was quickly deployed against other entities to advance similar goals. In one district, which included a Chinese laundry as well as two Japanese laundries and residences, residents petitioned for it to be designated an exclusively residential zone. In another, residents, alarmed that a "negro dance hall" might move in nearby, did the same.

These cases have frequently been cited as clear evidence that single-family zoning originated as a means of racial exclusion. The

Berkeley city councillor Lori Droste told a reporter in 2021 that she'd sponsored a resolution to end single-family zoning in the city because "these zoning practices originate[d] because Berkeley didn't want African-American dance halls or Chinese laundromats." The resolution passed. Later that year, Governor Gavin Newsom ratified a bill known as SB 9 that effectively ended single-family zoning in the state, overriding local rules to allow property owners to split their lots or convert their homes into duplexes. "The housing affordability crisis is undermining the California Dream for families across the state," he declared, "and threatens our long-term growth and prosperity."

Undoing Cheney's work, though, won't be that simple. Single-family districts might have been the most extreme element of the zoning scheme he devised, but his plan abounded in other designations that were just as effective in maintaining the city's economic and racial segregation. Limiting a neighborhood to two-family homes—or banning commercial uses—could be almost as effective. As it happens, neither of the cases cited by Droste as the justification for overturning single-family zoning had anything to do with single-family zoning. In both instances, residents petitioned for a Class V district—one that would allow every form of residential use, from single-family homes to frat houses to apartment buildings, but not commercial establishments like laundries or dance halls. Both times, the city's Civic Art Commission instead recommended a more restrictive residential zoning classification. Single-family zoning didn't create America's housing problems by itself, and simply rolling it back cannot fix them.

The supply of housing in Berkeley now lags far behind demand, as rising prices force out residents and homelessness surges. Cheney had assured Californians that restrictive zoning could create garden cities filled with affordable homes for ordinary workers. In fact, it created garden cities and then priced workers right out of them. The Elmwood Park home where he once lived is now worth roughly $2.8 million. In 2016, its owner listed a one-bedroom rental inside the house for $4,290 a month. Despite Cheney's best efforts, it had become, by his definition, an apartment building.

A few blocks farther down Piedmont Avenue sits the home of Phil Bokovoy. Like Cheney decades before him, he came to town because of the university; he arrived in 1983, as a graduate student in economics, and bought a home six years later. And like Cheney, Bokovoy is worried that too many people are now trying to crowd into the city with which he fell in love. In 2018, Bokovoy sued the university through a nonprofit he'd created, Save Berkeley's Neighborhoods, alleging that its decision to increase enrollment required an assessment of its environmental impact under the California Environmental Quality Act (CEQA) that it had failed to perform. The case made national headlines in 2022, when appellate courts affirmed a ruling by a California judge that adding more students could produce an adverse change to the environment. The university was suddenly faced with the prospect of admitting fifty-one hundred fewer students.

Cheney's belief that there was something un-American about apartment buildings echoes in Bokovoy's public remarks. While the lawsuit was pending, Bokovoy and other activists warned that a planned upzoning in the city would threaten "its unique 'garden city' character," which is what Cheney so treasured. "We'll end up like Bangkok, Jakarta, Kuala Lumpur—dense Asian cities where there's no transportation network," he warned in one interview. "Immigrants, who lived in crowded, dense places," he told my colleague Annie Lowrey, "do not want to have fourplexes next door to them," because "that's what they spent their lives trying to get away from." Although he sued the university for failing to plan for more students, he's also opposed past efforts to create the space to house them, objecting that the city "should be protecting the quality of life in our low and medium [density] residential neighborhoods." He argues that Berkeley has grown beyond its existing infrastructure; if the university must expand, he'd prefer it set up a satellite campus or house its students someplace else.

Bokovoy's core complaint, though, is premised on the old Puritan idea that Berkeley belongs to those who are already there. By admitting thousands of new students to compete for the existing supply of housing, his lawsuit alleges, the university will displace tenants, add to homelessness, and increase noise and trash. In a different lawsuit brought by a separate group, a judge recently ruled that a proposal to build new student housing on the campus had not satisfied the environmental impact standards set by CEQA, because the university had failed to consider the noise a larger student population would generate. Students arriving in Berkeley in search of better lives are treated, in these cases, as a literal form of pollution whose effects must be mitigated. (The second case prompted the legislature to intervene, stipulating that noise generated by people is not subject to CEQA review, and leading an appellate court to overturn the ruling.) Cheney had created single-family zoning because the courts could not be convinced that apartment buildings were a noxious use, meeting the legal standard of a nuisance. A century later, even as municipal and state governments were rolling back zoning, the courts were changing their minds about what constituted a nuisance. The economic rewards of moving toward opportunity remain undiminished, but the courts continue to find new grounds on which to block Americans from moving to take advantage of them.

But in 1915, all that lay in the future. Zoning was on the rise, driven by the fierce enmity many Californians bore their Chinese neighbors and the willingness of the state courts to abet it. Outside California, though, its fate seemed much less certain. If communities were going to be able to reassert their right to control who belonged within them, zoning would need to find a firmer legal foundation. The battle now shifted back to the East Coast, to the scene of Cheney's worst nightmares.

CHAPTER SIX

TENEMENTOPHOBIA

On a warm August evening, I find myself walking along a quiet block on New York's Lower East Side, trying to imagine what it looked like a century before. There's hardly anyone around to break my reverie. I find a middle-aged woman walking a small dog, straining on its leash; a pair of twentysomethings perched on a stoop, engrossed in their phones. Parents periodically pop out of their cars to pick up their children from a day care. Across the street, a trendy bar offers pork tacos and $21 barrel-aged Negronis.

Then, quite suddenly, I come face-to-face with a ghost. Sandwiched between a fourteen-story luxury apartment building and an aging six-story apartment block stands a little brick tenement, just three floors tall, with windows at the front and back. It's a remnant of the old Lower East Side, haunting the new. The building shows its age. The brickwork has been patched, and the walls bulge a little in places. A pair of antique-style sconces frame the door invitingly, but iron fence work and security cameras make it clear that strangers are unwelcome. I knock and ring the bells anyway, but no one answers.

Not so long ago, this building was packed with life, housing families crammed into its tight spaces. It once held a plumber's shop, full of pipes and gaskets and wrenches. Before that, it was home to a Hebrew school where a hundred immigrant boys gathered every day in the late afternoons to study what the public schools wouldn't teach them, but what their parents insisted they learn. And even before that, in 1901, you didn't have to ring or knock. The door was open, and after paying in the front parlor, visitors could visit the impoverished women standing in the doors of the rooms they rented to ply the world's oldest trade. "Fair complexion," a vice investigator recorded. "Age about 25 years. Weighs about 140 lbs. Height 5-6 inches. Jewish."

When reformers decried New York's tenements as agents of moral degradation, they had buildings like this one in mind. In fact, they singled out this specific building. And the Lower East Side was full of others just like it. A century ago, this street would have been crowded on a summer evening, filled with peddlers crying out their wares, shop fronts spilling out on to the street beneath their awnings, children dodging between the pushcarts, and weary parents trudging home from the sweatshops. The Lower East Side in 1910 was the strangest neighborhood that has ever existed in the United States. Nothing remotely resembling it had ever been built before, and nothing like it has arisen since. No neighborhood in Manhattan today is even a quarter as dense or compact. Had the Lower East Side been its own state that year, its population would have ranked ahead of Arizona, Delaware, Idaho, Montana, Nevada, New Hampshire, New Mexico, North Dakota, Oregon, Rhode Island, Utah, Vermont, and Wyoming.

In 1910, roughly three-quarters of the people living in New York City were first- or second-generation immigrants. They worked for low wages and crowded into cramped quarters, suffering disproportionately from infectious disease. They spoke with thick accents, if they spoke English at all. They ate strange-smelling foods, dressed in outlandish clothes, preserved bizarre customs, adhered to alien faiths, and lived in odd arrangements, taking relatives and boarders into their homes. Elite New Yorkers were uniformly concerned— a few on behalf of the immigrants but most worried that the immigrants were there at all. Something had to be done.

Much of this anxiety was focused on the Lower East Side, a neighborhood of extremes. It was, one contemporary demographer concluded in 1900, "probably the densest district in the Western world," outstripping the most crowded precincts of Prague or Paris or London. Think of it this way: A suburban neighborhood today might have four families on an acre, each in a spacious home with two parents and a couple of kids. By 1910, the Lower East Side had not 16 residents per acre but 619—the equivalent of stacking 155 single-family homes on that same amount of land. Only, since there was a limit to the stairs residents could climb, both the space each family occupied and the buildings they lived in were tightly compressed. The tenements in which immigrants lived, and often worked, offered a scant 102 square feet of space per person. Plumbing was scarce, and privacy nonexistent.

The eastern European Jews who made up the greatest portion of the Lower East Side's population were among America's strangest immigrant groups. Many of the people who came to the United States in those years were young men who intended to save up enough cash to return home to their ancestral villages. Eastern European Jews were perhaps twice as likely as other European immigrants to arrive in family units, husbands together with their wives and children, and they were much more likely to remain in the United States. By one estimate, between 1908 and 1914, three European immigrants went back to the old country for every four who arrived. Among eastern European Jews in those years, fourteen stayed for every one who returned; only the Irish, who were likewise fleeing oppression, rivaled their propensity to remain in the United States. Jews placed a particular value on geographic proximity to families, stores, and places of worship; densities on the Lower East Side were highest around synagogues. So they came as families, they came to live together, and they came to stay.

The tenement dwellers who so worried the social reformers of the Progressive Era and so aroused the xenophobes and the bigots would climb swiftly out of poverty over the ensuing decades. The very cultural traits that the reformers saw as pathologies would later be eulogized by the immigrants and their descendants as the enablers of their success. The extended families that migrated together and piled into overcrowded apartments? They were close-knit and resilient, seeking a better future for their children. That they were willing to live in unsanitary conditions, and to stay, instead of going home? This showed how deep their love was for the *Goldene Medina*, the land of opportunity, and how great their commitment was to their new nation. Their propensity for taking in boarders? It was a demonstration of their prudence and frugality, because they sacrificed short-term comfort to accelerate their savings and move up and out. Their insistence on clustering in tightly packed neighborhoods? It was evidence of the strength of their communities and the depth of their traditions. Their children would fight in two world wars, returning home to find middle-class jobs. Their grandchildren would climb into the professions. Their great-grandchildren, like me, would write books, like this one. A few decades ago, someone fixed up an old tenement and turned it into a museum, a shrine to America's first rung on the ladder of opportunity. In this country that worships economic success and anything associated with it, it is something of a wonder that no subsequent band of do-gooders has suggested building rows of tenements to propel new waves of immigrants to similar prosperity.

Given how it all turned out, it's hard to recover just how terrifying Americans found the sight of the Lower East Side a century ago— why they suffered from a severe case of tenementophobia. There was, of course, nothing magical about tenements and nothing ennobling about the suffering their inhabitants endured. But then, neither did they have the diabolical powers their critics imputed to them: to warp their inhabitants, to mire them in poverty, to trap them in ignorance. They were just apartment buildings. Today, the very same units reformers claimed would ruin the health and morals of their inhabitants rent for princely sums. What the Jews of the Lower East Side and their neighbors from Italy and Ireland needed to succeed were higher wages; less discrimination; fast, cheap public transit; antibiotics; and a little time. What they got, instead, was continued exploitation, discriminatory laws, and zoning.

But in 1910, when native-born New Yorkers looked at the Lower East Side, they couldn't see a neighborhood teeming with upwardly mobile immigrants who would soon disperse across the metropolitan area, enriching their city and its culture. They couldn't see a strange, anomalous place, born of a unique confluence of circumstances, never to be replicated. Instead, they saw a nightmarish vision of their future, a festering sore that was sprawling outward, destroying everything it touched, slowly devouring their city. They were sure that New York was destined to fill with endless rows of tenements, swallowing up the grass, blotting out the sun, driving out the native-born. Destined, that is, unless someone could be found to stem the tide. Edward Murray Bassett answered the call.

Bassett's life was built by mobility. He was born in Brooklyn, in 1863, and had lived in three separate houses there by the time he was seven. His father then moved the family upstate to Watertown so he could sell goods from a peddling wagon, moving from town to town. The family also kept moving, occupying five more houses before Bassett graduated from high school. Watertown was not large in those years, but it would afford Bassett some valuable connections. His family kept a cow in a pasture adjacent to that of the Lansing family, and Bassett grew close with their son Bert, a future secretary of state under President Wilson. Frank Woolworth tended the counter at the local dry-goods store, saving up to open his own shop; half a century later, Bassett's law office would be in the skyscraper Woolworth built in New York.

Bassett enrolled at Hamilton College, living in a boardinghouse in central New York, before transferring to Amherst. He befriended Arthur Rugg, a future chief justice of Massachusetts's Supreme Judicial Court, and, through his fraternity, Delta Upsilon, met Charles Evans Hughes, later chief justice of the United States. Then he returned to Brooklyn and attended Columbia Law School. Next, he headed west to Buffalo and together with his brother George founded Bassett Brothers, which would eventually design and build fifty-three waterworks plants. He continued to study law with some friends, using the law office of the newly elected governor, Grover Cleveland, who lent it to them in the evenings.

In Buffalo, he first landed at a residential hotel. Then he moved to a bachelor apartment building, and finally he and George rented the upstairs rooms of a family home together with two of their sisters. After the brothers married, they bought a strip of land and built five brick row houses, the two new families moving together into the house at the end of the row. With his first child on the way, however, Bassett needed more space. He rented an apartment in a single-family home that had been converted to house five families. By the time he left Buffalo at the age of twenty-nine, he had lived in at least sixteen separate places over the course of his short life, representing the full range of nineteenth-century housing. Each form of housing, from boardinghouse to residential hotel to apartment conversion to single-family home, met his needs at a different stage of his ascent. Mobility had brought Bassett into contact with the men who would make his career. And yet he would devote much of the rest of his life to constraining, or eliminating, it for others.

Returning to Brooklyn in 1892, he carried with him a bulging roster of contacts. He sent them all notice of his move. None were particularly surprised; Bassett had joined a massive migration toward the largest cities. "The bright young men seem to gravitate toward the great centers of population, where of course, the chances are greater for men of real ability," one of his old Hamilton College professors replied. Bassett had been hoping to turn his experience as counsel of the waterworks company into a lucrative corporate law practice, but he struggled to establish himself. Instead, he found that his frequent moves from one place to another had positioned him to bridge communities. He tapped his network—members of the Buffalo Club, friends from Hamilton and Amherst and his fraternity, business acquaintances from upstate—to send him their unpaid bills so that he could collect debts on their behalf in the city. As these relationships developed, a second opportunity opened to him. Correspondents who had extra cash wanted safe investments with good rates of return; Bassett, surrounded by people seeking mortgages, was happy to help broker their loans, exchanging their cash for a mortgage note. Not only was the practice reliable, but it also made him a particularly valuable person to know in Brooklyn, a conduit for the steady stream of dollars exiting smaller cities and flowing to new opportunities in the great metropolis.

By this stage of his life, Bassett cut a striking figure. He brushed his thick brown hair straight back up from his broad forehead, the pompadour bringing his height to a round six feet. He favored neatly tailored suits and high club collars. A small mole by the corner of his left eye did more to accentuate the appearance of genteel refinement than to spoil it. Only his piercing blue-gray eyes, set beneath high-arched eyebrows, betrayed his fierce intensity of purpose.

His offices were in a series of buildings in downtown Manhattan, mostly along Broadway. Even there, mobility played to his advantage; he later recalled that he never minded moving, because every time he sent out a note to all his contacts announcing a relocation, in came a flood of new business. He first bought a home not far from his father in Brooklyn, then settled with his family on Newkirk Avenue, in the still-developing neighborhood of Flatbush. He joined a variety of civic clubs, but unsurprisingly his forays into civic life reflected the frustrations of a new homeowner. He wanted better schools in the neighborhood and, in 1899, was appointed to the Brooklyn Board of Education, making him a prime dispenser of patronage jobs. From there, he won election to Congress as a Democrat in 1902, serving a single term. For a decade, he tried to improve the drainage along Newkirk Avenue and to have the street paved and accepted as a public thoroughfare by New York. That brought an appointment to a mayoral commission on streets, in 1906. And he fought for cheaper and more frequent transit service, to ease his daily commute to his offices on Broadway in lower Manhattan. That led his old friend Charlie Hughes, now the Republican governor, to appoint him, in 1907, to the Public Service Commission, which regulated public utilities like transit.

But if there was one cause that truly excited the passions of men like Bassett in those years, it was keeping their neighborhoods free from apartment buildings. Bassett had bet big on Brooklyn. He imagined a New York City that abandoned the verticality of Manhattan, with its spines of buildings running up the island, in favor of a circular pattern of development, with swift and cheap transportation routes spoking out into Queens and Brooklyn. One vision would lead to "congestion of traffic and of population," tall towers, long rides, and "comparatively unsanitary housing." The other, he felt, promised "smaller units of housing, shorter rides for working people ... sunshine and air, moderate rents, and in general, more wholesome and sanitary housing." He watched nervously as prosperous homeowners decamped for New Jersey and Westchester and Connecticut and Nassau, out to developments protected by restrictive covenants. And above all, he feared the spread of the Lower East Side and its immigrant-packed tenements.

In 1908, Bassett traveled to Germany, stopping at a conference in Düsseldorf on municipal administration. There he fell under the spell of Werner Hegemann, who would also strongly influence Charles Cheney. (The German roots of zoning were admiringly touted by American advocates right until the entry of the United States into World War I, when they suddenly discovered that zoning was not actually German in the slightest and never had been.) On Bassett's return to New York, at the urging of his friend Nelson Lewis, he joined the National Conference on City Planning. He realized that city planning "offered a vast field of progressive legislation," and just as important, its objects could be accomplished not through taxation but through the government's police power. By the time the Brooklyn Committee on City Planning was organized in 1912, Bassett was a logical choice to serve as its vice-chairman. "Brooklyn is known as a city of homes," he said, urging "loyal citizens" to take precautions to defend it against the tide of "tenements or diminutive houses" that spread along the spines of transit.

New York City, meanwhile, kept right on growing. Developers tore down old buildings and threw up new ones. They built fashionable districts that were swiftly superseded by newer and still more fashionable districts. Marching uptown along Manhattan's Fifth Avenue, which had long been a boulevard of opulent mansions and glittering commercial palaces, was a row of new steel-framed buildings, standing fourteen, eighteen, even twenty stories tall. But their developers had overestimated the demand for office space in the area and, instead, attracted the garment industry. Sweatshop owners leased space on the upper floors. The rent was pricey, but the proximity of these buildings to transit lines, hotels housing out-of-town buyers, and the temples of fashion for which they executed designs made it worth the cost. Here was Bassett's vision of transit alleviating congestion put into practice. The sweatshops were migrating out of the tenements of the Lower East Side and separating residences from industry while putting workers into comparatively brightly lit, well-ventilated spaces. And on their breaks, they could walk along the broad street, enjoying the sunshine and air. "In the morning, and especially in the noontime hour, the working people pour out on the street, five abreast, arm in arm eating their lunches," Bassett said. He should have been delighted. Instead, he was completely horrified.

So were the merchant princes of the Fifth Avenue Association. They had moved their stores to the neighborhood, displacing a residential district, but now they dreaded the "constant, seething turmoil of tearing down and rebuilding" and wanted the city to protect them from further change. Like the citizens of Modesto trying to push back Chinese immigrants, their first resort was force. They demanded police clear the sidewalks of the garment workers so that they wouldn't drive away wealthy customers. One observer described seeing the usual lunchtime crowd of "poor, hard-working people, most of them Russian Jews but nevertheless human beings and entitled to some consideration," getting swept up in a police raid, a hundred of them loaded into wagons and fined a dollar apiece for the crime of loitering. The noontime hour, though, was when the workers took their only break, when bosses from busy shops descended to the street corners to hire extra help for the afternoon shifts, when tailors peered into department store windows to study the latest designs. Even nightsticks and fines couldn't clear the sidewalks. Workers soon learned to shuffle forward when told to move along, and the special details of police officers accomplished nothing more than antagonizing them and arousing "class feeling." Next, the property owners met with union leaders, who agreed to move some of the hiring off the street. They posted flyers in Yiddish, English, and Italian, reminding workers that "customers who are visiting Fifth Avenue and buying from the shops located on it and the side streets object to loitering." But the workers were unpersuaded that the sidewalks of a public street should be reserved for their social betters.

The leaders of the Fifth Avenue Association appealed to the mayor, who asked them what else they expected him to do. They had no answer. They met again with industry officials and union officers and Jewish communal representatives. Then, in the winter of 1911, they pleaded their case to the Manhattan borough president, George McAneny, who appointed a commission to study the problem. A few months later, it recommended restricting the heights of buildings along Fifth Avenue to squeeze out the garment factories. But rather than proceed piecemeal—creating a special set of rules just to keep the merchant princes happy was bad politics—the Board of Estimate created the Commission on the Height, Size, and Arrangement of Buildings, to look at the question on a citywide basis. McAneny was the nominal chair, but Bassett led the advisory body that would do the work.

The Fifth Avenue Association's formal statement to the commission warned that the garment industry workers on Fifth Avenue had "utterly changed its former high-class character" and suggested that a height cap was a way to reclaim it. The deadly fire at the Triangle Shirtwaist Factory in 1911 had already led to reforms, reducing the number of workers per floor; limiting the number of floors would further cut down on the lunchtime crowds. Height limits would also constrain the supply of space in the neighborhood, driving up rents and forcing out manufacturers. The Fifth Avenue Association pulled in Frank Veiller, whose brother Lawrence was the driving force behind tenement reform, as an expert witness. Veiller testified that the "hordes of factory employees" were destroying the "exclusiveness of Fifth Avenue" and that only a height cap could save the property values. The Fifth Avenue Association presented the commission with a straightforward choice. The city could either respect the long-established right of its people to develop their property or use its power to defend the investments of some of its wealthiest citizens at the expense of the working poor.

Not every politician lined up with the wealthy. A wave of reformers dislodged the Democrats from city hall, and McAneny was succeeded by Manhattan's first Jewish borough president, Marcus M. Marks. Marks had made his fortune in the garment business and then served as founding president of the National Association of Clothiers. He told the members of the Fifth Avenue Association that while he sympathized with their efforts to preserve the brand value of their addresses, they had neglected the human side of the problem, the needs of the workers. "They want relief from your shops, they want to get out into the sunshine, and they want to talk things over together, and it is a natural and a healthy desire on their part, and you can't solve your problem without remembering that every one of them is a man with a heart and passions and ambitions, the same as yours," he said. But not even channeling Shylock's soliloquy from *The Merchant of Venice* helped him get through to the merchants of Fifth Avenue.

Even as some politicians recoiled, the work of the Heights of Buildings Commission ground forward, led by Bassett and aided by three staffers who would be integral to the spread of zoning through the United States. George B. Ford served as the secretary, Robert H. Whitten as the editor of the report, and Herbert S. Swan as the statistician. The commission's finished product, delivered at the end of 1913, ran nearly four hundred pages. The commission had been charged with examining whether the city should regulate the "height, size and arrangement" of new buildings and whether those rules should vary by zone. The report it returned, disguised in dry legal language and armored with appendixes, was an audacious gambit that far exceeded that mandate.

What the city really needed, Bassett and his colleagues insisted, wasn't just regulations that could limit the height, size, and arrangement of buildings. The city needed to regulate the *use* of private property, dividing industry and residences into separate zones. New York law didn't actually allow that, and Bassett himself acknowledged the legal consensus that such an effort would be unconstitutional on its face, but he was undeterred. He helpfully included a statute that could be forwarded to the state legislature, to allow his scheme to be implemented. In 1914, the state legislature adopted the law, and the city created the Commission on Building Districts and

Restrictions—a zoning commission—with Bassett as its chair and much of the staff and membership of the Heights of Buildings Commission reprising their roles. Bassett would spend the next two years gathering testimony, making maps, and laying out his vision for the future of the city and of the country. There was not much mystery about what he wanted. The question was whether he could find a formula that would persuade the public, and the courts, to go along.

———

Zoning was one idea for how New York could cope with its surging population—a city of 3.4 million in 1900 had expanded to almost 4.8 million a decade later—but it was hardly the only contender. There were three approaches under consideration, each representing a very different vision of the future: exclusion, expansion, and regulation. The United States could keep new arrivals out of the country, accelerate its growth to accommodate the influx of immigrants, or expand the reach of government to control the ways in which they labored and lived. These were not necessarily mutually exclusive options; the debate among Progressives largely concerned which to emphasize and to what degree. And while Bassett charged forward with his plan, other government commissions were pushing their own agendas.

Immigration restrictionism offered one solution to those who saw the Lower East Side as a nightmare and feared that tenements teeming with immigrants would devour the country. In 1906, nativists pushed Congress to impose literacy tests and other measures designed to cut off the flow of immigrants, prevailing in the Senate but falling short in the House. A divided Congress decided the problem needed more study, and so voted to create the Dillingham Commission to investigate the matter. In its 1911 report, spanning forty-one volumes of detailed descriptions and statistics, the commission's professional staff meticulously documented the enormous contributions immigrants were making to America. Immigrants, it concluded, were "impelled by a desire for betterment" and largely achieved it. Even so, the commissioners worried that America was afflicted with a surfeit of unskilled labor, an excess of young men seeking only to take their wages back home, and an overabundance of immigrants. It wanted to slow the pace of immigration, to allow for more effective assimilation and absorption. "The Commission as a whole recommends restriction as demanded by economic, moral, and social considerations," it concluded, endorsing a literacy test and ethnic quotas to make that happen. Before Congress could wrestle with the report, war broke out in Europe, sharply reducing the flow of immigrants across the Atlantic. But the Dillingham Commission's recommendations would be revived after World War I, forming the basis of the Immigration Restriction Act of 1921, which imposed tight quotas on the numbers allowed to emigrate from eastern and southern Europe. In 1914, though, it was far from clear that Congress would act.

Not everyone, though, favored restriction as the right solution. Nativism, bolstered by the pseudoscience of eugenics, might have been popular in large swaths of the United States, but enjoyed rather less support in New York. The city was hardly devoid of anti-Semitic or anti-Catholic sentiment, along with other xenophobias, but a platform of straightforward restrictionism was unlikely to get very far in a city heavily populated by immigrants. The city's wealthy elites and its native-born reformers instead argued over whether the city could grow its way out of its problems or whether growth itself had become the biggest problem.

A month before the Board of Estimate appointed the Zoning Commission, at the behest of the city's young, reform-oriented mayor, John Purroy Mitchel, the city had created a commission on taxation. At first glance, the two initiatives seem wholly unrelated. But Mitchel had asked the tax commission to look at a radical idea, backed by the followers of the political economist Henry George: taxing land instead of buildings.

The scheme, its supporters on the commission argued, would raise the cost of holding vacant land or leaving it incompletely developed, encouraging owners to build. "It would also tend to do away with the old ramshackle buildings in lower Manhattan and lower Brooklyn," they wrote, "and compel their replacement with commodious modern buildings." The construction boom would lower unemployment, and the flood of new units coming onto the market would lower rents. The plan would also lower taxes on single-family homes, stimulating their construction and "drawing people out of the crowded tenements in the slum districts" and into homes of their own. By attracting people and industries to New York, the land tax would also stimulate its growth.

Both proponents and critics agreed that the plan was likely to produce "a more intensive use of valuable lands and the development of a more compact city," but they split on whether to fear this outcome or hope for it. The Georgists argued that if the density of people per acre were to rise, it should be seen not as congestion but as efficiency—with tall new buildings allowing families to live in desirable areas while providing them with ample space, and office skyscrapers doing the same for workers. And if people truly objected to this, well, Bassett's commission could impose height limits that would spread the most intensive development over a somewhat broader area. The Georgists were confident in the city's future and its capacity to provide opportunities to the next generation of residents. The solution to congestion, they argued, was construction.

But most members of the commission were unpersuaded. They insisted that density itself was a menace. The final report included a long list of other objections to the scheme, but in the end much of the opposition boiled down to a simple set of facts. The land tax aimed to extract money from the city's wealthiest landlords and reduce the value of their holdings while lowering the taxes and rents of middle- and working-class New Yorkers. Even if it were phased in over a decade, as backers planned, ratifying the tax would instantly change the value of every parcel of land in the city, and the worst losses would be borne by the richest and best connected. It was the sort of plan that helped cost Mitchel the Republican nomination, making him a one-term mayor.

Bassett's zoning plan was, in its own way, far more radical than what the Georgists proposed. Georgists wanted to change the basis on which property was taxed; Bassett proposed to change the basis on which private property was held, allowing the city to decide what could or could not be built on any parcel. The genius of Bassett's plan, the indispensable ingredient of its success, was that it proposed this sweeping revolution in the service of a fundamentally conservative vision. Zoning could be carefully tailored to keep every neighborhood more or less as it was; existing buildings that ran afoul of its rules would be grandfathered in. Instead of asking New Yorkers to endure painful changes, as the Georgists had, Bassett promised a way to preserve the status quo. He told elite New Yorkers he could succeed where King Canute had failed; he would halt the onrushing tide of change. And they were primed to listen, because for more than a decade they had been trying to fend off the menace of tenements and failing.

At a housing conference in 1913, Lawrence Veiller made an astonishing declaration: Tenements had a "very bad effect on American life"; even "an apartment house of the highest type" couldn't provide "proper homes." The trouble, he continued, was that a disconcertingly large number of Americans liked apartments. Democracy couldn't be trusted; a referendum on banning such buildings was bound to be defeated. So, he advised the assembled regulators, it was best to take an indirect approach. "Do everything possible in our laws to encourage the construction of private dwellings and even two-family dwellings, because the two-family house is the next least objectionable type, and penalize so far as we can in our statute the multiple dwelling of any kind, whether it is [a] flat, apartment house or tenement house," he counseled.

This, he told his audience, was what he had done in New York. The secret? Fire safety. Everyone agreed that the police power covered building regulations aimed at reducing the risk of fire. "If we require multiple dwellings to be fireproof, and thus increase the cost of construction; if we require stairs to be fireproofed, even when there are only three families; if we require fire-escapes and a host of other things," then, he continued, each of the rules could stand up in court, "and at the same time we have made it difficult to build apartment homes." Just in case anyone thought he was genuinely concerned about saving families from the threat of lethal conflagrations, he added one more piece of advice: "Allow our private houses and two-family houses to be built with almost no fire protection whatever."

It was a remarkable confession, a public admission that the cause to which Veiller had devoted the previous fifteen years of his life had largely been a sham. His CV told the story of one of progressivism's most successful movements. He had organized the Tenement House Committee and mounted the Tenement Exhibition that awakened the public to the dangers of inadequate housing. He wrote the report for the Tenement House Commission that was then set up to examine the problem and authored the Tenement House Act of 1901 to put its recommendations into law, imposing new requirements on old buildings and defining the rules for "new law" tenements. Next, he served as the first deputy commissioner of the Tenement House Department, enforcing the regulations he had conceived. To take his crusade national, he had started the National Housing Association, which convened the conference at which he was speaking. The prematurely balding Veiller sported a neatly trimmed mustache and a pointed beard. He stood just five feet five, but he was a giant in his field. No man in America was more closely identified with a single issue; Lawrence Veiller was Mr. Tenement Reform.

More remarkable even than Veiller's confession, though, was that it caused no stir in the room. The tenement reform movement presented itself as championing the downtrodden, rescuing the city's poor from the depredations of rapacious landlords, and giving them housing that would elevate their condition. But although some champions of tenement reform were earnest in their efforts, no one who had paid the slightest attention to the movement could have had any doubt as to the actual aims of many reformers. The influx of immigrants to New York City was the problem; eliminating affordable housing was the solution.

Veiller's exhibition, and the statistics he collected, proved beyond doubt that conditions in some tenements were horrifying, and in many others, extremely trying. To Veiller, this was persuasive evidence that the buildings themselves "helped to produce the epidemics of poverty and disease," turning New York into a "City of Living Death." Veiller compared the sights and sounds of the neighborhood to Dante's description of hell; he mused that benevolent despotism might prove more capable of addressing their problems than democracy; he fantasized about burning the tenements to the ground, rejecting the idea only because he was unsure what might replace them. He bemoaned the "abnormal increase of population through immigration" bringing a "vast horde" of workers to compete with the native-born, driving down wages and the standard of living. And he ticked off a doleful litany of the imagined consequences of overcrowding: "the destruction of home life, the weakening of the parental influence, the falling off of religious faith, the changed relation of the sexes, the absence of privacy, the intrusion of strangers upon the family life, the use in common of facilities of living where propriety and decency demand their restriction to a single family, the constant sight and sound of debasing influences from which escape is impossible." It's something of a wonder that he failed to blame the rise of jazz on the existence of six-story apartment buildings, too.

An essay on immigration, included in the Tenement House Commission's report, presented the buildings as an agent of natural selection, that "forces out or kills off" the better sort of immigrant, leaving each generation more degraded than the one before it. New York's governor, Theodore Roosevelt, much impressed with Veiller's exhibition, told the crowd that improving tenements would "cut at the root of the diseases which eat at the body social and the body politic." The exhibition, and the report that followed, stand as singular triumphs in the field of mistaking correlation for causation.

Reformers like Veiller associated the apartment building with everything they disliked about immigrant life, and the single-family home with everything they valorized about America. If native-born Americans had grown up in farmhouses, then surely getting immigrants out of apartments was the first step toward Americanization. And if cities were full of sin and temptation, then surely the apartment building—that most urban of dwellings—was partially responsible. "The tenement house is an impediment to God's plan for the home," William B. Patterson, a leading Methodist preacher, proclaimed, "and no matter to what high degree of physical healthfulness we may raise the tenement, this basic fact will remain."

Veiller was particularly appalled by the practice of taking in lodgers to help pay the rent. Tolerating the "lodger evil," he warned, would lead to "the breaking down of American standards of living, of morality, of civic and social responsibility, and of even liberty itself." Noting that the practice "prevails among the Jews in the larger cities," among other groups, he wrote that it could lead to "the downfall and subsequent degraded career of young women, to grave immoralities—in a word, to profanation of the home." That immigrant families took in unmarried men offended Victorian notions of privacy and propriety.

If overcrowding was the problem, though, the most obvious solution was to build lots of new, cheap housing. Some progressive reformers did push hard in this direction. Various nonprofits sponsored model tenements, although these usually reflected middle-class ideas about the value of the features they included, like larger and airier bedrooms. Commercial developers, compelled to meet the actual demand of the housing market, found that few immigrants were willing to pay enough to justify the increased expense of building such apartments. Other advocates pushed for the construction of public housing, although the rapid erection of market-rate tenements undermined their case for its need. A third solution was to disperse housing around the city, using public transit to make the commute between a Brooklyn home and a Manhattan factory as short as the walk from a Lower East Side tenement. Each of these approaches started from the assumption that new arrivals in the city needed to be housed and set as its goal the provision of affordable shelter.

Veiller, instead, did everything in his power to make housing more expensive. Immigrants continued to pour into the city in the years immediately after the passage of the Tenement Act, but newly constructed tenements became increasingly unaffordable. The cost of making the improvements to old-law tenements mandated by the law, and increasing competition for the remaining affordable units, combined to drive up prices, setting off rent strikes in 1904 and 1907. "The fact is that the new-law tenements . . . are beyond the reach of unskilled wage earners," one reformer complained in 1919.

The Jews on the Lower East Side who could afford it took advantage of improving transit to relocate to Harlem, or across the river to Williamsburg. But many were tied to their jobs in the garment trade and could neither move nor afford new-law buildings. For them, the principal effect of Veiller's reforms was that they paid even more to live in the same apartments.

For New York's most impoverished residents, housing conditions were frequently horrifying. In 1890, when the reformer Jacob Riis published *How the Other Half Lives,* his photographs of lightless hallways, narrow air shafts, privies heaped with refuse, trash-strewn courtyards, and crowded bedrooms shocked elite New Yorkers. In the worst of the tenements, often constructed for some other purpose and later converted into apartments, the air was fetid and the water foul. Such buildings were death traps when they caught fire, and their lack of sanitation or ventilation accelerated the spread of disease. But it was also true that reformers hunted for the most appalling conditions they could document, to dramatize their cause. One inspector testifying before a state committee was asked if he had found "several adults" indecently sleeping in a single room. He told them he had not—only ever a man and wife. Overcrowding, he explained, was produced not by the nature of the buildings but by crushingly low wages that left families unable to afford adequate space. Unsatisfied, the chair asked him for the worst example of overcrowding he'd encountered. The inspector had once found eleven people in two rooms, he reported, with the windows nailed shut at the top and the night too cold to open them at the bottom. That was more to the committee's taste. The example went into its final report; the observations on wages did not.

For most tenement dwellers, however, the conditions were difficult but not degrading. Instead of picking out just the worst examples, the Dillingham Commission took a comprehensive look at more than ten thousand households in poor, congested urban neighborhoods. Its report criticized reformers for painting a grossly inaccurate picture of tenement life by focusing on a relatively small number of extreme cases. In fact, "a large majority of the immigrants in cities lead a decent, hard-working life, in homes that are clean, though in many cases poor." The streets might be filthy, but only because cities were failing to provide basic services; the apartments, tended by their residents, were largely tidy. The overwhelming majority of New York's tenements, despite their reputation, were in comparatively good condition. Modern researchers have noted that the infant mortality rate in the Tenth Ward—the most crowded segment of the Lower East Side, packed with Russian Jews—was among the lowest in the city. In the decades of peak immigration, even as densities rose in New York, childhood mortality fell. New York's tenements grew more crowded and more sanitary at the same time.

Moreover, tenement life was a way station, not a permanent condition. Roughly half the foreign-born heads of households the commission surveyed had immigrated within the previous decade—which is to say, roughly half of the families living in tenements a decade before had already moved on to better housing, replaced by these new arrivals. Immigrants put up with crowded conditions because they were determined to live within their means and accrue savings. Generally, the report found, they moved to more spacious quarters as soon as they could afford to do so. While the report recommended some degree of regulation, it found in the tenement districts not a crisis in need of resolution but what later scholars would term "zones of emergence"—neighborhoods launching one group of immigrants after another into American life. "Well-regulated tenement houses," it concluded, "are better adapted to the needs of a crowded city than are private houses converted for the use of several families."

Even the much-ballyhooed "lodger evil" was not at all what it seemed. Low wages made it all but impossible for an adult male, working in an unskilled job or in the garment trade, to earn enough to rent an apartment for his family. Some supplemented their income by putting their wives and children to work. The solution preferred by others, particularly Russian Jews, was to take in lodgers; the labor of the women and children could then be used to provide room and board to the lodgers, bringing the family much-needed cash, without forcing wives to work outside the home or removing the children from school. Both the families and their lodgers could save more of their earnings, bringing closer the day when they could move out and acquire homes of their own. The crowded conditions of the Lower East Side, it turned out, were the result partially of poverty, and partially of inadequate supply of affordable housing, but also of the strategic choices made by immigrants.

The pioneers on the western plains, staking their claims, erected crude sod houses and one-room log cabins—dwellings that offered little light, poor ventilation, no running water, overcrowded conditions, and dismal fire safety. No health inspector working for Veiller could possibly have given a passing grade to a little house on the prairie. But just like the farmers, who were willing to endure difficult conditions on their arrival if it brought them closer to achieving lasting financial security, New York's immigrants were prepared to use tenements as a stepping stone on the way to their goals.

In fact, before Veiller ever entered the field, tenements were already undergoing a startling transformation. In the middle of the nineteenth century, most tenements were structures converted from other uses, filtering down to house the poor. But as immigrants began developing new buildings—Jews, in particular, found working for themselves in real estate a useful means of bypassing employment discrimination—the structures they produced bore ever less resemblance to Veiller's caricatures. These amateur developers used the growing abundance of manufactured materials to encrust building facades with elaborate ornamentation, offering residents the trappings of respectability. They competed for tenants by layering on the latest amenities; landlords offered stoves, hot and cold running water, ranges, sinks, flush toilets, bathtubs, steam heating, dumbwaiters, and gas lighting. Seasoned immigrants delighted in relating tales of greenhorns, arriving in New York and being unable to grasp how to use these miraculous new technologies—finding hot water available on tap, for example, and searching beneath the sink for the fire that must have heated it. Floor plans added parlors and then dining rooms at the front of the buildings, both of which were lit by natural light and gave families space to gather. If bedrooms were still small and dark and crowded, that reflected their secondary importance as rooms in which few waking hours were spent. These buildings reversed the floor plans of the model tenements, to reflect the actual priorities of immigrants and not the preferences of elite reformers. Ground floors generally contained shops, producing a bustling commercial street where residents could buy necessities and save time and carfare.

What Veiller and his various reform groups had failed to grasp was that the tenement was a machine for social mobility, a remarkably efficient technological solution to the challenges of immigrant life. Immigrant entrepreneurs were busily transforming the stock of buildings, tearing down dilapidated structures that had been built for some other function and then turned into tenements, and erecting new ones, purpose-built as multifamily housing. The entrepreneurs who developed them kept wealth within their communities, and the immigrant tenants enjoyed upgraded accommodations and made the city prosper. In the century after Veiller all but regulated the cheapest tenements out of existence, cities like New York would experiment with a wide array of other approaches to housing their working classes, including public housing developments, public-private partnerships, rent control, and vouchers. None proved half so effective at expanding the housing stock, or providing affordable rents, as the tenements fashioned by immigrant entrepreneurs.

Market forces alone would not solve all the problems of housing, of course. As standards of living rose, government regulation helped ensure that older buildings were upgraded or well maintained and that newer ones were built to safeguard the health of their residents. Some Progressive Era reformers focused on these sorts of rule changes, motivated by genuine concern for the poor. But to truly succeed, those regulations needed to be tuned to encourage mobility, by fostering large-scale construction of the types of housing that New Yorkers were actively seeking out. They needed to allow for tenements and residential hotels and boardinghouses and all the other varieties of nineteenth-century housing that kept dwellings affordable and made homelessness comparatively rare. Instead, Veiller had written his codes to restrain mobility and to make it unprofitable to develop new housing for the working poor. Veiller's reforms, one leading builder of model tenements complained in 1912, were "the chief cause of high rents," producing shiny new buildings that no workingman could actually afford and making it all but impossible to construct low-cost units.

The only way to make sense of such reforms is to believe the confessions of the men who authored them, who were frankly hostile to immigration, apartments, and mobility. As much as some reformers were disturbed by the wretched conditions in the worst of the tenements, they were perhaps even more disconcerted by the attractive conditions in the best of them. As the historian Zachary Violette has argued, a converted structure could be dismissed as a temporary expedient; a brand-new tenement, its facade encrusted with decoration, its rooms filled with eager tenants, offered physical evidence that immigrants and their cultures were taking up permanent residence. While Veiller defined tenements as a problem, immigrants were busily turning them into a solution. And, although Veiller had jacked up the price of apartment living, he had only slowed the spread of apartments, not arrested it entirely. As immigrants achieved greater financial success, they began to move uptown and toward the outer boroughs. Regulation alone couldn't halt the march of the tenements or the people they housed. So Veiller joined another reform movement, becoming a member of Bassett's Heights of Buildings Commission.

By the time Bassett's commission delivered its recommendations, New York's moneyed classes were primed to embrace them. Here, at last, was a tool to control immigrants and their un-American ways; to stabilize real estate investments; to protect exclusive districts from the encroachments of the working classes; and, above all, to impose order and rationality on the city's organic growth.

Take George T. Mortimer. A real estate man, Mortimer was simultaneously the second vice president of the Fifth Avenue Association and the chair of the commission's committee on Fifth Avenue. Such conflicts of interest were essential to the design of the commission, which was less an impartial body than an exercise in coalition building, structured to garner broad support for its preordained conclusion. Mortimer, who managed some $40 million worth of Manhattan skyscrapers, might have seemed an unlikely convert to the cause of height limits and zoning. He was president of the Equitable Office Building Corporation, managing a slab-sided forty-story structure stretching the length of a whole block, erected over the vociferous protests of neighboring property owners. He quickly came to understand, though, that Bassett's scheme could be a particular boon to real estate management, which depended less on developing new towers than on squeezing cash out of those that had already been built. If zoning were enacted, no one would be able to build new structures quite as large as the ones he managed. Not only would this swiftly increase the value of his buildings, but it would slow the pace of change in the neighborhoods that surrounded them, stabilizing that value for the long term.

That was precisely what concerned rival landlords. "They stole my light and air from me," one owner of a lot adjoined by skyscrapers complained, "and now the game is to keep my buildings down to protect the theft." But most property owners quickly grasped that zoning promised to line their own pockets at the expense of the city's workers and renters. Manhattan's residential population peaked in the census of 1910, just before zoning went into effect, when immigrant entrepreneurs were still able to build cheap housing close to the centers of manufacturing. When the enumerators returned a decade later, they found the city still growing rapidly, but the growth had been displaced toward the outer boroughs, while Manhattan itself was shrinking. Zoning had turned space in Manhattan into an artificially scarce commodity, precisely as Bassett intended. Mortimer himself would eventually proclaim that "the zoning system is the best thing that ever happened to real estate in this city."

The early public debates and hearings over zoning attracted mostly planners and property owners and reflected these divides. Most of those who testified against zoning were fearful it would hurt the value of their property, or leave them footing a larger tax bill, while many of its enthusiastic supporters expected it to benefit their holdings or cut their taxes. Voices taking a stand against zoning on grounds other than self-interest were scarce, and testimony from the vast class of renters whose lives these bills would alter was all but nonexistent.

When a national zoning commission produced a bibliography on the topic in 1922, it included just three critical perspectives. One of these came from the acid pen of Bruno Lasker, a social worker at the Henry Street Settlement on the Lower East Side. Its inclusion on the list shows that the planners were perfectly aware of how critics saw their work. Lasker charged that zoning, in practice, amounted to class-based segregation:

> Whence, to ask a very simple question, do so many of the zoning commissions derive their sanction for dividing the physical make-up of the city into use districts that distinguish between the residential needs of different classes? . . . Why, in this country of democracy, is a city government, representative of all classes of the community, taking it upon itself to legislate a majority of citizens—those who cannot afford to occupy a detached house of their own—out of the best located parts of the city area, practically always the parts with the best aspect, best parks and streets, best supplied with municipal services and best cared for in every way? Why does it deliberately "segregate" the foreign-born who have not yet become sufficiently prosperous to buy or rent a home under building regulations which preclude the possibility of inexpensive development and construction?

In a vision grounded in the possibilities of growth and expansion, Lasker called for a more inclusive planning process, greater involvement by organized labor, and a new focus on civic unity. The solution to neighborhoods like the Lower East Side, where Lasker worked, was not to wall them off but to allow their residents to integrate into the rest of the city.

The apostles of zoning were alive to the threat posed by such critiques. Charles Cheney rose to the defense of the planning profession, penning a rebuttal titled "Removing Social Barriers by Zoning." The true aim of zoning, he insisted, was equal opportunity, giving the "poor man and the foreign-born" the same right to live in a neighborhood safeguarded by restrictions as the wealthy. Cities in the western United States were largely free from tenements, he noted, and zoning would preserve the preponderance of single-family homes within them so that workers could have access to the same mode of housing enjoyed by the affluent.

But Lasker's charge stung because he was right. Cheney had previously admitted as much, boasting about zoning's roots in anti-Chinese discrimination and its utility in excluding "the less-desirable and floating renter class." Even its advocates recognized this purpose. "Perhaps the earliest known instance of zoning," Dr. W. A. Evans offered in 1924, finding a precedent in medieval Europe, "were the establishments of ghettoes in which the Jews were required to live." Now, in an unsettling echo, zoning was being deployed in New York to push Jews back into the Lower East Side. The new law helped price many clothing manufacturers out of their lots along Fifth Avenue and prevented new ones from moving in. The final push came in the form of a boycott, with merchants refusing to buy from manufacturers unless they moved back downtown. Soon, wealthy housewives could shop at noon without having to walk past the Jewish garment workers who had labored for long hours and meager pay in terrible conditions to produce the things they wanted to buy. "Fifth Avenue has been saved," Bassett exulted, "and the 'Save New York' movement has gone along and helped press back the garment workers farther south than they were before."

But Bassett, ever the careful legal strategist, told his colleagues that unless zoning was in general use, their reforms would never stand up in court. Only by spreading zoning through the country before the inevitable legal challenges ripened could their achievement be safeguarded. So they established a national zoning committee, supported by donations from the beneficiaries of their work. The Fifth Avenue Association chipped in $100 that first year, and the Save New York Committee was good for $1,000. Bassett became its chief counsel, a title that disguised the fact that within a couple of years the committee was just Bassett and his secretary. He drew a salary of $4,000 and didn't bill for consultations in New York but made a steady additional income by consulting on the endless questions he received from elsewhere. He proved an untiring evangelist for zoning, speaking in forty-four cities, helping to frame enabling acts in twenty-two states, and consulting with dozens of municipalities. When he wrote columns or pamphlets, he mailed them out to planners around the country. His office became a clearinghouse of information, connecting planners to each other and spreading new ideas. He had help spreading the new gospel from a small band of devoted apostles from across the country. Just five of them—Charles H. Cheney, George B. Ford, Robert H. Whitten, Harland Bartholomew, and Herbert S. Swan—wrote fifty-two of the seventy-eight zoning ordinances in effect across the country by 1921. But the case of another advocate, Jefferson Cleveland Grinnalds, who was not among Bassett's disciples, may be even more illuminating.

Grinnalds was a surveyor and topographic engineer, who in 1921 secured an appointment as assistant engineer for the City Plan Committee of Baltimore and quickly parlayed it into new opportunities. He spent the spring of 1921 blasting out form letters to the mayors of small cities in nearby states, like a latter-day Harold Hill selling zoning instead of boy bands. "Dear Sir," read a typical entry. "Is the quiet enjoyment of any of your homes ever disturbed by the location of a garage or automobile repair shop in a residential neighborhood?" Whenever he secured one speaking invitation, he wrote to nearby municipalities to say he'd be in the neighborhood, to see if he could land more. By the fall, Baltimore had created a zoning commission, and Grinnalds was appointed secretary. He spoke at conferences, wrote for journals, and traveled to meet with leading figures in the field. Men like Grinnalds saw in zoning the chance to turn themselves from mere technicians, making measurements for others, into respected experts, telling others what to do.

The man who really transformed zoning from one more strange idea of big-city progressive reformers into a national faith, though, was Herbert Hoover. The consummate technocrat, Hoover was the secretary of commerce for both the Harding and the Coolidge administrations and brought his crusade for standardization to bear on so many topics that one exasperated Treasury official complained he was acting as the "Secretary of Commerce and Under-Secretary of all other departments." He wanted to find the one best way of doing things, and so eliminate waste and inefficiency. At different lumberyards, for example, you might buy an "inch board" that was anywhere from ⅞ of an inch thick to 1¼ inches thick, depending on the manufacturer; building plans had to be adjusted accordingly. Hoover put an end to that. He appointed a lumber industry committee which determined that, henceforth, an inch board would measure ²⁵⁄₃₂ of an inch. The Department of Commerce couldn't enforce such standards, but that wasn't the point. Hoover operated by convening experts, getting them to produce recommendations, and then encouraging their broad adoption.

Hoover wasn't just concerned about lumberyards. An immigration restrictionist, he worried about "the dumping of great hordes of people into our slums" and the resultant "misery of tenement life and its repercussions on each new generation," evils that he thought planning could cure. His loathing of apartment buildings was paired with a love of the single-family home, "the foundation of a sound economic and social system." The homeowner, he believed, was happier, more productive, and more virtuous. Zoning, he knew, could hold back apartment buildings and mixed-use developments, preserving solid tracts of single-family homes.

The trouble was, in much of the country, local governments had no legal authority to put zoning regulations into place. So Hoover appointed an advisory committee on zoning to draft standard state enabling acts, which, when ratified by their legislatures, would delegate zoning authority to local governments. Frederick Law Olmsted joined, lending his fame to the committee, and Lawrence Veiller and Nelson Lewis would lend their expertise. Grinnalds got hired on as a consultant, but the work of drafting the statute would largely fall to Edward Bassett.

The committee managed to produce a preliminary draft by the end of 1922. By the time the final version was printed two years later, Hoover could boast that eleven states had already used the draft version to pass enabling acts. By the end of 1925, some 421 municipalities had enacted zoning codes, covering more than half the nation's urban population. And much to Bassett's surprise, zoning had spread beyond the cities, because suburbs and rural counties adapted his framework to suit different needs. Given the opportunity, it turned out that most everyone was eager to enact rules that would enshrine the status quo and exclude other Americans from seizing the same opportunities they already enjoyed. Zoning had gone national.

"I prefer to think of Iowa," Herbert Hoover began his memoirs, "through the eyes of a ten-year-old boy." Most of us remember the world of our youth that way, through the hazy glow of nostalgia. Hoover was born into a nation that was three-quarters rural and sat down to write his memoirs in a land that was two-thirds urban. The migration from the farm to the city was the defining experience of the generations born in the second half of the nineteenth century— a group that included every president from Teddy Roosevelt to Dwight Eisenhower—and it imbued Americans with a deep nostalgia for the world they had willingly abandoned. They had grown up in farmhouses, then left them behind in search of opportunity. But they associated those freestanding homes with their childhood, with family, with community, with tradition—with virtue. If the tenement became the embodiment of all the changes they found unsettling, the single-family home became the avatar of everything they cherished.

But look at Hoover's Iowa not through the eyes of a child but with the sober gaze of an adult, and it appears in a very different light. Hoover was born in 1874 in a crude board-and-batten cottage divided into two rooms. The smaller, measuring less than a hundred square feet, was for sleeping; he eventually shared it with his parents, older brother, and younger sister. The other, about twice as large, was for everything else. There was also an enclosure on the porch, where a hired hand sometimes slept. The cottage had no plumbing; there was an outdoor privy at the back of the small lot. The only heat was a wood-burning stove. His father's blacksmith's shop, with its sooty forge, stood nearby; playing barefoot in the yard one day, Hoover stepped on a hot iron shard that branded him for life. Five years after Hoover was born, his family moved to a two-story frame house a block away; the property they vacated would house four more families over the next decade.

Crowded sleeping quarters, an adult boarder, inadequate heat, a lack of basic sanitation, poor air quality, industrial hazards, peripatetic residents—there was hardly a charge leveled against tenements that could not with greater justice have been entered against Hoover's own birthplace. There was no inherent virtue in a single-family home. But when Hoover returned to Iowa as an old man to visit his birthplace, he saw not its inadequacies but the chances it had afforded his parents. "This cottage where I was born," he told the crowd, "is physical proof of the unbounded opportunity of American life." And he was right.

Where did that opportunity take him? By the time Hoover wrote his memoirs, he was rich enough to live anywhere he pleased. He did not, however, move back to a board-and-batten cottage, or even to a spacious single-family residence in West Branch, Iowa. For the last twenty years of his life, Hoover chose to reside in Manhattan, in a suite on the thirty-first floor of the Waldorf. Similarly, Lawrence Veiller, who dreamed of leveling his city's tenements, did not return to his native New Jersey. He wrote his reports while living with his wife in a series of rental units in Manhattan, including at the Madison Square, "an exclusive and luxurious Apartment Hotel."

What matters is less that so many who extolled the moral virtues of the single-family home were hypocrites—although they undoubtedly were—than that they did not see their own hypocrisy. Yes, they had touted the single-family home as an inculcator of independence and responsibility and hard work; a ward against socialism and communism and anarchism; a guard against immorality and promiscuity; a panacea for communicable diseases; a solution for juvenile delinquency and crime; and above all, a powerful engine of assimilation to American values. But these prescriptions were for ailments from which they believed themselves immune. The maladies they were intended to address were brought on by immigration and internal migration—the arrival in the nation's burgeoning industrial cities first of large numbers of eastern and southern Europeans and later of white and Black laborers from the American South. The single-family home was supposed to foster the habits and values that would turn these impoverished new arrivals into respectable citizens. Elite reformers like Veiller and Hoover could live in luxury apartments without fear of moral degradation, because they were already thoroughly respectable.

There was, of course, no shortage of reasons that Americans often preferred to buy and live in single-family homes. The promotional pamphlets distributed by Hoover listed many of them. A homeowner could never be asked to pay more rent or to vacate the property. He could alter the house to suit his needs, and ultimately profit from any improvements. The home could serve as a giant wooden piggybank, holding the family's savings in the form of equity. Standing apart from other dwellings, it offered privacy. Perhaps it had a lawn on which the children could play, or a plot of land for a vegetable garden. Above all, it offered pride and a sense of security, a chance to put down roots. For these and other reasons, millions of Americans purchased houses, without needing Hoover or Veiller to persuade them.

But homeownership came at a steep price. At the most basic level, mortgages were difficult for workingmen to secure, and the cost of owning, on a monthly basis, was generally higher than the cost of renting. Hoover's pamphlet advised that a family used to paying one-sixth of its income in rent might pay one-fourth of its income to own a home. The biggest costs, though, were measured in lost opportunity. A manual for savings and loan associations was more cautious than the Commerce Department, warning that homeownership was not for everyone. "The mobility of our urban population in America is extraordinarily great," it advised, ascribing part of this to "restlessness and discontent," but admitting that most celebrants of Moving Day were going to a better home, a better job, a better commute, or a better neighborhood. In those circumstances, the manual warned, homeownership became a handicap. When factories shuttered or offices moved or neighborhoods changed or families expanded, renters could simply relocate. At best, homeowners faced steep transaction costs to sell one home and buy another. At worst, they might be stuck with a house worth less than they paid or a dwelling no one at all wanted to buy.

That's why, when Hoover solemnly proclaimed in 1923 that "the love of home is one of the finest instincts and the greatest of inspirations of our people," he was only 45.6 percent correct; the rest of the American population rented (although not all by choice). In the rapidly expanding country, huge numbers of new houses were being built, but so were apartments. He was particularly alarmed to discover that over the preceding two decades, the percentage of homeowners had actually declined. Some Americans were shut out of the housing market. But many others had weighed the costs and benefits and decided that—at least for their present stage of life—renting made more sense. An annual lease on a modern apartment in a good neighborhood, sitting above useful shops, with a streetcar running right to the office, was cheaper, less risky, more convenient, and, most important, more flexible than homeownership. They might still dream of owning a home; they understood the appeal. There was nothing Hoover could tell the residents of tenements about the glories of homeownership that they didn't already tell themselves a hundred times a day. But in the short term, most chose to prioritize the pursuit of opportunity, even if that meant that—like Hoover himself—they would have to live in a rented dwelling a while longer.

Housing reformers, though, saw the choice between renting and owning, between the apartment and the house, not just as an economic decision but as a moral one. Some, like Hoover, tried oratory and exhortation. Others, like Veiller, tried criticism and vilification. Their efforts were unavailing; the spread of the apartment continued unabated. Instead of snapping up ersatz farmhouses in neat little rows, Americans demonstrated a preference for the diversity of urban life, mixing together social classes, jumbling offices and stores and residences. Rhetoric alone wouldn't suffice to resegregate these populations and functions. Only the force of law could accomplish that.

———

Now our story shifts back to Ohio because, a century after the Buckeye State helped inaugurate the freedom to move by giving its people the right to become residents of any community they chose, it would play a critical role in the process of unraveling it. Ohio had been among the first states to see its population swell overnight with migration to its farmland, and among the first to see that wave pass on and its rural precincts shrink. The population had shifted to follow first the canals and then the railroads. Where these transit lines converged at a harbor along the shore of Lake Erie, the city of Cleveland grew enormous, first as a hub of commerce and then as a hothouse of industry. Men flocked there to make their fortunes. John D. Rockefeller arrived in Cleveland in 1853; three decades later, he was the richest man in the world. By 1900, the city had swelled to hold almost 400,000 people. Over the next decade, it added nearly 200,000 to that tally, and the value of its land and buildings more than doubled; by 1920, Cleveland had a population of almost 800,000.

Residents found this growth at once exhilarating and disorienting. Immigrants from southern and eastern Europe settled in ethnic enclaves, drawn by factory jobs. Black and white migrants moved there from the South in the enormous flow of population that, taking its name from the journey of the Puritans in the seventeenth century, would be called the Great Migration. Members of both groups wanted the same things as other new arrivals—the chance to work hard, to raise their families, to build a better life—but were met with hostility, exclusion, and even violence. Cleveland had produced a broad middle class, and its members began migrating in turn, leaving the center of the city to the newer arrivals and heading out along the streetcar lines to the suburbs. And it wasn't just the wealthy. Manufacturers followed the railroad tracks out of the city, seeking open sites with good access to transportation to build the enormous new facilities their industries required. Workers moved along with the jobs, but they were also drawn by the chance to have a house to call their own, a little more sky, a patch of grass.

The Village of Euclid sat just to the east of Cleveland. It stretched along Lake Erie for four miles at its northern end, a pair of railroads ran east to west through its center, and beautiful hills rolled along its southern edge. It had a population of scarcely three thousand in 1920, but some of its leaders were determined to reap the bounty of Cleveland's economic boom. On January 1, 1922, Charles Zimmerman took office as mayor. Two days later, the village hired Fred Pease as engineer, and a week after that, retained David Christopher as the village solicitor. Together with James Metzenbaum, a member of the village council, they would be the driving forces behind a remarkable expansion.

Over the next three years, the tiny village invested a staggering $4.5 million in infrastructure, doubling its population. Near the lakeshore, it constructed a grand boulevard, with paved roads bracketing an eighty-foot median, all of it illuminated by sparkling new electric lights. In the south, it paved the western end of Euclid Avenue to connect it with Cleveland. The village set to work on roads running north to south to tie these districts together, a wide avenue near the tracks to bear heavier traffic, and water mains and sewers running to the undeveloped lots. The goal was a city painted in three broad stripes, with prosperous residential districts along the boulevards in the north and south sandwiching an industrial district along the tracks in the center. It was an extraordinarily ambitious scheme, and it paid off handsomely—particularly for its authors.

The engineer, Fred Pease, was the biggest winner, and his presence was a crucial clue to what Euclid was really up to. His eponymous firm designed the garden community of Shaker Heights, catering to members of Cleveland's elite as they moved out of the city and into its eastern suburbs. He was then retained by eight nearby villages and the city of Cleveland Heights to replicate that success, and he billed handsomely for his services. Instead of drawing a salary, he charged 4 percent commission on all public works spending and then hired his own firm to build major projects like Euclid's incinerator and its sewage plant, further padding his profits. Euclid paid him more than $170,000 in commissions alone during the first three years of the arrangement—more than $3 million in contemporary dollars—and by the end of the decade he'd pocketed more than $1 million in commissions from various Ohio jurisdictions.

No Ohio village hired Pease at these rates simply because it needed an engineer; what Pease offered was the tantalizing promise that he could transform their communities into the next sought-after suburb. And while Shaker Heights had used deed restrictions to secure its exclusivity, ensuring it would remain a neighborhood of stately single-family homes without Black or Jewish residents, Pease now had a new tool in his kit. Shortly after he was hired, Euclid used the state's new enabling statute to set up a zoning commission. By May, it was holding regular hearings, with Zimmerman, Metzenbaum, three other members, and Christopher and Pease in attendance. Pease guided the process, drawing on his knowledge of other communities to suggest rules for lot sizes, height caps, and uses. The commission secured a pamphlet from Hoover's advisory committee on zoning, a copy of Bassett's zoning report from New York, and various ordinances from around the country. Pease himself drafted the map, putting all the pieces together. And in November 1922, the village adopted a zoning ordinance.

Much of the Euclid map showed the sort of straightforward segregation of uses familiar to municipalities from Berkeley to New York. The streets along the lake, where Zimmerman lived, were restricted to single-family residences. Below that came a broad swath of land zoned for two-family homes, with major streets set up as commercial corridors. Next, along the tracks, lay the industrial land, running in its broad strip from east to west. And south of Euclid Avenue, the land was zoned for single-family homes on large plots, with several developments already fully planned, complete with the curving streetscapes popularized by Shaker Heights. The plain intent of the map was to produce, on the hills at the south of the village, an extension of the other wealthy suburbs on the adjoining heights—what the city later described as a "fine residential district." The portion of Euclid Avenue running through Cleveland had been home to Millionaires' Row, as impressive a stretch of mansions as existed anywhere in the country. Now those millionaires were migrating east, and Euclid was setting up a district, backed by the force of law, where the city's wealthy elite—or at least its aspirational middle classes—could gain all the pleasures of exclusivity.

The trouble was the factories. They promised to make the village rich: pulling in workers, furnishing customers, sprawling over acres of highly taxable land. But who wants a mansion across the street from a factory? Not, apparently, Metzenbaum, whose spacious Euclid home fronted on Euclid Avenue. So, the ordinance established a buffer zone along the north side of the avenue, stretching back about 750 feet, in which a variety of uses—mostly residential—were permitted, but industry was barred. If factories were permitted to approach the avenue, the village later explained, residents to its south would face "the very pall of the smoke" and the noise and other damaging effects. That would leave "one of the most valuable parts of the entire village" and its "many large and very extensive residence allotments" blighted and "decimated in value."

The Ambler Realty Company, which had been holding a sixty-eight-acre lot stretching from Euclid Avenue north to the tracks, swiftly filed suit, claiming that placing its lot in the buffer zone had reduced the value of its property. More than a dozen other property holders in Euclid backed the suit, paying to retain Newton Baker, a former mayor of Cleveland who had served as secretary of war during World War I. Here was a test case tailor-made for the skeptics of zoning, and the realization of all Bassett's worst nightmares. For the first time, a comprehensive zoning statute would face a challenge in federal court. But instead of New York City's carefully crafted ordinance, which had taken pains to reflect existing uses and carefully avoided single-family zoning, the courts would be considering Euclid's effort to preserve a district for upscale development by reducing the ability of adjacent property owners to fully develop their own land.

Bassett's personal connections, which had been so crucial in building momentum behind zoning, had also helped protect it against legal challenges. In 1920, the Massachusetts Supreme Judicial Court—which, in that era, often set national trends—ruled that a pending bill authorizing zoning did not violate the state constitution. The chief justice was Arthur Rugg, Bassett's college friend with whom he'd stayed close. In 1924, as single-family zoning was being struck down in state-level courts across the country, Rugg authored a landmark opinion defending it. "It may be a reasonable view that the health and general physical and mental welfare of society would be promoted by each family dwelling in a house by itself," he wrote, citing the increase of fresh air and play space for children. A delighted Bassett instantly proclaimed it "one of the foundation stones of modern zoning."

But the state courts were one thing. The real question, as Bassett had understood from the beginning, was whether zoning could withstand a challenge at the Supreme Court. Bassett was racing against time, working to make zoning so ubiquitous that by the time it reached the highest tribunal, the justices would have little choice but to sustain it. He was still giving speeches, mailing out court rulings, organizing conferences, and working with the Commerce Department. And then, all of a sudden, the clock expired.

Euclid v. Ambler wasn't a particularly complicated case. Despite the village's protests to the contrary, witness testimony made clear that carving up the Ambler tract and zoning parts of it for residences had depressed its value, reducing the market price of the front portion of the lot by as much as two-thirds. The witnesses also made it clear that the developments to the south of Euclid Avenue were struggling. The developers of Indian Hills, south and farthest to the west, had laid out all the requisite infrastructure for a couple hundred lots. "They tried to make it a high-class residential district," one real estate investor testified, "and failed in it." Directly across from the Ambler site was Euclid Villas, laid out in 1922 as the village was drawing up the zoning ordinance; the elegantly curving streets of the development bore names like Parkview and Buena Vista Drive. Perhaps Industrial Overlook would have been more fitting; one realtor testified that buyers would "question your sanity" if you dared to tell them it was a "high grade residential section" while it presented a view of factories below. Only a few dozen homes were sprinkled over the hills, mostly modest residences for skilled industrial workers.

Euclid called Robert Whitten, who had relocated to Cleveland after his work for Bassett, as an expert witness on zoning, but he stumbled, because he hadn't grasped the actual issue at stake. Poor Whitten still clung to the idealistic notion that zoning was a matter of determining the best use of the land. Under cross-examination, he affirmed that the fact that the Ambler parcel was worth three times as much for industrial uses as for residential should have been a "vital consideration" in deciding how to zone it, implicitly conceding that the village had abused its authority by zoning it for residences just to protect the view. An attorney for Euclid tried to repair the damage, leading Whitten through a series of hypotheticals. *If* the public interest, health, safety, and welfare were at stake, that could trump purely economic considerations. *If* to the south of Euclid Avenue "there is a high bluff which renders that property available only to the higher class of residents," then surely "it is desirable to secure a strip of residential property north of Euclid and between Euclid and the balance of the industrial property." But Ambler's attorney, sensing blood, went in for the kill. He got Whitten to concede that if he were on a zoning commission, he'd have wanted a far more thorough investigation before removing the parcel from industrial use.

By the time the case went to Judge David Westenhaver, a protégé of Baker's, the facts were not much in dispute. The constitutional question, though, remained very much in doubt: Could the police power be used to impose zoning, when there was no actual nuisance to abate? In Westenhaver's view, zoning ordinances violated the Fifth Amendment's takings clause, which required the state to compensate individuals if it seized their property, and also the Fourteenth Amendment's due process clause, which prohibited seizing property without due process of law.

A government, Westenhaver conceded, could burden property holders with a costly rule if, on average, it left them all better off. But, he continued, Euclid had instead imposed its aesthetic preferences on private property owners. The ordinance, he thundered, was an effort to place a "strait-jacket" on land and regulate "the mode of living" of its future inhabitants, to "classify the population and segregate them according to their income or situation in life." Westenhaver was no champion of the oppressed; he had famously sentenced the socialist leader Eugene Debs to a decade in jail and was just as racist as most of his peers. "The blighting of property values and the congesting of population, whenever the colored or certain foreign races invade residential sections, are so well known as to be within the judicial cognizance," he wrote. Even so, the Supreme Court had recently struck down a Louisville zoning ordinance that had segregated the city on the basis of race. If the Louisville statute had been upheld, he said, it would have spread across the country and led to cities "segregating in like manner various groups of newly arrived immigrants." However sympathetic he might have been to that impulse, he was not prepared to affirm its constitutionality. Americans, he maintained, had the right to sell their property to whomever they chose, to develop it as they saw fit, and to live wherever they wanted. "The true reason why some persons live in a mansion and others live in a shack, why some live in a single family dwelling and others in a double family dwelling . . . is primarily economic," he continued. How could Euclid pretend that designating some sites for spacious single-family homes, and others for modest two-family houses or apartments, was a necessary use of the police power and not just a bald effort to impose economic segregation?

The case went up to the Supreme Court, as everyone had known it would. It was argued, then mysteriously sent back for reargument, as filings and amicus briefs piled up. A morose Bassett told supporters of zoning to brace for a blow. The Euclid ordinance was "not a fair test" of zoning, he complained, because some of its provisions were so clearly unfair to many property owners, and because it attempted to designate a residential community on land that "naturally and actually" was industrial. The court was dominated by a bloc of conservatives, later dubbed the Four Horsemen, who had spent the previous few years using the due process clause to invalidate a remarkably wide array of social legislation in nominal defense of property rights. Zoning looked next to fall.

There were two ways, though, to think about the system that Bassett and his allies had erected. The first was as a progressive defense of the general welfare, limiting individual property rights to protect the public good. On those terms, Euclid might win over the court's progressives, but it was bound to lose before its conservative majority. But zoning could also be thought of as a conservative measure, defending the sanctity of the family against encroachments, allowing communities to choose their own members, and keeping out undesirable populations. In framing Euclid's case, Metzenbaum had been careful to avoid this approach; he insisted Euclid was acting to protect the general welfare. The civic planner Alfred Bettman was not so reticent. He asked his friend Chief Justice William Howard Taft for permission to file a lengthy amicus brief and quoted extensively from various commission reports on the topic from around the country. Zoning, he argued, was best thought of by analogy to the law of nuisance, although, he rushed to add, it should not be limited by the traditional definitions of nuisance. Just as homeowners put the furnace in the cellar rather than the living room, he wrote, zoning finds the right place for each use.

In the end, the law was sustained by an unlikely coalition. The court's progressives, led by Louis Brandeis, were generally willing to uphold social reforms as defenses of the general welfare, but they couldn't constitute a majority on their own. The decision in *Euclid v. Ambler* was instead written by George Sutherland, one of the Four Horsemen, and it embraced the logic advanced by Bettman. Sutherland zeroed in on the constitutionality of excluding apartments from certain residential districts, adapting from Bettman's brief the familiar litany of complaints about their presence. When erected in neighborhoods of single-family homes, he wrote, "very often the apartment house is a mere parasite," cashing in on the elevated value produced by its environs even as it erodes it, and therefore apartments come "very near to being nuisances." And a nuisance, he claimed, "may be merely a right thing in the wrong place—like a pig in the parlor instead of the barnyard." It was such a wonderful line—a clear improvement on Bettman's living-room furnace—that perhaps not everyone noticed the logical sleight of hand.

To call an apartment "very near" to being a nuisance, after all, was to concede that apartments were not, in a legal sense, actually nuisances. Sutherland borrowed this language, helpfully supplied by Bettman, from a decision handed down in 1925 by California's Supreme Court sustaining single-family zoning. There was ample precedent for banning "near-nuisances" under the police power, that court had found; after all, hadn't California previously sustained the exclusion of Chinese laundries on just such grounds? Homeownership promoted personal investment in family, child rearing, school, church, and community; it safeguarded "manhood and womanhood"; it protected the "civic and social values of the American home," the court had ruled in *Miller v. Board of Public Works*. Single-family zoning, then, was a means of promoting the welfare of the community.

Even the nation's leading expert on the police power, Ernst Freund, found the Supreme Court's logic a little tough to swallow. Freund had no problem with the goal of exclusion, but objected to the hypocrisy of trying to defend single-family zoning as a legitimate use of the police power. "Everyone knows that the crux of the zoning problem lies in the residential district," he wrote. The difficulty, as Freund acidly observed, was that the advocates of zoning were dishonest about their goals. If single-family zoning was "conducive to health, and to cultivation of all kinds of civic virtues," he asked, then why didn't the government force the long-suffering children of the obscenely wealthy to dwell in such neighborhoods, removing them from "the blighting influences of hotel life"? But no one was suggesting that life in a luxury residential hotel was degrading. Freund charged that zoning was less a defense of the general welfare than an effort to turn the police power, which historically could only "operate irrespective of class distinctions," into a means of enforcing such distinctions. He suggested that zoning advocates instead create a new legal theory to advance their cause. Sutherland, for his part, preferred the redefinition of an old legal principle to the invention of a new one. If the court was to alter what it meant to own private property, it would do so on the pretense that it was simply applying old principles to novel problems. Like many radical changes, zoning gained public acceptance by declaring itself a defense of tradition.

Forty years before, the California Supreme Court had ruled against Hang Kie, allowing the nation's first zoning ordinance to drive Modesto's Chinese residents back into Chinatown. It had later pointed to his case as the crucial precedent as it sustained single-family zoning, which would be used to drive newer immigrants out of fashionable districts. And the Supreme Court of the United States, in turn, borrowed both the language and the logic of the California ruling in order to sustain zoning nationwide. Using the tools of housing regulation and zoning, local jurisdictions could now legally segregate themselves on the basis of class, and in the United States that meant they could largely segregate themselves on the basis of ethnicity and race as well. The counterrevolution against the freedom to move had begun in Modesto, expanded into cities like Berkeley and New York, and then taken hold in suburbs like Euclid. Zoning could now easily pass the legal test for any exercise of the police power; it had come into general use. By the time the court ruled on *Euclid* in 1926, tens of millions of Americans were already living in communities with zoning ordinances. Even the justices commuted to work through a city that had been zoned by an act of Congress. Bassett had won his race against time.

The zoning ordinance was upheld. Ambler never managed to develop its land, but even so Euclid's efforts to create enclaves of affluence at either end of the town fell flat. In 1942, the federal government seized Ambler's vacant plot and leased it to the Cleveland Pneumatic Aerol Company to churn out landing gear for bombers. After the war, GM's Fisher Body division acquired the massive building in which the landing gear had been built. Workers flooded into Euclid, many of them eastern European immigrants, moving toward the jobs its sprawling factories provided. Acres of housing sprang up around the plants. By 1950, the population had reached forty thousand; by 1970, it had topped seventy thousand.

Euclid had tried to use zoning to make its southern hills the exclusive preserve of the middle class, and now, in an ironic twist of fate, that dream had finally come true. In the postwar boom, Euclid Villas filled out at last, with handsome ranch houses lining Buena Vista Drive. But what Zimmerman and his colleagues had never imagined was that the owners of these homes would be the very factory workers whom they had worked so hard to exclude, pushed up into the middle class by unionization and postwar prosperity. Once again, the best cure to the problems associated with poverty proved to be not limiting where the poor could live but raising the incomes of the poor high enough to allow them to exercise their mobility.

Zoning alone, in its early twentieth-century guise, was rarely enough to stop the movement of the population, or to jam the wheels of opportunity. But the 1920s brought a broad revolt against diversity as a series of federal laws sharply curtailed foreign immigration, a raft of new zoning laws attempted to do the same to domestic migration, and restrictive covenants spread as a means to exclude unwanted groups. Many Americans—particularly those who were white, educated, and affluent—wanted more control over their communities. They sought tools that they could use to defend their privilege and to keep their social inferiors someplace else. They drew on the New England tradition of autonomous towns functioning like members-only clubs, with the premium it placed on consensus and homogeneity. All would be well, they believed, if they could just keep everything and everyone in the proper place.

CHAPTER SEVEN

AUTO EMANCIPATION

"I had to roll out of my bed, crawl on my knees in my living room, because I was scared that bullets was going to come through my house." Thelma Price's voice rises in indignation as she speaks. The sixty-four-year-old had watched a young man walk into a party at her neighbor's apartment with an assault-style rifle. Later that evening, the shooting started.

As she finishes, she looks me in the eye. "But I love my city. I'm not going nowhere, so I don't care what they do."

Flint, Michigan, wasn't always like this. Thelma's parents grew up in a different century and a different world. They came to Flint after the war, in the Great Migration. Her father came from Arkansas; he'd heard about the jobs at the General Motors plants from relatives who had preceded him. Her mother came from Mississippi and found work at the Holiday Inn. Together, they had twelve children. Thelma rattles off the names of the streets on the north side where they lived growing up: Baltimore, Philadelphia, Carlton, Harvard, and Home. She pauses. "I'll never forget when we moved on Russell Street; that was our best house. Five bedrooms."

She graduated from high school and found work at a restaurant. After she had her first child, she got jobs at a succession of small plants making auto parts. She commuted to Brighton, to Milford, to Ann Arbor, but she never left Flint. She laughs at the very idea. "I couldn't give Flint up. I love it here. This is all I know." Her family is here. Her five children live in Flint. So do all eight of her grandchildren, and her four great-granddaughters. Her church is here. House of Prayer Missionary Baptist, up on Carpenter Road, is looking for a new pastor, but not quite satisfied with the current crop of candidates. "I've seen a couple of them I know would be good for our church," she confides, "but who am I?"

She has her complaints, of course. She'd like more of the abandoned houses torn down. There was a stench in her neighborhood recently, traced back to a decrepit wood-frame building. Inside, the authorities found three dead pit bulls, victims of a dogfight staged on the premises. "I don't care what kind of breed the dog is," she says. "Y'all not supposed to do that." And she's upset that the young men are trading up from pistols to assault-style weapons, which the police seem helpless to stop. "I wish they could get some of the guns off the street." The shootings seem to be getting worse. "I don't feel safe here like I used to," she says, "but that's all right, because I stay at home."

Some relatives have moved away in search of opportunity, just as Thelma's parents did by coming to Flint. Two nephews are thriving in Tennessee, and her mom's two sisters went down to Oklahoma City and Allen, Texas. "They keep trying to get me to come down there. I'm looking at the cost of living. You know, I'm just going to stay put. I'm good."

Because that's the other thing about Flint. Her second daughter pays $800 a month in rent. Thelma laughs again. "I told her, 'That's because you're living with all that pretty, luxury stuff—y'all got all that fancy stuff.'" At the Rollingwood Manor Apartments, Thelma pays just $198 for her HUD-subsidized unit. That rent ties her to Flint as tightly as anything else. Where else is she going to find that?

"They could blow us off the map, and I'm still going to be in Flint. I love Flint."

In the first half of the twentieth century, Flint, Michigan, was a beacon of hope, drawing workers with the promise of well-paying jobs and a better life. African Americans came north, escaping the violence, humiliations, and grinding poverty of the Jim Crow South, in the hope of building brighter futures for their children. I've come to Flint because, as much as any other place in America, it has illustrated the power of mobility to remake lives. Today, though, the jobs are largely gone. Flint is racked by violence and poverty. More than half the city's residents have left, but most of those who remain, like Thelma, are Black. And that's the other reason I've come to Flint: to find out what happens when a population is deprived of the freedom to move.

When GM began to close its local plants in the 1980s, it devastated Flint. "It was a slow-motion Katrina," Dan Kildee tells me. "That was the storm that no one could push back against, no one could defend, and it emptied this place out." General Motors was born in Flint in 1908; Dan Kildee was born in Flint in 1958, to a large Irish family. Sixty years after its founding, GM directly employed some seventy-five thousand workers in the Flint area, and the city itself held almost 200,000 people. And today, sixty years after that, nine GM jobs out of ten are gone. "It's not just the loss of 60 percent of the population; it's the loss of 90 percent of the wealth. That's"—he trails off, and sighs heavily—"that's a nightmare."

Dan made a name for himself here by creating the Genesee County Land Bank. Speculators were snapping up the thousands of tax-delinquent houses in Flint but leaving the dwellings derelict, fueling crime and fires. Instead of allowing properties to be sold off to speculators, the Land Bank took possession of tax-delinquent properties itself, rehabilitating those for which there was a plausible resale market and tearing down the rest to clear the lots, removing the blighted structures. Even in the boom years, the urban fabric of Flint looked moth-eaten as developers leapfrogged past each other, selling lots on the next block before the first was fully built out, leaving vacant parcels scattered along rows of houses. Now, though, in large swaths of the city, it's not the periodic vacant lot that catches the eye but the occasional remaining house.

"One of the weirdest moments for me was taking ownership of the house that I lived in until I was four," Dan says. A decade ago, he went back to the house on New York Avenue and sat in a cold drizzle on the porch, listening to the church bells ring. He could almost hear the factory whistle sounding through the old neighborhood, see the swarms of workmen carrying lunch buckets on their way to the plants. Talk to anyone of a certain age in Flint for long enough, and the ghosts of Flint's golden age pay their visit. Dan kicked in the door and walked into the eight-hundred-square-foot, single-story house, past his parents' room, past the bedroom he shared with his brother. He had come to say goodbye. The Land Bank tore down the small blue house, and all that remains is a grassy lot.

Dan's grandfather came to this neighborhood on the east side from rural Michigan in the early 1920s. He'd been a lumberjack, but the Michigan forests had been cut, and the future lay not in harvesting wood but in turning it into things. In Flint, where factories once fashioned logs into carriages, they began fashioning them into cars. He got a job on the Buick assembly line—brutally hard work before the union arrived, but work that paid. He died of a heart attack at fifty-seven. Dan's father struck out on his own, setting up an electrical supply company to peddle goods to the automakers. And Dan followed his uncle into politics. He was elected to the school board at eighteen, dropping out of UM-Flint to focus on his career. (He went back to school decades later to earn a degree.) His next stop was the Genesee County Board of Commissioners; then he won a race for county treasurer, where he created the Land Bank; and, finally, he succeeded his uncle in Congress.

Wealth, he tells me, is more mobile than poverty. After the factories left, many of Flint's most affluent citizens departed, too. The evisceration of the city's tax rolls gutted its ability to provide even basic elements of civic infrastructure, making it hard to attract new investment and deepening the crisis of poverty. But the shuttering of the factories didn't cause Flint's inequalities; it merely exacerbated them. "The first wave of migration was racial avoidance," Dan points out. In 1940, Flint was already the third most segregated city in America. After the war, white families moved out to the suburbs, where Black families were mostly barred—by federal lending guidelines and overt discrimination—from following. Even as the laws and practices that once enforced segregation have changed, those basic spatial patterns persist today. One recent study of segregation in the United States ranked the Flint area just behind Mobile, Alabama.

When, decades before, Flint offered opportunities, a wide array of families came to pursue them. Everyone had to work hard for what they achieved, and some, like the Kildees, made enough money to keep moving. "When my dad was a little more successful, he bought a house on the west side," Dan remembers, "which, for him, was like moving to Beverly Hills. You know, it was like a fifteen-hundred-square-foot Cape Cod. It was a mansion to them." But the majority of Black families remained confined to the neighborhoods where they first landed, struggling to build wealth. Like Thelma, many Black residents of Flint love their city. But their choices, like hers, have been constrained by a web of discriminatory laws and policies that stretch back to the first arrival of their ancestors on these shores. And if you want to understand Flint today—if you want to understand the contemporary United States—you need to go all the way back to Virginia. Because if mobility has been the key to producing American success, then limiting mobility has been the key to producing American inequality.

———————

No group has better loved the most foundational American freedom—to live where you desire, to stay if you want, to leave when you choose—than the community to whom it has most often been denied. Africans were ripped from their homes and sold into slavery, then brought across the Atlantic against their will. They were torn apart from the families they loved and sold down the river. If they left without permission or tried to stay against instructions, they were cruelly punished. Enslavers were obsessed with controlling the movement of the people they held as property. They formed slave patrols, combing the countryside. They established a pass system, requiring written permission for enslaved people to journey away from home, and jealously guarded the literacy it required. The exercise of the basic human right to move at will was transfigured into a crime, and those who dared to claim it were branded fugitives.

After the American Revolution, white southerners joined the westward movement of the population, seeking opportunity. But many of those who migrated voluntarily refused to extend that privilege to others. Some 225,000 whites left the Chesapeake in the two decades after the Revolution, but they forced 98,000 enslaved people to accompany them. In those same years, another 100,000 enslaved people were sold from Virginia alone. White farmers who moved out along the southern frontier prospered, but that prosperity fed their appetite for enslaved labor.

The slave system disfigured the American South and stunted its growth. Along the frontier, many white men found opportunity and social mobility. But as land was claimed and cleared, the familiar hierarchies of the planter aristocracy reasserted themselves. South Carolina, where more than half the population was enslaved, gives us a glimpse into how a mature slave state operated. Almost half the white families in the state were slave owners, coercing enslaved people into the backbreaking labor necessary to grow cotton and other cash crops. Those who lacked the wealth or inclination to buy land and the people to work it, though, found the state stultifying, with few towns or cities, little industry or commerce, and scant opportunity for new arrivals. Of 300,000 white people in South Carolina on the eve of the war, just 10,000 had come there from abroad, and fewer than 15,000 from elsewhere in the United States. Almost 200,000 white native-born South Carolinians, meanwhile, had left for places like Georgia, Alabama, and Mississippi. The slave system found mobility of all kinds threatening to its hierarchies of race and class, and for white people who sought opportunities—whether younger sons of wealthy planters or members of the much larger class of small farmers—the best choice was often to leave.

It was mobility—specifically, the defiant exercise of the freedom of movement—that ultimately brought down the slave system. Human beings are difficult to hold in bondage, even if half a continent has been turned into a vast, open-air prison. As long as some place of refuge where people can claim greater freedom and opportunity exists, no system of repression can wholly immobilize a population.

"Throughout the South," Frederick Law Olmsted reported in 1860, "slaves are accustomed to 'run away.'" By the eve of the Civil War, the historians John Hope Franklin and Loren Schweninger estimate, perhaps fifty thousand enslaved people were running away each year. The overwhelming majority of such escapes were short-lived, lasting days or weeks. But all of these efforts at self-liberation raised the cost of maintaining the system. Planters paid for tens of thousands of newspaper ads offering substantial rewards, and slave patrols and search parties absorbed time and effort. Only a small percentage of escapees ultimately secured their freedom, but planters found even that small northward flow intolerable.

The South set out to eliminate the sanctuary the North presented by introducing the Fugitive Slave Act. Passed in 1850, the legislation required northern states to cooperate in the return of escaped slaves. Many in the North had been comfortable profiting from southern agriculture without facing their own complicity in slavery. Now, though, they were being asked to enforce the limits the South had placed on Black mobility. When Anthony Burns, who had escaped from slavery, was seized in Boston, it galvanized the city. "We went to bed one night old-fashioned, conservative, Compromise Union Whigs," Amos A. Lawrence, heir to a fortune made by turning southern cotton into cloth, later recalled, "and waked up stark mad Abolitionists." The law accomplished what centuries of brutality and exploitation had not, radicalizing northerners against slavery and setting the country on the path to war.

By the time the first shots were fired at Fort Sumter, the North and South were a study in contrasts. They had adapted the same English laws to a new land, but with starkly different results. The North had come to embrace the freedom of movement, however imperfectly, and prioritize the construction of voluntary communities. People flowed west to cultivate new land; they flowed toward county seats, turning them into centers of commerce; and they flowed to urban centers, where industry boomed. The greater opportunities presented by a mobile society, both economic and social, swelled the populations of the free states with immigrants and internal migrants. Virginia, the country's largest state in 1790, was by 1860 ranked fifth largest—behind Pennsylvania and New York, but also

Ohio and Illinois. If the North enjoyed a bigger population, an ampler harvest, and a much larger industrial base, it was less because of natural advantages than deliberate political decisions.

The North had one other critical advantage in the war: Black mobility. It had not set out to abolish slavery, but by the thousands enslaved people liberated themselves and sought refuge behind Union lines. Unwilling to return them to involuntary servitude, but reluctant to absorb them into northern communities, the federal government erected camps to house them. Freedmen, as they were known, had grasped partial freedom but were still denied their full rights by a government that regarded them not as citizens but as a pool of potential labor. They gravitated toward urban areas, seeking food and medical care and work. Their mass migration depleted the southern labor force and, eventually, swelled the ranks of the Union army. By the war's end, a quarter of the blue-clad soldiers were immigrants, and one in ten was Black.

Northern visions of a reconstructed South varied widely, but most centered on the idea of free men, Black and white, voluntarily contracting for their labor—exercising their freedom of movement between places and employers to pursue opportunity. This was, to say the least, frightfully naive. Most southern visions were different. The Yankee writer John Townsend Trowbridge was traveling through South Carolina by stagecoach shortly after the war, when he criticized the postwar Black Codes, the repressive legislation enacted by southern states to roll back the freedoms brought by the end of slavery. "All we want," one of the other white passengers, from South Carolina, countered, "is that our Yankee rulers should give us the same privileges with regard to the control of labor which they themselves have."

Trowbridge asked him what he meant. In Massachusetts, the South Carolinian explained, laborers must sign annual contracts. Employers who hire away another man's laborer can be fined. If a laborer leaves before the end of the term, he can be jailed. Trowbridge, who had been living in Massachusetts for the previous two decades, was only too happy to explain that none of this bore the slightest resemblance to the truth.

"How do you manage without such laws?" exclaimed his incredulous companion. "How can you get work out of a man unless you *compel* him in some way?"

Trowbridge recounted the story for its entertainment value, but his New England ancestors would not have gotten the joke. In colonial America, enticing servants or apprentices to leave was a serious offense, as was running away. Their masters could go to court to force their return or to recover damages; in Massachusetts, enticers were sentenced to be whipped or to sit an hour in the stocks, or were fined. By the nineteenth century, though, the Mobility Revolution had swept across the North, and enticement was relegated to a civil offense—and seldom enforced, at that. As Trowbridge explained to the men in the coach, employers competed for labor by offering attractive terms and incentives, and laborers protected their own rights by moving about.

Having ruled over a system of coerced labor for centuries, many southern planters found it hard to imagine such an arrangement. More than that, though, they were unwilling to accept the essential premise of free labor, bargaining with workers as legal peers. But freedmen wanted to control the conditions under which they labored, to work the same hours as other free workers, and to keep their wives and children out of the fields. Most planters yearned for the days of slavery; they wanted a labor force that would cost them as little, and work as arduously, as it had then. Their racism left them unable to imagine that treating Black workers as northerners treated their hired field hands—wooing them with competitive compensation—could bring to their farms northern levels of productivity and prosperity. Immediately after the war, many southern states did exactly what the South Carolinian proposed, criminalizing the act of enticing tenant farmers to leave one farm in favor of another for better terms. They also passed vagrancy laws, allowing adults deemed to lack a residence or steady employment to be bound out as laborers for fixed terms, and apprenticeship laws, which operated in much the same way with respect to children. Convict laws allowed counties to take anyone sentenced to serve time or unable to pay their fines—no matter how trivial the charge—and hire them out, too. If the freedom to move was the first and most essential liberty, planters were determined to curtail it.

Most northerners felt as Trowbridge did. The South's Black Codes provoked a fierce political backlash, producing a more aggressive effort at Reconstruction, and the federal government struck down or repealed many of their provisions. Southern landowners soon pursued other strategies to control their workers. They tried recruiting European immigrants, fronting their passage to the United States in exchange for a fixed-term contract, but found the workers tended to melt away as soon as they received their first paycheck, unwilling to labor under plantation conditions. Planters rented out their land to tenants, but they also made sharecropping agreements with farmers, both Black and white, giving them land to farm in exchange for a portion of the crop. They frequently colluded with other landowners in the neighborhood, whether in formal compacts or informal agreements, robbing tenants of the leverage they needed to negotiate better terms. And most diabolically, they advanced necessities to their tenants on credit, often far above market rates; it wasn't unusual for farmers to remain indebted even after the crop was in, so they would have to roll over the balance of their debt and stay tied to the land for another year. Unscrupulous landlords and employers frequently manipulated the books to keep them in debt, overcharging for purchases or failing to credit their full share of the crop. Lynchings spiked every year around the time accounts were settled. Indebted workers who tried to move off the land were chased down and arrested, often on pretextual charges; employers would then pay their fines, deepening their debt. Those trapped in this cycle of debt peonage had little recourse.

Wealthy southerners used violence, collusion, and repressive laws to erect a brutal regime of white supremacy throughout the South, seeking to immobilize Black workers. But in the first decades of the twentieth century, as the system hardened into Jim Crow, Black workers began to leave anyway. When employment agents recruited Black workers across state lines, threatening to promote the mobility of labor, states swiftly imposed prohibitively expensive license fees to fend off the danger—to little avail. For all its horrors, it turned out, southern racism wasn't the primary force that had pinned Black workers to the countryside, forcing them to labor for little gain. No, that force was *northern* racism.

When the Civil War ended, many Black families were eager to head north, but those who did found few opportunities. Northern employers who reached out to the Freedmen's Bureau in those early years to recruit Black workers uniformly offered far less than what they paid white workers, and few were willing to accommodate families. In the North, Black workers were also largely shut out of trade unions, blocked from the professions, and excluded from skilled occupations. Most northern employers preferred to hire European immigrants, who squeezed Black workers out of the few opportunities they had left. The cultural norms and legal mechanisms of bigoted exclusion proved incredibly potent. The grim irony is that in the segregated South, a broader range of roles was open to ambitious Black men and women, who met demand from their own communities. A Black shop owner could sell to Black customers; a Black doctor or dentist could fill his practice with Black patients. If most of the other available jobs in the South were unappealing, at least Black workers there faced little competition from the surge of immigrants who were vying for unskilled and semiskilled jobs in the rest of the country. The South as a whole, excluding Texas, actually saw a decline in its foreign-born population following the war as immigrants abandoned its moribund economy and ossified social hierarchy.

When workers in a particular area pressed for better conditions, or dared to leave home in search of opportunity, planters turned to repressive laws and violence. Some did leave—a notable exodus to Kansas in the 1870s showed that movement was possible, when a destination presented itself, but most Black people in the South found themselves stuck without a reasonable alternative. "Cast down your bucket where you are," the Black educator Booker T. Washington urged in a speech in 1895, counseling Black southerners to accommodate themselves to their situation. "Whatever other sins the South may be called upon to bear, when it comes to business pure and simple it is in the South that the negro is given a man's chance in the commercial world."

The country as a whole, though, was speeding up. Railroads crisscrossed the South, followed, at the turn of the century, by automobiles. Communications improved. The occasional Black farmer or laborer who migrated out sent word about the opportunities that beckoned elsewhere, or cash to enable relatives to follow them. Nearly 400,000 Black soldiers served in World War I, and those who returned south brought back elevated expectations. They had risked their lives for their country, seen what was possible in northern cities and in France, and wanted the same basic rights that other Americans enjoyed. Even southern racism undermined political support for preventing Black migration; poorer southern whites often viewed Black farmers as competitors, and many were only too happy to see them depart.

What ultimately tipped the balance, though, was a different form of exclusion. World War I choked off the flow of European immigrants even as it ramped up demand for industrial labor, and then legislation barred the gates to the United States more permanently. Big corporations wanted workers who would willingly accept low wages to perform dirty, repetitive, and dangerous jobs, and immigrants were no longer available. Instead, they looked south, advertising in newspapers, sending recruiting agents, and spreading the word. And once jobs were available, Black workers came.

Over the course of the twentieth century, some 28 million southerners moved north or west, infusing the rest of the United States with southern culture. Their migration proceeded in two phases, surging with the start of World War I, falling off with the onset of the Great Depression, and then coming back even stronger with the onset of World War II. Between 1910 and 1930, roughly 1.25 million Black migrants left the South; another 4.9 million Black migrants departed between 1940 and 1980. They were part of a broader movement of southerners toward jobs and economic opportunity; some 2.4 million southern whites left in the first phase, and almost 11 million in the second. All of these Americans were moving toward opportunity, leaving behind an impoverished agricultural region where per capita incomes badly lagged behind the national average for burgeoning centers of industry where incomes exceeded it.

The largest portion of the migrants—some twenty million people by the end of the century—were white, although less than half would settle permanently outside the South. Instead of forming ethnic enclaves, white southerners scattered throughout northern cities and assimilated quickly. Although Black Americans formed a smaller portion of the total, close to eight million, they migrated out of the South at higher rates, and some two-thirds relocated permanently. They tended to come from deeper within the South, and if it was economic opportunity that finally opened the door to their migration, it was not only material improvement that they sought by moving. The arrival of these Black migrants in cities with negligible Black populations was instantly visible, in a way that the arrival of southern whites was not. They clustered tightly together, sometimes out of personal necessity, more often because laws and discrimination confined them to certain neighborhoods. Though they sought the same thing everyone around them had sought, their mere presence provoked a fierce backlash. White northerners, whose distinctive commitment to mobility had been the font of their prosperity, looked at their new Black neighbors arriving from the South and seemed to have second thoughts. But still, Black southerners came, moving to cities likes Flint, Michigan, where jobs were abundant. And one of them was J. D. Dotson.

John Dotson, J.D.'s grandfather, was born in 1825 in Mississippi. By the time John's son, Kennand, was born, just after the end of the Civil War, John, like so many freedmen, had taken refuge in a city, in Baton Rouge, Louisiana. But when the federal government made a concerted push at the end of the war to revive southern agriculture in an effort to encourage freedmen to return to farming, John headed back to Mississippi to become a sharecropper outside Vicksburg. Kennand also farmed, and J.D. worked on the farm as a child. Like many sharecroppers, Kennand picked up cash seasonally, working in a local sawmill. At some point, though, he decided to seek better opportunities. The 1920 census found Kennand and his family well up the Mississippi River in Phillips County, Arkansas, where the wartime demand for rifle stocks had produced a boom in the hardwood lumber industry. He worked on the farm of George E. Blackburn, a white landowner, along with his son J.D. and his son-in-law, Lawson Truly.

It was a perilous time to be a Black migrant in Phillips County. As large planters drained and developed land along the river, the balance tipped away from smallholders, and the share of white farmers who owned their own land dropped from three out of five to less than one in five. Migrants like the Dotsons flooded in so that by 1920 more than three-quarters of both the white and the Black farmers in the county were born outside Arkansas. All of these changes angered many of the poorer white residents. Black farmers, too, had their grievances; many were tired of being cheated by landowners and hoped to capture more value from rising cotton prices.

Near the town of Elaine, not far from the farm where the Dotsons worked, some Black sharecroppers hired a lawyer to negotiate a better deal with their landlord. On September 30, 1919, a hundred Black farmers gathered at a church for a meeting of the Progressive Farmers and Household Union of America, a small organization trying to organize farmers and sawmill workers. Agents of the white landowners surveilled the meeting. One anonymous informant later alleged that these white men fired at the church and drove off many of the farmers. Then the agents of the landowners saw an approaching car and opened fire again, killing one occupant and wounding another. The car, though, did not hold more Black farmers, but instead a railroad security officer and a deputy sheriff, both white. Whoever fired the shots, the white citizens of Phillips County blamed the Black farmers. In response, white vigilantes rampaged through the countryside, killing, capturing, and torturing Black residents with wild abandon. The actual death toll is impossible to establish, but some estimates place it in the hundreds, which would make what was known afterward as the Elaine massacre one of America's deadliest instances of racist violence.

One of the Black men imprisoned after the riot was, like the Dotsons, a laborer on the Blackburn farm. Whether the Dotsons themselves had attended the meeting, or whether they had been caught up in the ensuing violence, they did not linger in Phillips County, joining the more than five thousand Black residents who left Phillips County over the decade following the slaughter. J.D., by one later account, drifted through Chicago and Kankakee in Illinois, and Mount Royal, New Jersey. At some point, perhaps radicalized by the massacre, he joined the Communist Party. In interviews and documents, J.D. offered various accounts of his origins—he was from Louisiana, or Memphis, or Vicksburg—but made no mention of his time in Arkansas. If Dotson's silence was purposeful, it was not unusual. Mobility offered the chance for endless new beginnings; migrants often invented or embellished useful pasts for themselves, or concealed the things they would rather forget.

The violence of the Red Summer of 1919 was not restricted to Arkansas. Race riots took place in dozens of towns and cities across the country, including in northern cities like Chicago. Some accelerated the northern movement, while others amounted to a backlash against it, a reminder that mobility was not uncontested.

The Dotsons were part of an extraordinary exodus. As industrial jobs were finally opened to Black workers, they did exactly what other Americans have always done: they moved toward opportunity. On average, Black migrants from the South were better educated, likelier to have lived in urban areas, and less likely to have worked in agriculture than those who stayed behind. But that average conceals an interesting split. Those most likely to leave were the sons of those at the bottom and the top of the social structure—impoverished farmworkers and unskilled laborers, or those in white-collar and skilled blue-collar trades—while the semiskilled workers or tenant farmers in the middle were likelier to stay behind. Migration, in other words, skewed either toward those with the resources to pull it off or those with the least to lose. But it was a good bet for both groups. When two brothers made different decisions, on average, the brother who migrated earned twice as much as the one who stayed, even though migrants were generally consigned to the most unpleasant and poorly paid positions when they arrived in the North. And the migrants gave better lives to their children: their kids were likelier to graduate from high school and likelier to earn more than the children of those who stayed. But for all that, migration was deeply traumatic. For many, it meant surrendering the dream of becoming a self-sufficient farmer, sundering ties of family and community, and taking a leap into the unknown.

The Dotsons landed in Flint, Michigan, the heart of the burgeoning automobile industry. "Every job I applied for, I was told was a white man's job," J.D. recalled. Standing a full six feet tall, he was lean and strong from his years of farmwork. By 1925, he had landed a job at the Buick foundry. The work was hot, dirty, and unreliable, and it was all the company would offer Black workers. "They had one man who would come around with one of them old pint milk bottles, rinse it out and give you water," Dotson recalled. "We could drink water with one hand, watch for the boss, and keep working with the other hand." The heat was often overwhelming. "I see many a man would get so hot up there he'd fall down, and they'd have to carry him out on a stretcher." And supervisors were unsympathetic. "If you tell 'em you were sick, they say, 'Die and prove it!' If you say you was too hot, they say, 'Fall down and I'll believe it.'"

The auto industry was a fickle employer. In boom years, as cars rolled off the line, there was plenty of overtime. But when inventory built up, or the plants needed to retool for new models, the factories shut down—furloughing workers, who were out of luck. Moving could provide a hedge against this inconstancy. "When there wouldn't be no work here," Dotson remembered, "I'm a cook for trade and I would go out of town and cook. And when the shop would call back, I'd go back and work them three or four months, whichever it was, and then go right back on the road." Dotson rose to be a labor foreman, supervising the truck drivers at the plant, and threw himself into the Communist Party and labor organizing. In Elaine, the faintest whiff of socialism and a faltering effort at organizing had provoked a brutal massacre. In Flint, Dotson and other activists faced violence, harassment from police and FBI agents, and periodic dismissal. But in Michigan, he found he could fight back. He was active in unionizing campaigns at Buick and played a role in the famed 1936 Flint sit-down strike at GM that opened the way for the United Auto Workers (UAW) to organize the industry. He led a "flying squadron" for the UAW, which was sent to hot spots to brawl with toughs the company had hired to break up organizing efforts.

April 1940 found Dotson with four other members of a United Auto Workers committee on the sidewalk outside Buick's corporate headquarters, in the winter chill of Michigan. They had come to present a request, but they'd just been chased out of the lobby before they could make it. Union solidarity didn't preclude racist taunts.

"Send the eight-ball in," one of them said. Dotson, the lone Black man among them, entered the building. He talked his way into the office of Harlow Curtice, the most important GM executive in Flint.

"Well, what you come here for, boy?" the president of Buick demanded.

"You know John L. Lewis is coming to town," Dotson replied. Lewis led the Congress of Industrial Organizations, the fledgling labor organization that included the UAW. He was coming to Flint for the first time since the strike and planning a massive rally at the IMA Auditorium, followed by a grand parade through the streets of the city. Curtice knew he was coming; he knew it with all the certainty of an incipient migraine. "Well, what do you want me to do about it?" he asked.

"We would like to get them your cars to drive."

Curtice was incredulous. "You mean to tell me that you got guts enough to ask for a car to bring a labor leader to town?!"

That was exactly what Dotson had come to ask. But faced with defeat, he decided to bluff. Ford, he lied, had already promised all the cars he needed. "We can get five Lincolns out of Detroit to bring John L. Lewis to town," he said. In other words, Lewis and his entourage could roll through the birthplace of General Motors, cheered by thousands of Buick factory workers, in the latest, fanciest models manufactured by its archrival.

That was too much for Curtice. "No, you won't!" Buick would provide the cars, he insisted. And so it did. Lewis drove from Detroit to Flint between two carloads of state police. Dotson met him at the city limits with automobiles from the company he was there to organize. Curtice had been outwitted by a Mississippi sharecropper's son who had taken one of the few jobs made available to Black workers in the Buick plants and turned it into a platform for change. Dotson was a man whose life summed up all the possibilities of mobility in America—and, for Black Americans in particular, the limits of mobility.

If Flint was not the promised land, at least it was more promising than the South. The city offered strong schools, good wages, and a thriving community. What it lacked, above all, was decent housing. In 1930, all of the Dotsons lived on East Pasadena Avenue, just west of the Buick plant, in a single-family house, which had been subdivided into three units. J.D. and his first wife lived in one unit, paying $40 a month in rent—about a third of what the average auto industry worker earned at the time. His mother and father moved in with his sister and her husband, along with two adult boarders, also paying $40. A third family of four paid $20. Twelve adults, crammed into a single wood-frame house, paying a total of $100 a month. It was a common solution to the city's housing crisis; in the 1930s, a sixth of the houses in that neighborhood contained multiple families. A contemporary housing survey described the neighborhood as "a deteriorated residence section, more than a third negro," mixed together with immigrants from central, eastern, and southern Europe, and home to gambling, prostitution, and other vices. But those who grew up there remember it differently, as a close-knit working-class neighborhood where everyone struggled and everyone helped each other out, the sort of community where all the neighbors knew all the kids.

A new single-family frame house in Flint that year cost just over $4,000, and newspapers advertised enticing deals with no money down. But much of the city and its surroundings were effectively off limits to Black workers. Over his first decade in Flint, Dotson bounced around the same few blocks on the north side—East Dartmouth, East Pasadena, East Gillespie, back to East Pasadena—looking for adequate and affordable housing. In the only areas where he was allowed to live, there just wasn't enough of it to go around.

As the auto industry boomed, Flint was growing faster than housing could be erected. The city's population tripled to 39,000 in the first decade of the twentieth century, then approached 92,000 by 1920, and 156,000 by 1930. The growth both thrilled and terrified Flint's elite. They wanted their city to be the automobile capital of the world, but like other wealthy Americans of their era they suffered from tenementophobia, fearing their city might come to resemble the apartment-choked metropolises of the East.

In 1917, Flint's wealthy citizens brought in the city planner John Nolen to impose order on the city's dynamic growth. Nolen arrived in a city where thirty-one hundred factory employees were unable to find homes for their families. Men would come while the factories were open, putting up with crowded and cramped conditions to save money, and then return home each winter as the factories shut down for months to retool for the new model year. The exodus created an annual traffic jam on the roads leading south through Missouri, a novelty at a time when cars were still uncommon. "Flint was a city or town of boarding house citizens," one local later recalled. Those who couldn't stand to be separated from their loved ones made difficult compromises; 98 families were living in tents, and 651 in tar-paper shacks.

But as desperate as the situation might have been, there was one potential solution in which Flint's leaders had no interest. "Flint is now practically free from the three-decker or other multiple dwelling, and the tenement row type of building which produces the congested, over-populated city district and excessive land values in low grade residential property," Nolen wrote in his 1920 report, to general acclaim. "By legislative oversight Flint can keep under control all such development." He proposed that Flint adopt a zoning ordinance that limited apartments to the narrow business districts lining a handful of major streets, because of "their undesirable influence on residential property." Nolen's goal was to confine business and industry to designated areas and remake the residential portions of the city into a garden suburb, filled with single-family homes, from which all other uses would be excluded.

In an unusually bald statement of the self-interest at the heart of the zoning movement, Nolen told an Akron audience in 1919 that "to protect what we have got, we must have zoning." He asked them to imagine "a quiet residential street improved with private dwellings," onto which a tenement house suddenly intruded. Zoning, he said, could make restrictive covenants permanent and ward off the menace of apartments. Owners of single-family homes would see the value of their property rise, he promised, and new houses in their neighborhoods would be "of a higher type and better finish." Zoning, in other words, could segregate a city by social class, preserving the property of those who "have got" it at the expense of those who hadn't. And that wasn't the only kind of beneficial segregation that Nolen promised zoning could produce. "It is in most respects a distinct advantage to the negroes to be separated from the white population provided the areas in which they live are suitable in location and character," he wrote in his plan for Asheville, North Carolina—embracing the standard rationalization that racial segregation was in the best interest of Black Americans and the lie of separate-but-equal accommodations.

Flint was primed to buy what Nolen was selling. He found an eager champion in the industrialist J. Dallas Dort, who led the City Planning Commission. And, in 1919, as Nolen was producing his report, GM itself took action, setting up the Modern Housing Corporation to help solve the city's housing crisis. Employees could buy a home and, after five years of service, receive an $800 credit toward its cost. During layoffs and shutdowns, no payments would be due. The 950 homes GM built in Civic Park and Chevrolet Park were equipped with baths, hardwood floors, gas ranges, electric lights—and restrictive covenants. Attached to the property deeds, these covenants stipulated that only single-family homes could be built on the property and barred residence by anyone "not wholly of the white or Caucasian race." Each proposal underscored the two ways that Flint's leaders understood their problem. They wanted a city of single-family homes, not apartments. And to the extent they could, they wanted to keep it white.

The city did not immediately adopt a zoning ordinance, though. As in New York, some wealthy Flint residents who had purchased lots hoping to develop them commercially feared they would be zoned residential. And zoning itself was still on shaky legal ground; Nolen's report arrived before Michigan had even passed its state enabling statute. Nonetheless, Dort pushed the plan forward in an extended series of hearings over the next few years. The Planning Commission received more than fifty requests from landowners hoping to pursue commercial development, for changes that would zone their parcels less restrictively, and granted almost all of them. If any renters were worried that zoning would further constrict the supply of housing and drive up prices, their testimony went unrecorded. And in 1927, with Michigan's state enabling statute now on the books and the Supreme Court's ruling in *Euclid* removing lingering doubts about its legality, Flint enacted a zoning statute.

By 1930, the basic parameters of Flint's housing market were in place. Zoning restricted most of the city to single-family homes and a portion to two-family dwellings. Continual revisions to the city's building code drove up the cost of any new construction. Black families crowded together into the existing houses in the few neighborhoods where they were allowed to live, paying extortionate rents for substandard conditions. But white migrants had another option. Flint itself still had tens of thousands of vacant lots already hooked up to the city's sewer, water, and electrical systems, many of them close to shopping, factories, and schools, but the new regulations had put the cost of building homes on those lots well beyond the reach of almost all working families. Instead, many moved out beyond the city limits.

The communities of white migrants that sprang up just outside Flint, though, bore little resemblance to contemporary notions of suburbia; they were for those too poor to afford homes within the city. Migrants could buy lots on the urban fringe for a dollar down and a dollar a month and put up cheap tar-paper shacks or crude wood-frame dwellings, just beyond the reach of the tightening zoning and building codes of Flint. State building regulations theoretically applied to these areas but were seldom enforced. In 1937, Genesee County considered a building code to prevent anyone from building "a tar paper shack beside an expensive house," but the measure was defeated. There was no zoning in Genesee County outside Flint. Many residents were uncertain whether Michigan was a temporary stop or a permanent home. "Well, we don't know," one woman said. "My husband sort of talks about going back, and maybe we will later." The tar-paper dwellings seldom had toilets or running water, and although the lots offered workers the chance to garden as a hedge against layoffs, they also bred social isolation. "You hardly even know the neighbors next door," one resident complained.

The difficult conditions faced by white southern migrants weren't confined to the urban fringe. In the city itself, their homes were

slightly less likely to have basements and twice as likely to lack running water as the homes of their Black neighbors, whom they outnumbered by roughly four to one. Local elites looked down on them;
in Detroit, the public health department identified southern children in the schools by their dialect and—because they were "notorious as an anti-vaccinationist group"—by their immunization status.
As late as 1956, a pair of state investigators found "considerable un-
happiness on the part of northern, native whites with southern
whites." But white southerners were hired for better-paying plant
jobs than their Black counterparts, and they were allowed to settle
both throughout the city and along the urban fringe. Within a generation, more than half of white southern migrants had intermar-
ried with northern-born whites or immigrants.

Barred by housing rules that constrained their geographic mobility and confined to lower-paying jobs, Black workers, who had migrated from the same places as white workers, could not follow
them up the ladder of opportunity. On the eve of the Depression, the
city's relatively small immigrant population—about 14 percent of
residents—and the 4 percent of residents who were Black Americans lived side by side in a handful of neighborhoods close to the
factories, filled with aging single-family homes. Black residents
earned more than they had in the South, but when housing costs ate
up roughly half their gains, they found themselves with few options.
They couldn't build cheaply, they couldn't build up, and they couldn't
move out. The policy choices made by Flint's elite left them kettled
in a handful of districts, paying high rents for aging homes. But as
bad as things were, the federal government was about to make the
situation far worse.

CHAPTER EIGHT

THE HOUSING TRAP

The Great Depression hit Flint hard. As auto sales faltered, the city suffered, and migration slowed and then reversed. Roughly one in three southern whites in the city headed back home between 1930 and 1934. Black migrants were likelier to stick it out, perhaps because fewer had family farms waiting for their return; only one in five headed out of Flint. But although the situation in the city was grim, it still offered better prospects for both Black and white migrants than most other places. A detailed study of white men who came to Flint from elsewhere in Michigan between 1930 and 1935 found that they were several times more likely to jump an occupational bracket—from clerk, say, to manager—than those who remained in their hometowns. But where were they to live?

The Depression had turned housing into a national crisis. Falling incomes and mass unemployment left millions struggling to pay the rent or the mortgage. And as borrowers defaulted and banks went bust, the production of new homes fell sharply, putting laborers out of work. To revive the housing sector, President Franklin D. Roosevelt came up with a multipronged approach.

In 1933, the government created the Home Owners' Loan Corporation (HOLC) to refinance existing mortgages. In the 1920s, most primary mortgages were for short terms—loans of three to five years were common—and many required only interest payments.

Lenders demanded down payments of up to half the property's value to insulate themselves from risk, and assumed appreciation would build further equity. In a highly mobile nation, few borrowers worried about paying off their loans. They assumed they would move before the loan expired, and if they stayed, they could always refinance for another few years. Plunging incomes and property values shattered this model. Borrowers went to bed with the imagined security of homeownership and woke up the next morning in a house now worth less than they owed, paying far more each month for the mortgage on their houses than their neighbors were paying to rent their own. Defaulting, previously unthinkable, became a rational response, and the bad loans threatened to demolish what was left of the banking sector.

The HOLC aimed to solve this by making monthly mortgage payments as cheap as monthly rent, removing the incentive to default; for the same number of dollars they would have to pay to rent, people could own their homes. To pull that off, it stretched out the term of the loans to fifteen years, cut the interest rates, and required borrowers to pay down the principal. This strategy staved off default for some 80 percent of the loans it handled while putting owners on a path to paying off their debt entirely. The HOLC introduced another big change to the mortgage market. Congress worried that standard loans, which covered only half the present value of a house, might be too small. Someone who purchased a house for $6,000, for example, might try to refinance their $3,000 loan, only to discover that their house was now worth just $4,000. So it authorized the HOLC to lend up to 80 percent of the current value. The HOLC had simply set out to stabilize the housing market. But the key features of its refinancing program would help revolutionize it.

The HOLC produced detailed maps of America's neighborhoods, distilling the prejudices and practices of local real estate agents and lenders into a simple color-coded scheme. The areas they considered most hazardous for lending were highlighted in red. But although these redlining maps would later become notorious, there is little evidence they had any effect on the lending decisions of the HOLC; they merely recorded a landscape of discrimination but did not create it. The HOLC's mission was to refinance existing loans, and that's exactly what it did.

The agency refinanced loans in all sorts of neighborhoods, from Black and white borrowers alike, in roughly the same proportions that banks had made them. Nor did it confine itself to exclusively residential areas. A third of the HOLC's loans in the New York area went to houses that included some business use—perhaps a ground-level store or a dentist's office. And despite taking on so many loans in the redlined areas that its own maps and guidelines suggested were dangerously diverse, the agency didn't amass huge losses in its effort to rescue a million mortgages. Instead, it turned a modest profit.

The second prong of FDR's approach, the Federal Housing Administration (FHA), followed in 1934. In many ways, its goals were more modest than those of the HOLC, but its effect on American life would be as profound as that of any program the federal government has ever undertaken. The FHA aimed to step in and restore the market for private mortgage insurance, safeguarding lenders against the risk that borrowers would default, in order to give them confidence to resume lending. But instead of simply replicating what private insurers had once offered, the FHA adopted many of the HOLC's innovations. The loans it backed were to be amortized; they would be paid back over twenty years; and they could cover up to 80 percent of the value of the house. (These were later amended, in some cases, to twenty-five years and 90 percent.) The National Housing Act also required the FHA to ensure that mortgages were "economically sound" and to "encourage improvement in housing standards and conditions."

Leave it to Congress to require the impossible. The government was supposed to offer cheaper mortgages stretched over longer terms than any home loan or savings society had dared to extend, and to do it without accepting a higher risk of default. In a country as restless as the United States, with a population forever on the move, how could the FHA be sure that the value of a particular home wouldn't dip more than 20 percent, or that prices in a particular neighborhood would remain high for the decades it would take to pay back a loan?

A local bank might know enough about a borrower to extend him credit on the strength of his personal integrity; an immigrant home-loan association might rely on the social pressure of a tight-knit community to compel repayment. That sort of nuanced, individual approach wasn't available to the FHA. If it was going to insure loans on a national scale, the agency decided, it would need to map the country, assigning one of four grades to every neighborhood it contained. Once it had assigned a grade to a neighborhood and insured property loans on that basis, it was, quite literally, invested in keeping that neighborhood exactly the way it was.

The FHA, in effect, declared war on diversity, on mobility, on change itself across the entire country. It gave the federal government a stake in turning a mobile nation static, in freezing the status quo. After more than a century in which it had used its power to expand mobility—extending frontiers, improving transportation, and easing the flow of the population—it now set itself to the task of persuading Americans to settle down and stay where they were. And that was not all. Because the FHA wanted everything sorted into nice, clear buckets, it set out to permanently segregate the nation's land, dividing it according to use, class, and race. It was one of the great turning points in American history, and no one at the time even realized or, perhaps, even intended it.

The burgeoning economy of the United States had been built around the remarkable mobility of its people, who could move to communities they selected in pursuit of jobs, relocating in response to shifts in the labor market. The same held true on more local scales as towns and cities constantly reshaped themselves around emergent needs. The result was a disorderly jumble of uses and populations as old buildings were put to novel purposes and new arrivals moved in alongside longtime residents. Americans had long celebrated this dynamism as a key national strength.

But dynamic communities were definitionally unpredictable and for a lender risky. The FHA preferred stasis. Its underwriting guidelines penalized neighborhoods that mixed residences and retail, old homes and new, small homes and large with low ratings. The rules were aimed at the "prevention of the infiltration of business and industrial uses, lower class occupancy, and inharmonious racial groups"—an explicit endorsement of racial and economic segregation. The highest ratings were reserved for areas with "adequate and properly enforced zoning regulations" or "effective restrictive covenants," which "provide the surest protection against undesirable encroachment and inharmonious use." Covenants should separate single- and two-family homes from apartments or shops, and limit the occupants of any neighborhood to "the race for which they are intended." The rules also required a range of expensive infrastructure, from sewers to sidewalks. The goal, the FHA explained, was "to assure a homogeneous and harmonious neighborhood." But homogeneity doesn't produce harmony, blending distinct parts into a pleasing whole; it merely produces monotony.

At one level, the FHA was simply ratifying the practices some real estate developers were already using in their fashionable new suburban developments. But by writing these practices into its guidelines, the agency effectively took the preferences of a small number of affluent, native-born white homeowners and turned them into federal policy. Private lenders soon adopted the FHA's requirements for their own loans. Over the next couple of decades, the FHA would profoundly reshape the American landscape. Families that wanted adequate housing generally had to move out of the urban core and into new developments, often outside the city limits, in order to find it. Before the FHA, metropolitan areas were dominated by renters; two decades after its arrival, America had become a nation of homeowners. Or at least the parts of America that qualified for FHA loans. The Americans who couldn't qualify for FHA loans—because they lived above their workplace, because they didn't earn enough, or because of the color of their skin—got left behind.

The third prong of FDR's approach to the housing crisis was to create public housing—codified as the Wagner-Steagall Act in 1937. "There are nearly forty million people"—a third of the country— "who are of such low earning capacity that they cannot get credit," FDR explained to reporters. The average FHA borrower, he pointed out, earned nearly three times as much as the average family. What about everyone else, stuck renting a deteriorating home or apartment? The answer he landed on was public housing. Local authorities would construct housing, using annual federal subsidies, and make available "decent, safe, and sanitary dwellings for families of low income," the act stipulated. To avoid competing with the private sector, the average cost per unit needed to be lower than that of commercial developments, the incomes of tenants were capped, and, as a general rule, one unit of substandard housing needed to be destroyed for each new unit that was created. "We must restrain our enthusiasm for the ideal," the administrator of the U.S. Housing Authority cautioned, and focus on "the necessity of careful economy." In practical terms, that almost invariably meant building row houses and apartment complexes instead of single-family homes. And local authorities could control where these new units would be placed.

Taken together, these federal programs established a new logic of housing. White middle-class families could use FHA loans to buy single-family homes in new suburban subdivisions, if they exceeded the minimum income. Working-class families could apply to rent apartments in public housing developments, as long as they didn't exceed the maximum income. Low-density sprawl and class-based segregation became a matter of federal policy. And federal dollars flooded toward the rapidly expanding and politically powerful middle class, while working-class families received only a comparative trickle. Between 1935 and 1964, the FHA financed 6.4 million single-family homes, but its Section 207 program financed just 219,000 apartments over the same span.

Where Hoover had simply encouraged the adoption of zoning, FDR effectively imposed it on the entire country. If communities wanted to attract new residents, or even just find buyers for existing houses, they needed to please the FHA, and that meant enacting zoning for the first time, or revising existing rules to meet the FHA's stringent standards of spatial segregation. Most of the urban fringe of Genesee County, Michigan, found itself redlined by the FHA, lacking both the amenities its loans required—from sewers to sidewalks—and the zoning ordinances the agency demanded. Though monolithically white, the suburbs of Flint had been economically diverse;

affluent enclaves sat near stretches of self-constructed migrant dwellings. But to qualify for FHA loans, communities rushed to incorporate themselves, to raise taxes and construct amenities, and to pass zoning ordinances. At the behest of the federal government, metropolitan areas began sorting themselves economically as the middle classes moved out to new suburban subdivisions, where building and zoning codes imposed new standards. The working classes, meanwhile, were increasingly shunted back to the urban core. And the effects of this confinement compounded over time; jurisdictions that couldn't meet FHA requirements suffered from depressed property values, which in turn made it difficult for them to invest in the infrastructure the FHA required.

White southerners who had migrated to Flint to take advantage of the abundance of wartime industrial jobs continued to cluster on the urban fringe, although some now qualified for FHA loans. The UAW found that half of the autoworkers were commuting at least ten miles to work, and a fifth were driving thirty or more each way. For some, of course, the trade-off was worth it. But others told the surveyors they would happily move into the city, if only housing could be found. The FHA, however, had made loans for urban housing development so difficult to obtain that almost any new private construction would have to take place outside the city limits. Of the 24,000 vacant lots in Flint in 1947, only 188 were rated "excellent" by the FHA.

Black workers in the Second Great Migration that followed World War II poured into the few neighborhoods where they were permitted to live, filling the aging housing stock past its capacity to absorb them. Frank Williams, for example, moved to Flint with his mother from Faith, Arkansas, around 1942, when he was only three. His grandfather had a job at a Chevrolet plant and also bused dishes at a local Walgreens lunch counter. When his mom arrived in Flint, she joined her father at the Walgreens and then found a factory job at AC Spark Plug. Frank's grandfather had rented the first floor of a single-family frame house, wedged next to a coal yard, with train tracks running along the back. He slept on a bed in the living room, near a potbellied stove, while Frank's mom slept on a small couch and

Frank slept nearby. In the dining room slept his grandfather's sister, along with her husband and her two children. There was no bathroom, just a toilet that froze up in the winter.

As bad as the wartime crowding could be, peacetime made it worse. In 1946, the Urban League of Flint warned that the end of the war would not be the end of the city's housing crisis; the advent of the mechanical cotton picker would accelerate the northward movement of the southern population. "When people cannot make a living in their home communities, they will eventually be forced to move to other communities that offer greater opportunities.... Hundreds and thousands of these displaced workers will think in terms of 'cousin Joe' who went up to Michigan to work in the shops. These migrants will be colored as well as white. This is a problem that Flint will have to face. The help of every fair minded Negro and white person will be needed to expedite their adjustment."

In 1947, Frank's mother married Garland Jones, a war veteran, and they bought a home of their own. Everyone was doing it. That year alone, Americans constructed 1,265,100 new houses, and 542,000 of them were purchased with veterans' benefits using the GI Bill. But the GI Bill, like the FHA, operated through local lending institutions that weren't willing to make loans in Black neighborhoods. Even though Jones was a veteran, he couldn't get a mortgage to purchase his house on Florida Avenue. Restrictive covenants, meanwhile, blocked qualified Black borrowers from purchasing houses in the surrounding areas. A 1937 map from the HOLC assigned the Jones neighborhood the lowest available grade of D, with the annotation "Undesirables—aliens and negroes." The FHA maps haven't survived, but presumably rated it the same way.

So Jones, like many aspiring Black homeowners, made a desperate gamble. He bought a house directly from a seller, on a "land contract," without taking out a mortgage. For white veterans, buying a house meant acquiring a financial safety net. Unlike renters, they slowly built equity, which could act as a cushion in hard times. In an auto town like Flint, with seasonal layoffs for plants to retool and mass unemployment during recessions, a safety net was no small thing. Buying a home on contract was more like walking a tightrope.

If Jones stumbled twice in a single year, making his monthly payments even a day late, he'd fall to his financial doom.

Many sellers, in fact, were counting on buyers to stumble. They kept the deeds until the last payment was made. If they had the chance, they could simply repossess the house, instantly wiping out all the money buyers had paid over time, and sell it to the next desperate family, in a cycle of cruelty and misery. Not only did Jones have to shoulder more risk, buying the house on contract; he also had to pay handsomely for the privilege. He put $200 down and promised to pay an additional $6,000 in monthly installments at 6 percent interest. In the white neighborhood across the tracks, veterans were putting together VA benefits and FHA loans to buy similar homes for $4,000 to $4,500, for no money down, with mortgages as low as 4 percent. Even though Jones managed to walk the tightrope, he ended up paying roughly 80 percent more, simply because he was Black.

Jones's story was not unusual. In the decade after the war, America built more than 13 million homes, and there were more than a million Black veterans eligible to buy them. By the educated guess of one sympathetic Veterans Administration official, though, "less than 30,000 colored veterans . . . benefited from the provisions of the G.I. loan program" over that period. The few who did secure loans still faced an impossible situation. Since few lenders would extend loans in Black communities, qualifying for a mortgage often meant buying a home in an otherwise white neighborhood. One veteran in the Detroit area who managed to use his loan encountered "organized efforts to prevent my occupying my house on the grounds that I am of the colored race." It was the old, familiar logic of "warning out."

Flint's building and zoning codes and FHA redlining left the city poorly equipped to provide desperately needed housing in the postwar years, even for white workers. Most new housing in the area went up in subdivisions on undeveloped land near the city limits, or in the suburbs, and much of it was too expensive for ordinary factory workers. "Our market in Flint is for $5,000 and $6,000 homes. All of us know that," the Flint builder Robert Gerholz said in 1948, complaining about regulations. "We've got to somehow provide decent housing for those who cannot afford to pay the higher figures." Multifamily buildings offered to bring down the cost per unit, but Flint remained committed to being a city of single-family homeowners, even though its primary industry—with its low-paying jobs, seasonal layoffs, and repeated booms and busts—was almost uniquely ill-suited to that model. "Typically, dwelling units have been bought on mortgage by incoming workers, under-maintained during the short period of tenure, and returned to the housing market during periods of economic depression or recession," Flint's Department of Community Development reported in 1959. It recommended increasing the supply of rental housing to accommodate the surges and downturns of the auto industry.

But if the segregation of Flint by land use and social class could be painful for white migrants, its segregation by race was a catastrophe for its Black residents. In 1950, the census tract in Flint with the highest percentage of nonwhite residents also had the most people per unit, the lowest monthly rent, and a D grade from the FHA. Almost 40 percent of its housing units were rated as dilapidated or lacked a private bath. Black residents of Flint were fighting "an uphill battle against overcrowding, slum housing, fantastic housing shortages, and an almost unbroken pattern of housing segregation," the journalist Charles J. Wartman charged in a series of reports in 1958 and 1959. Again and again, investigations sought to understand the origins of Flint's slums. And again and again, they pointed back to racist policies and discrimination. "Flint is the most segregated city in the Northeast, North Central, and West," an Urban League report concluded in 1966.

On January 10, 1855, the Boston industrialist Amos A. Lawrence, the man who claimed he and the rest of Boston "went to bed one night old-fashioned, conservative, Compromise Union Whigs" and after the kidnapping of Anthony Burns "waked up stark mad Abolitionists," sold off some land near his mansion in Brookline, an affluent suburb of Boston. He wanted cash, but he also wanted neighbors of his own kind. One parcel of land went to Franklin G. Dexter, son of a leading Boston attorney and a respectable member of the Brahmin elite, to build a home. The other two parcels went to Ivory Bean, a developer. The deed Lawrence wrote out for Dexter was fairly standard, conveying the land without restrictions for $8,000. But although Lawrence hadn't been able to resist the temptation of greater profit—he charged Bean $11,400 for one parcel, and $13,100 for the other—he was clearly nervous about what the developer would build next door to his estate. So Lawrence included a fairly standard nuisance covenant, barring the use of the land by a list of tradesmen, including butchers, varnish makers, soap boilers, and sugar bakers. And he included another, quite extraordinary, clause, barring "occupation by any negro or negroes nor by any native or natives of Ireland."

Nuisance covenants were already common in property deeds by the mid-nineteenth century, barring harmful activity from a lot, restricting its use to dwellings, or mandating setbacks from the street. But Lawrence's clause is the earliest known example of racial restrictions in a property deed. It had been just six months since Lawrence had waked up a stark raving abolitionist; he was, at the time of the sale, pouring his fortune into keeping Kansas a free state and would shortly arrange a vital shipment of Sharps rifles to abolitionist settlers in the state. But hating slavery was one thing; living beside Black neighbors something else again. Bean erected a pair of elegant homes on the land, touting their location in a neighborhood "of the highest respectability." There is no evidence Lawrence's restrictions were ever enforced, nor that they would have been upheld by a court. But they marked an ominous beginning.

The first known effort to actually enforce such restrictions came several decades later, on the opposite coast. In 1886, Alex Gandolfo, who operated a grocery store in one of Ventura, California's, first redbrick commercial buildings, bought the land it sat on from a man named Steward. Gandolfo's store backed on to "Chinese Alley," a crowded row of tenements and, the city inspector alleged, opium and gambling dens. As part of the transaction, Steward recorded in the deed that neither the land he sold to Gandolfo nor the adjacent plot could be sold or rented "to a Chinaman or Chinamen." Some time later, Steward sold the rest of his land to Fridolin Hartman, a German immigrant who operated a hotel and a brewery across the street. Hartman, in turn, rented two of the lots to a pair of Chinese restaurateurs, Sam Choy and Fong Yet. (Census records suggest that Fong, like many operators of small businesses, moved into the building that held the restaurant.) In November 1890, Gandolfo sued Hartman, Choy, and Fong on the grounds they had broken the restrictions. When the case found its way to federal district court, however, the judge was having none of it. "Any result inhibited by the constitution can no more be accomplished by contract of individual citizens than by legislation, and the courts should no more enforce the one than the other," he wrote. "This would seem to be very clear."

It should have been perfectly clear. Only somehow, it wasn't. Steward wrote his racially restrictive deeds just as anti-laundry ordinances were proliferating, just as Modesto was inventing zoning, just as towns throughout California were resorting to violence to drive away their Chinese neighbors. Just like zoning, racially restrictive covenants appear to have developed as a tool of anti-Chinese xenophobia and then been quickly adapted to suit other bigotries. A real estate trade journal in 1890 cited a deed for a property on Mott Street, in New York's Chinatown, that barred leases or sales to "any of the Mongolian or African race." By 1906, a self-help manual for real estate development written in Los Angeles noted that "high-class subdivisions" there had "pretty generally adopted" clauses restricting sales to "members of the white race," as if the practice had become so widespread in a few short years as to elide the need for further explanation. As time went on, some deeds would include long lists of noxious races; in Washington, D.C., one deed barred anyone "of negro blood or extraction" and also "Armenians, Jews, Hebrews, Persians and Syrians." Most often, such restrictions targeted Black Americans. But all these rules were intended by communities to warn out people they deemed unfit to belong. That they were, legally, "covenants" was no coincidence; they revived the old covenantal logic of New England's exclusionary towns.

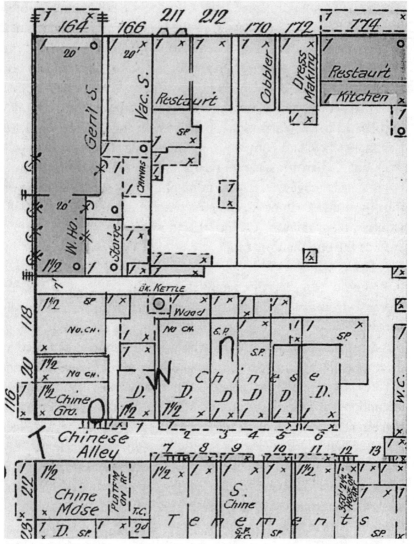

This map of Ventura in 1892, the year that *Gandolfo v. Hartman* was decided, shows the first effort to enforce a racially restrictive covenant. Gandolfo's grocery is on the upper left. The restaurant is on the lots labeled 211 and 212, between a vacant storefront and a cobbler. Chinese Alley is at the bottom of the map.

LIBRARY OF CONGRESS, GEOGRAPHY AND MAPS DIVISION, SANBORN MAPS COLLECTION.

Deed restrictions, though, were a decidedly imperfect mechanism of exclusion. If you wanted to enforce them, you had to sue, and to do that, you needed to be a party to the contract. Neither the buyer nor the seller was likely to object to their own transaction. Developers, of course, could put restrictions into the deeds of new subdivisions; some existing neighborhoods persuaded property owners to join binding compacts and accept onto their property mutually enforceable contracts. Even then, going to court was expensive, time-consuming, and uncertain. These covenants might best be thought of as an example of what legal scholars term the "expressive function" of law, intended more to communicate norms and beliefs than to generate routine enforcement. And at that, they were distressingly effective; new neighborhoods throughout the country were effectively segregated, even where no legal action was ever taken to enforce restrictive deeds. Even so, many cities and towns wanted more powerful instruments of exclusion. So, at the same time these restrictions were spreading, communities turned to a new zoning tool.

In 1910, Baltimore's city council adopted a singularly odious ordinance, designating one section of the city as the only place to which Black people could move. Within that territory, whites could not move to majority-Black blocks, and Black people could not move to blocks with a white majority. Hailing it as a "progressive step," the former city councillor William Ogden declared it would "keep our people together, our population solid, and let us live where we want to live." But Ogden's "we" was meant to include only the city's white citizens, and not its Black ones. The flawed statute even outraged many white residents in the designated area; one moved out of his home for renovations, only to realize that he had tipped the white majority on his block into a minority so that moving back would be a crime. Twenty-six criminal cases were filed in the first month. In the face of adverse judicial rulings and public criticism, the council was forced to revise the statute repeatedly. And although promoters had promised all would benefit from the law, restraining Black mobility predictably drove up rents and crowding within the area that the law had turned into a ghetto. Despite all this, cities throughout the South quickly embraced the scheme. Within the next few years, explicitly racial zoning ordinances were adopted from Asheville to Richmond, Atlanta to Birmingham, and St. Louis to Louisville.

The newly formed NAACP, founded in 1909, took up the fight against segregation in opposition to these ordinances, with mixed results at the state level. But in Louisville, the organization concocted a particularly clever test case. The local head of the NAACP contracted to buy a piece of property from a supportive white realtor and then had the realtor sue to force him to complete the purchase. The question it placed before the courts, then, was not whether it was constitutional to stop a Black man from buying property but whether a city could abridge a white man's right to dispose of his property as he saw fit. In 1917, the Supreme Court held in *Buchanan v. Warley* that racial zoning deprived whites of their property without due process of law. The NAACP's success catapulted the fledgling organization into the foreground of the civil rights movements. And although cities continued to pass such ordinances, state and federal courts swiftly struck them down.

That left restrictive covenants as the primary means of mandating residential racial segregation, and so, despite their shaky legal foundation, they continued to proliferate. In 1926, the same year the Supreme Court decided that zoning was constitutional in *Euclid v. Ambler,* the related case of *Corrigan v. Buckley* came before the court. It involved a twenty-one-year restriction in Washington, D.C., against selling to Black buyers. The justices sneered that the "alleged constitutional questions [were] so unsubstantial as to be plainly without color of merit and frivolous," and that the Fourteenth Amendment could not be applied to a contract among private parties. Taken together, the court's rulings on these two cases offered a road map for racial segregation: use the power of municipal government to segregate on the basis of land use and economic class and rely on private contracts to segregate on the basis of race. This was the legal framework in place when the New Deal began, and it's what the FHA demanded developers and communities adopt and enforce.

Not until 1948 did the Supreme Court reach the conclusion that had been "very clear" to the Ninth Circuit in 1892. In the case of *Shelley v. Kraemer,* it held that racial restrictions in private covenants were unenforceable in court; discriminatory contracts between private individuals might be legal, but the government could play no role in upholding them. This decision did nothing, though, to strip the language out of deeds, nor did it stop developers from adding restrictions to new properties, unenforceable though they might have been. Often, they were used as marketing tools, touted in real estate advertisements to reassure white buyers. And by the time the court struck down racial covenants in 1948, it was, in many respects, too late. Cities like Flint had already sorted themselves by race and class, and those divisions would prove incredibly difficult to erase.

In 1966, Michigan's Civil Rights Commission heard testimony from Black federal employees who had tried to rent in Flint. In small apartment buildings, one employee said, the vacancy would disappear between the time he called and the time he arrived; in large ones, they'd simply lose his application. Newly hired Black teachers would have to cancel their contracts because they couldn't find any place to live. One Black buyer was told by a realtor that it was "against their national code of ethics to introduce a foreign element into a neighborhood"—as, indeed, it had been until 1950. But even when codes of ethics changed, covenants became unenforceable, and FHA guidelines were revised, the racist attitudes they had enshrined remained stubbornly hard to alter.

All across the country, as members of racial and ethnic minority groups sought to move into neighborhoods that offered attractive housing, excellent schools, and access to jobs, they faced similar challenges. In response, they began to campaign for fair housing laws, which would bar discrimination in renting or selling real estate. Advocates of discrimination, for their part, drew on the legacy of the sovereign community to argue that American neighborhoods should be allowed to operate as members-only clubs. Fair housing laws, a New Yorker complained, would "force us to give up our basic rights to choose our neighbors and have thrust upon us undesirable people whether we wanted them or not." Orville Hubbard, the mayor of Dearborn, Michigan, opposed an integrated housing project with a resolution declaring, "We have the right and want to choose our own neighbors." A Chicago man complained that he "woke up one morning and we were the only white family on the block," and he, too, wanted to "choose my own neighbors." But the clearest articulation of these ideas came in a 1952 broadside published by America Plus, a short-lived anti-civil-rights group in California. "The roots of America are in its neighborhood," it said. The people of each community should have "the right, by majority vote, to say who they *preferred* as neighbors." Touting the freedom of choice, the group proposed a Second Bill of Rights, including the right of property owners to select their own tenants and neighbors.

But by the mid-twentieth century, such overt defenses of racism had begun to run the risk of discrediting those who made them. The America Plus article referenced the case of Sing and Grace Sheng, a Chinese American couple who, in 1952, tried to purchase a home in San Francisco's Southwood neighborhood. After being threatened by some white residents, the Shengs challenged the neighborhood to put their purchase to a plebiscite—and, devastatingly, lost by a vote of 174 to 28. America Plus hoped to make that sort of procedure routine by putting a referendum on the California ballot legalizing discrimination, and civil rights advocates feared it would succeed. The Sheng case, though, drew critics who worried the neighborhood's exclusion of a Chinese American couple had embarrassed America on the Cold War stage in the middle of the Korean War. Instead of boosting America Plus, the vote proved the group's undoing; it faced wide condemnation, and its efforts to back a referendum failed.

Progress toward formal legal equality was uneven, at best, and white neighborhoods continued to deploy violence and threats to exclude minorities. But as the historian Martha Biondi has argued, the fight to secure geographic mobility by striking down residential restrictions in the immediate postwar period led Black communities to organize politically and provided the infrastructure on which the rest of the civil rights movement was built. In 1968, after a long and bruising battle, and by a narrow margin of thirty votes out of the forty thousand cast, Flint voters became the first in the United States to approve an open housing law, banning discrimination in sales or rentals. The federal Fair Housing Act followed in 1968. These laws, too, had important expressive functions—they were attempts to signal that racist discrimination was no longer legally or socially acceptable—but again, enforcement was spotty.

And there was another problem. In the postwar years, white homeowners had moved into neighborhoods populated exclusively by single-family houses and built wealth using veterans' benefits, federally guaranteed mortgages, and tax advantages. Most Black residents of cities like Flint hadn't had that chance. Their houses, if they owned them, had lost value over time. The majority of Flint's Black residents rented and had built no equity. The FHA had required communities to segregate themselves economically in order to qualify for loans, and although it gradually became a less central player in the housing finance market, the zoning statutes it had required remained on the books. Flint's more affluent neighborhoods and the suburbs that surrounded the city generally barred multifamily construction and demanded large lot sizes that produced lower densities and higher prices. So even where overt racial discrimination faded, economic segregation tended to produce the same result.

Flint's urban renewal program in the 1950s both highlighted and exacerbated these inequalities. When federal funds first became available, Flint's Black communal organizations clamored for inclusion in urban renewal, hoping to sweep away dilapidated housing from their neighborhoods and replace it with adequate dwellings. Flint's planners were equally eager to demolish Black neighborhoods, but notably less committed to helping their residents move up. They approved the demolition of Flint's two most prominent Black neighborhoods, St. John Street and Floral Park, in order to run an interstate highway through the heart of the city. By the time the city designated St. John Street for urban renewal in 1970, most of the white immigrants in the once vibrant melting-pot neighborhood had left. Of fifteen hundred households, just sixty of them were white. Many residents were scheduled to be relocated into new public housing developments built nearby, but the city failed to supply nearly enough housing for all the people the highway had displaced. The project ripped the heart out of Flint's two historic Black neighborhoods, leaving a highway like an ugly, unhealed gash running through the center of the city.

Like those of most industrial American cities of its era, the boundaries of Flint had initially expanded along with its population. The city annexed surrounding land in 1871, 1910, 1918, and 1920, generally with the eager support of residents who wanted to gain access to municipal services. To find factory sites large enough for its gargantuan postwar plants, General Motors was forced to develop land beyond the city limits, but expected that these sites, too, would soon be incorporated into the city and asked for sewer and water hookups in advance. But as the historian Andrew Highsmith documents in his masterful history of Flint, GM had failed to grasp how much Flint had changed. The once undesirable fringe had begun to coalesce into suburbs filled with middle-class white families, while the urban core was increasingly filled with poor Black families. In 1958, GM pushed a plan for New Flint, incorporating much of the surrounding area into a single metropolis. But those on the increasingly affluent fringe had no desire to share their wealth with the Black and immigrant families stranded in the urban core.

Strident suburban opposition sank the plan. Flint would manage to annex some small industrial strips, but in the postwar years communities on the metropolitan fringe would incorporate as independent cities rather than agglomerate into Flint. Instead of becoming a single integrated metropolis, the Flint region acquired a core of industrial sites and dilapidated dwellings inhabited disproportionately by Black migrants and European immigrants. Surrounding them, and constricting their expansion, were suburbs developed with the bounty of postwar government funding programs.

From time to time, the injustice of these suburbs provoked revolts. In the 1970s, three justices of Michigan's Supreme Court took a long look at how zoning operated in practice—a system in which variances that waived the usual restrictions, intended as rare exceptions, were fast becoming the rule—and concluded that it was effectively a set of one-off administrative decisions and not a body of precedent. As a result, it decided, landowners should be able to challenge whether any individual zoning rule applied to their property was reasonable. When the flourishing Flint suburb of Grand Blanc tried to block a mobile-home park because the land was zoned for single-family use, the justices refused to rule in their favor. "The real question presented by this appeal is whether zoning in Michigan is a popularity contest to be won by the most organized and vocal of proponents or opponents," the court's decision began. Zoning, after all, needed to be grounded in the police power. "We cannot possibly see how a mobile home park vis-a-vis single family residences can possibly affect Grand Blanc Township's morals, health or safety," the justices wrote, adding that "the only 'welfare' we can possibly see here is that Grand Blanc Township residents like single family residences better than they do trailer parks." But the familiar pattern held. Once again, a court had looked closely at zoning and struggled to find any legal principle that could legitimize it. And once again, popular pressure prevailed. Within a few years, the court abandoned its ruling. Zoning was very much a popularity contest, and its advocates were more organized and vocal than the less affluent people they aimed to exclude.

Through the 1970s, Flint continued to see its middle and professional classes migrate out toward new housing tracts and its tax base of factories and shops follow. The Black residents of Flint were largely left behind. By 1981, a new assessment noted that "there is no housing shortage per se in the City of Flint." The problem, instead, was that the existing housing stock was decaying and frequently unaffordable to the poorest residents. The situation worsened dramatically as the 1980s progressed and GM moved toward automation, shuttering its factories and shifting production out of Michigan. Once a city with too few houses for all of its workers, Flint became a city with too few workers for all of its houses. The city gained a Black majority and continued to generate a rich and vibrant cultural life. But while people once came to Flint in search of opportunity, now they were more likely to seek it by moving away.

On an August afternoon, I walk along a chain-link fence, searching for the ghost of J. D. Dotson. The Buick foundry where he worked is now an endless expanse of cracked pavement, sprouting weeds, and port-a-potties. The house where he lived on East Pasadena is gone, too, replaced by a church. There are no more homes on his block—just overgrown lots and two decrepit shells of houses, one of them blackened and cracked by fire. If these Craftsmen were in good condition, their front-facing, low-gabled roofs painted in pastels, they'd fit right into a fashionable neighborhood. Instead, numbers are spray-painted onto them in bright yellow, identifying them to maintenance crews as teardowns. There are so many houses like these slated for demolition that the Genesee County Land Bank can't find the funds to knock them all down.

An abandoned home on East Pasadena Avenue in Flint, marked by the Land Bank for clearance.
PHOTO TAKEN BY THE AUTHOR.

Down the street I find Moe Wright sitting on a folding chair, because it's too hot to sit in a car. His grandfather came to Flint to work at General Motors when his dad was a young boy, and both his father and his uncle retired from GM. By the time Moe graduated from high school, those jobs were gone, and he was ready to look elsewhere. "When somebody said they were moving, I'd say, 'Okay, well, I'll move with you, go down there, and see what's going on.'" A friend inherited a house in West Palm Beach, and he stayed with him. "I liked Florida," he said, but when his friend moved back home and Moe had to rent an apartment in Florida on his own, "the expenses got kind of a little too high for me." He lived with his cousin in Dallas for a year, but his cousin tired of the heat and returned to Flint. He lived in Syracuse, New York, with his son and his girlfriend, but when he took his five-month-old son home for a visit to Flint, the boy was diagnosed with kidney cancer. His girlfriend, he said, didn't want to deal with a sick child. So he and his son stayed in Flint.

Today, his son is fourteen and enrolled at a local charter school. Moe points across the street to the Berston Field House, designed by John Nolen's firm a century before, where his son was taking a boxing class. He dropped him off, and he's waiting for the class to finish. In Flint, they are surrounded by a network of support. "My friends and family won't ever let me down," he said. "You got good neighbors here." And if the auto plants are largely gone, not all the opportunities have vanished. "Work is easy to find," he told me. "A lot of people say there ain't no jobs, but there are jobs." Last summer, he applied for three jobs and got called back the same day by all three. One business told him he could swing by that afternoon and hired him on the spot to work in a warehouse for $14.70 an hour.

Statistically, the odds are stacked against Moe's son. The Harvard researcher Raj Chetty's data tell us what life was like for the kids born between 1978 and 1983 who grew up in the census tract where Moe and I sat. By age thirty-five, only 15 percent were married. They worked hard, just as Dotson had in the previous generation, but had far less to show for it. Seventy percent were employed, but they earned, on average, just $15,000 a year. And even that dismal statistic is inflated by the small number who moved away from Flint. Two-thirds of those surveyed still live in the metropolitan area, and they earned an average of just $13,000. Choose a hundred census tracts at random across the country, and in ninety-nine of them, kids of this generation—my own generation—grew up to earn more than children raised near East Pasadena Street.

So why does anyone still live here? Moe's youthful migrations form a familiar pattern, following friends and family toward opportunity, just like his grandfather coming to Flint. He'd have stayed in

Florida but was squeezed out by the high cost of housing. He was in Texas for a year, but when his cousin moved back, Moe had no place to stay. Even in Flint, there were few opportunities. He doesn't tell me about it, but court records show that before his son was born, he sold drugs for cash. He might have stayed in Syracuse, but his son's medical crisis pushed him back to Flint. Here, even if his job doesn't offer the security or pay that his father enjoyed at GM, it's enough to secure housing in Flint's depressed real estate market and to provide for his son. Moe's left eye is fixed in a squint, and he tends to turn away as he's talking, but whenever he mentions his son, his head comes back around and a grin breaks across his face. Looking at his smile, it's hard not to believe that he and his son will somehow beat the odds.

But Moe's desire to stay in Flint is unusual. Many Flint residents, like so many Black people living in the South in the early to mid-twentieth century, have decided that leaving offers them their best shot at opportunity. Between 2010 and 2020, amid a crisis that rendered the tap water unsafe to drink, Flint lost another fifth of its population, shrinking down to about eighty thousand inhabitants. Some of those who remain have good jobs and many options. They love the city's rich culture, they're invested in its institutions, they're tied closely to its vibrant churches. But many face a harsher calculus, weighing the uncertain gains of moving elsewhere against the high costs of housing in the cities with better jobs.

"The truth is I'm trapped here," Rodney Brown tells me. We're sitting together in an archive, sorting through old clippings from *The Flint Journal*. Brown grew up in Washington, D.C., and moved out to Flint in 1999 for a job at the local PBS station. He fell in love with the work, and the city. Two years later, the station shut down, and he discovered that the door had swung shut behind him. Soaring housing prices in D.C. had placed his native city beyond his reach. "I could never afford it where I used to live," he says. So, he put down roots, organizing a local film festival, teaching at the community college, partaking of the cultural life of Flint and Detroit. The city's low cost of living, he tells me, makes it possible to be an independent filmmaker. Even if he won the lottery tomorrow, I'm not convinced that

Brown would actually leave Flint; I've seldom met a man more obviously in love with his adopted city. But he's clearly bothered that the housing market has made the choice for him.

One evening, in the southeast corner of Flint, I meet Carolyn Schannon. She is sitting on a glossy-red mobility scooter beside her fifteen-year-old grandson, Elijah. She owns a home a few blocks from where we're talking. "Been there over forty years," she tells me proudly. "And I'm giving it to my grandson. I've seen him grow up there; his mother grew up playing around there. It's my legacy." In her neighborhood, the statistics aren't quite as grim as in other parts of Flint. Almost half the kids in Raj Chetty's study who grew up in Carolyn's neighborhood moved out of the metropolitan area. Largely as a consequence of that greater mobility, their adult outcomes are in the twelfth percentile; that is, out of every hundred Americans, only eighty-eight ended up better off—a grim statistic, but not the ninety-nine out of a hundred that prevails in some other Flint neighborhoods. Elijah wants to be a veterinarian, but Carolyn, who's highly invested in her community, isn't quite sold on the idea.

"I wanted him to stay here around the city, and I wanted him to be a police officer or an attorney"—she turns toward Elijah—"so you can help your people"—she turns back to me—"but he wanted to do dogs."

"Yeah, I don't want to risk my life making teacher's wages. Nothing against teachers. Plus, I want to surround myself with something I love."

Only, Elijah's not sure he can do it in Flint. "You know, it's not all about money, but I want to go where it's a good area for a veterinarian, like Ann Arbor."

And Carolyn, reluctantly, agrees. "He could even be a veterinarian for the stars in L.A., or Culver City, or somewhere in California"—her tone grows wistful—"where everybody got a dog, or two dogs, and they love them and they've got money to spend to get them fixed up." She gives me a rueful smile. "Around here, the dogs probably just live 'til they die."

CHAPTER NINE

A PLAGUE OF LOCALISTS

On the final day of 1939, Fred Edwards got into his car in California and drove out to Texas, where Frank Duncan, his brother-in-law, had been working on a WPA project. He loaded Duncan, his wife, and their infant son into the car and brought them back to California, to the hills near Marysville, where he hoped the climate would allow the health of Duncan's wife to improve. A short time later, unable to find work and with his meager savings exhausted, Duncan applied to the Farm Security Administration and went on the relief rolls. A special investigator for the state controller accused Edwards of having violated a law against transporting an indigent person—Duncan—into the state of California. "I don't know what it's all about, and I never heard of the law," a baffled Edwards told reporters. Backed by the ACLU, he decided to fight the charges; he couldn't believe it was a crime to help an American move from one state to another in search of opportunity. He was handed a six-month suspended sentence, and the case was appealed up the line to the U.S. Supreme Court. The justices would decide a question debated for centuries: Did Americans possess the freedom to move from one place to another?

The law Edwards violated had existed in some form since 1860, a decade after California attained statehood; twenty-seven other states carried analogous provisions on their books. All were rooted in the old-world notion that everyone belonged to a specific place, which was responsible for their upkeep should they become a public charge. Community members felt they had the right to exclude interlopers to avoid assuming any obligation to them. That had seemed an obvious truth in the colonial era and still did at the time the Constitution was ratified.

The Mobility Revolution had challenged the notion that communities should select their members with the counterclaim that people ought to be able to select their communities. But when the dust bowl created an enormous wave of migrants, Californians, fearful that a flood of Okies would descend on them, reverted to that older conception of belonging. In 1936, Los Angeles sent police to the state line to turn away indigent migrants, even though they were American citizens, dropping their blockade after some months only when it grew prohibitively expensive to enforce.

By the time Edwards's case was decided by the court in November 1941, though, the public mood had changed again. The country was moving to a war footing. The economy was rebounding; help-wanted ads replaced unemployment lines in California, where factories were desperate for laborers. Frank Duncan moved off the relief rolls, taking a job at a chemical plant producing war matériel. Worried that inhibiting citizens' freedom to move would hinder the mobilization of industry, a House committee on war industry migration filed an amicus brief in support of Edwards. Striking down the law now seemed both necessary and patriotic.

A federal circuit court judge in 1823 had affirmed, as a fundamental freedom, "the right of a citizen of one state to pass through, or to reside in any other state." In 1900, the Supreme Court, in upholding a tax on emigrant agents, acknowledged in passing "the right to remove from one place to another according to inclination." But the justices searched the text of the Constitution in vain for any reason that the long-standing privilege of state governments to turn people away might be unconstitutional. The framers had generally incorporated the guarantees of the Articles of Confederation into the Constitution but declined to preserve its promised right of "ingress and regress" between the states. Undeterred, the court struck down the California law unanimously anyway. Writing for a five-justice majority, James Byrnes argued that the law was a restraint on interstate commerce—adding, for good measure, that the logic of Elizabethan poor laws should no longer apply in a country that offered state and federal relief.

Justice Robert Jackson concurred in the result but not its rationale, rejecting the idea that people could be reduced to objects of commerce. He insisted that the right to migrate from state to state was one of the "privileges and immunities" guaranteed by the Fourteenth Amendment: "If national citizenship means less than this, it means nothing." And he was particularly offended by the idea that a state could exclude a migrant on the basis of poverty, which was, he wrote, "constitutionally an irrelevance, like race, creed, or color." He decried the law's effort to "divide our citizenry on the basis of property into one class free to move from state to state and another class that is poverty-bound to the place where it has suffered misfortune," writing that it was "at war with the habit and custom by which our country has expanded." A second concurrence, written by Justice William O. Douglas and joined by two of his colleagues, likewise pointed to the Fourteenth Amendment to affirm a right of free movement. The law, he warned, "would prevent a citizen because he was poor from seeking new horizons in other States. It might withhold from large segments of our people that mobility which is basic to any guarantee of freedom of opportunity."

In *Edwards,* the court ratified a public understanding that had slowly taken hold over the previous two centuries: that the freedom to move is a fundamental American right. The opinions are striking for their focus on basic principles rather than legal precedents. The justices were articulating an American understanding and then reading it back into the Constitution, because they could not imagine the nation without it. Upholding the law, as one wire service story put it, would have "convert[ed] the United States into 48 'concentration camps,'" their populations confined within their borders. All the Okies like Duncan were trying to do, after all, was what Americans had always done. "The early California pioneers had nothing when they came here," Earl Warren, then the state's attorney general, pointed out. "They came here to seek opportunity, and that is the reason the present migrants come."

The *Edwards* decision seemed to confirm the final triumph of American mobility. It arrived just as the Depression came to an end and Americans took to the road again. "There has been more movement of people in the United States since 1940 than in any other period of the same length in the history of this country," the Census Bureau reported in 1944. People were moving away from the rural Midwest and South and toward the industrial cities of the Midwest and New England and the states along the Pacific coast. After the long winter of the Depression, it was a welcome thaw. "No doubt, war and war industries have had a major effect in spurring the migration of Americans, but moving about always has been one of the principal and favorite occupations of the American people," as one newspaper observed.

Never had it been so possible for so many Americans to choose where they wanted to live. The needs of a growing economy, the successes of the civil rights movement, and the assimilation of European immigrants combined to loosen both formal and informal barriers to mobility. In the three decades from the end of the war to the late 1960s, about one American in five moved each year, according to the Census Bureau—about two-thirds within a county, and a third over longer distances. If it didn't approach the extraordinary mobility of the mid-nineteenth century, it was still a remarkable resurgence. New highways shrank the time it took to travel between destinations. There were roughly twenty-six million cars in America in 1945, fifty-two million in 1955, and seventy-five million a decade after that. Motor homes and RVs marched down the highways like processions of ants. Leonard Shoen, a U.S. Navy veteran, started renting trailers in 1945 for one-way moves, and a decade later his U-Haul company had some ten thousand trailers and trucks on the road.

Popular culture reflected these shifts. From *On the Road* to *Shane* to *The Wild One* to *The Price of Salt*, the films and books of the 1950s told stories of Americans in motion, of rebels and antiheroes marked by their inability to find a place to settle down. The popular sitcoms of the era, like *Leave It to Beaver* and *Father Knows Best,* offered an idealized version of suburban life that today feels nostalgic. At the time, though, they depicted a novel mode of living, which many Americans had either recently adopted or still aspired to attain. By the final season of *I Love Lucy,* even the glamorous urbanites Lucy and Desi had departed their Manhattan apartment for suburban Connecticut.

The resurgence of mobility revived other aspects of American life that had fallen off during the Great Depression. People sought out churches and clubs and lodges as they tried to construct community in their new surroundings. Between 1940 and 1945, rates of membership in American voluntary associations saw their largest recorded surge. Church membership ticked up, too. Just as the golden age of American voluntary associations in the late nineteenth century had been driven by the remarkable number of Americans moving from one place to another, its revival in the postwar decades was, too. Despite becoming sharply more likely to be living next to new neighbors, and to have moved to an unfamiliar place themselves, Americans expressed more trust in each other and more faith in institutions than they had during the immobile years of the Great Depression. Mobility again proved the wellspring of American community, mixing and recombining the population and stimulating the creation of fresh ties.

All this moving about also helped businesses thrive. In the first fourteen months after V-J Day, some 10.7 million Americans—aside from men in uniform—moved across county lines, mostly to take up new jobs. A company called Welcome Wagon paid thousands of women to make house calls on new arrivals, dispensing advice, samples disguised as gifts, and abundant coupons. "Being strangers in the city, they have not established buying habits, and are responsive to helpful suggestions given by the Hostesses," an ad explained. Workers left stagnant regions filled with declining industries that offered few opportunities and headed toward rapidly growing cities. They gravitated toward newer sectors—aerospace, home appliances, automobiles—whose growth was turbocharged by the influx of workers. As Americans moved, the economy boomed.

And then, right as mobility seemed to achieve its greatest triumphs, the backlash commenced in earnest.

———

The first source of resistance to mobility was opposition to desegregation. Flint's experience was in some ways extreme, but it stood in for a broader pattern. All over the country, middle-class white families moved out of their rented apartments in the city and into single-family homes in the suburbs. Their new neighborhoods were typically residential monocultures, maintained by the zoning rules and restrictive covenants demanded by government lenders. Suburbanites commuted back to their jobs in cities' business districts in their new cars, on huge government-funded highways that sliced through older neighborhoods. The working poor were left behind, as were Black families and others barred by discriminatory rules from following.

In part, the movement of the white middle class—the children and grandchildren of the European immigrants who had seemed ineradicably, unassimilably different—toward suburbia was driven by growing affluence, which put the dream of the single-family home within reach of more families. In 1943, the magazine *The Link* asked soldiers what they were fighting for. "I am fighting for that big white house with the bright green roof and the big front lawn," one entry began, "the house that I lived in before Hitler and the Japanese came into my life." So evocative was the essay, written by a Sergeant Thomas N. Pappas, that it was reprinted by *The Saturday Evening Post* and then by other publications throughout the country. It captured, *The Daily Missoulian* editorialized, no less than the American way of life. But the essay captured more than readers might have realized. By 1946, Pappas was a captain stationed in Germany, still dreaming of home, when his parents wrote to tell him they were selling that big white house with the bright green roof. His desperate plea changed their minds, at least temporarily, but his parents were far from alone; a survey that year showed that one in three Americans wanted to move. What most Americans had been fighting for wasn't nostalgia for the home they'd grown up in but the dream of their next home, the one they would move to when the war was over.

All those people on the move required new places to live. During the Depression, construction began on fewer than 100,000 new houses per year, on average, not nearly enough to keep up with the increase in population. And the existing houses were largely in the wrong places. As the population shifted toward the booming manu-facturing cities where wartime industries were centered, prices spiked. The shortages were sometimes a spur to ingenuity: A man in York, Pennsylvania, bought five scrapped trolleys, connected them, and made them into a dwelling for himself, his two adult children, and their families; the bowed fronts of the streetcars served as bay windows. In Plattsburg, Missouri, a couple purchased an abandoned gas station and moved in. Emergency government programs con-structed workers' housing, much of it temporary, but most of those who moved were left to make do as best they could, like the south-ern migrants in Flint forced to build tar-paper shacks.

In 1940, America was still a nation of renters—some 56 percent of households leased their dwellings—so the federal government stepped in with a nationwide rent-control program to keep costs in check. Where it was enforced, landlords resisted by taking their properties off the rental market and selling them, exacerbating the rental crisis. It was soon painfully clear that rent control was failing; the only realistic solution was for the federal government to support the construction of an enormous quantity of new housing where it was needed most. The government could have met the demand for rentals by investing in public housing projects or providing cheap loans to real estate developers to build multifamily apartment build-ings close to centers of employment. Instead, as the war came to an end, it chose to subsidize the purchase of freestanding single-family homes.

Millions of Americans used FHA and VA loans to buy houses. In 1944, America built 114,000 new homes; in 1950, it built 1.7 mil-lion. Even in the few places where private developers tried to build large numbers of apartments, they found that cities had layered on zones and code requirements, making it difficult to build up. It was much easier to meet demand by buying up open land on the periph-ery of major cities and building subdivisions filled with rows of houses. By 1950, the census reported that America had become a nation of homeowners, with 55 percent of households living in dwellings they owned.

Cities, meanwhile, were slashing municipal services, cutting budgets as their tax base migrated to suburbia. Many urban residents found themselves stranded on islands of poverty—unable to follow their former neighbors. Some offices and stores and factories also remained, but these were mostly providing services that suburbanites wanted but preferred to be sited far from their homes. Urban planners watched the creep of the blight they had helped create and urged the wholesale clearance and replacement of declining city neighborhoods. And in the suburbs, town officials and commercial developers worked hard to keep the city, its problems, and above all its people from migrating outward.

As restrictive covenants were struck down by the courts, and overt discrimination was banned by civil rights laws, these leaders turned instead to zoning. Racial segregation might no longer be legal, but economic segregation could still come close to achieving the same result. Zoning rules mandating minimum lot sizes and restricting development to single-family homes effectively set a minimum price to move into town. Homeowners tended to back these restrictions, or even to demand them. They watched the spread of decay in the cities with alarm. The small down payments and amortizing loans of the FHA had turned their houses into their primary vehicles for savings and their most valuable assets. If property prices declined, families that had only just climbed into the middle class could find themselves wiped out. Local governments spent the postwar years dreaming up new ways to help their residents keep tight control of their communities, with an expanding web of rules and regulations, all aimed at the same result: turning towns back into members-only clubs.

This hostility to change was a fundamentally conservative impulse, but on its own it merely slowed the progress toward greater equality. For almost three decades after the war, the gap between the nation's most prosperous regions and its poorest continued to shrink. Civil rights laws continued to advance. Many communities continued to diversify. And year after year, about a fifth of Americans continued to move. But there was a second backlash to the nation's rapid growth in the postwar years, and it was rooted in progressive concerns. Its authors were dissatisfied with the status quo; they believed they were pushing for dramatic change, rather than fighting against it. But the changes they implemented would do more to restrict the ability of Americans to move toward opportunity than two centuries of conservative opposition had accomplished.

The postwar decades might have been a golden age of American prosperity, but not everyone experienced them that way. By the beginning of the 1960s, a flood of bestselling books thrust festering social problems into the public consciousness. Michael Harrington's *Other America* focused attention on the depth and persistence of poverty; Betty Friedan's *Feminine Mystique* highlighted domesticity's often-stifling effect on women; and James Baldwin's *Fire Next Time* pointed to the violence and oppression of racism. But it was three other books that, by mounting versions of the same critique in different spheres, had a particularly profound effect on the years that followed. Jane Jacobs published *The Death and Life of Great American Cities* in 1961. The following year brought Rachel Carson's *Silent Spring*, a warning on the harms of pesticides. And in 1965, Ralph Nader's *Unsafe at Any Speed* showed that automobile manufacturers had failed to take even basic measures to save lives.

These three books were rooted in skepticism of America's relentless pursuit of profit and growth, and in horror at its unaccounted costs. They also helped to crystallize a potent critique of governmental failure, as the legal scholar Paul Sabin has argued. The New Deal had worked hard to curb corporate power by bringing business leaders to the table with unions and regulators so that they could be forced to work in the national interest. But that alignment between big government, big business, and big labor, these critics now claimed, had produced a power structure in which no one was defending the public.

Jacobs showed how the professional planners bulldozed their way through neighborhoods, both figuratively and literally, ignoring the accrued wisdom of local communities and the vibrancy of urban life. Carson detailed how the Department of Agriculture had encouraged local agencies to spray the landscape with pesticides, "drenching millions of acres with poisons." Unaccountable bureaucrats had brushed off concerns about health and the environment, prioritizing the profits of corporate agriculture. Nader leveled a similar critique of the auto industry and its regulators. One chapter of his book went after Chevrolet's Corvair for its swing suspension and the company's penny-pinching refusal to add a mechanical fix to prevent the rear wheels from folding under the vehicle while making sharp turns. He also documented how, in the pursuit of profit, Detroit had neglected to invest in basic safety features like seat belts or in emissions controls.

During the Progressive Era at the beginning of the twentieth century, reformers had seen empowering government bureaucracies as the solution to America's greatest challenges. They pushed to insulate government from partisan corruption by creating a civil service, delegating power to appointed commissions, and recruiting professionally trained experts. By the 1960s, reformers concluded that they had succeeded only too well, that career bureaucrats had become insulated from public accountability and captive to professional orthodoxies. The emergent New Left amplified these critiques. In the Port Huron Statement, the 1962 manifesto of Students for a Democratic Society, the leading lights of the New Left called for making the public sector genuinely public "and not the arena of a ruling bureaucracy of 'public servants.'" State agencies, for example, claimed the right to spray pesticides on private land without being accountable for harms. "Under such circumstances," Carson plaintively asked Congress in 1963, "what is the citizen to do?" She wanted the government to impose new rules and safeguards, but she also wanted something else. Carson recommended "that machinery be established" to allow the private citizens harmed or inconvenienced by spraying to seek redress. Arm individuals, in other words, with the ability to challenge the decisions government agencies had made in their name.

Carson died the following year. But that call was taken up by Nader. *Unsafe at Any Speed* turned Nader into a cultural icon. He recruited seven law students to investigate the Federal Trade Commission (FTC). The students, dubbed "Nader's Raiders" by a *Washington Post* reporter, charged that the agency had been captured by the corporations it was supposed to regulate. When the FTC report produced major reforms, Nader was deluged with applications from hundreds of law students, and set up new teams to investigate a wide array of other governmental agencies. One group was led by Robert Fellmeth, who had co-authored the FTC report, then followed it up with a second headline-grabbing investigation, this one into the Interstate Commerce Commission. "You know, as a twenty-one-year-old kid, it was kind of nice to be able to testify for the United States Senate," Fellmeth told me. For his next target, Nader picked out land and power in California.

Nader wanted to use direct democracy to rein in bureaucrats, who couldn't be trusted to act in the public interest. One of Nader's Raiders, David R. Zwick, put the matter particularly plainly to Congress in 1971. "We need laws which are essentially 'government-proof,'" he said. Zwick wanted to eliminate bureaucratic discretion and to arm ordinary Americans with the right to challenge government decisions in court. Nader and his Raiders sought to take power out of the hands of government and return it to the people. That was the approach that Fellmeth applied to California as his team investigated local authorities and state agencies for signs that they had been corrupted by developers. "Always blame the one you're studying," Fellmeth told them. They were studying government, and that's where they assigned the blame.

No state embodied the promise of American mobility better than California. Throughout the twentieth century, most people living in California had been born someplace else. In the 1920s and 1930s, California was the fastest-growing state in the country. "California may keep right on urging homemakers to come here," the *Long Beach Press* urged in 1921, "in full assurance that if millions of them came, this commonwealth would not be overcrowded." And millions did. The state's population increased by more than half in the 1940s, by nearly half in the 1950s, and by a quarter in the 1960s. Over the half a century between 1920 and 1970, California's population quintupled, from 3.4 million to 20 million. Construction boomed to keep pace with the new arrivals. Between 1950 and 1960 alone, California increased its housing stock by more than 50 percent, constructing nearly two million new units. All that development kept the state affordable, despite the surge in population. By 1970, the median house in California sold for $24,300. That was roughly in line with the national average, and just two and a half times the median income. Adjusted for inflation, that translates to about $197,000 today. But as effective as it was at creating opportunity and fostering equality, the boom in development worried many Californians.

The Nader group's finished report on land use stretched more than twelve hundred pages, later abridged into a somewhat more digestible form and published as a book. In its introduction, Nader recited a litany of problems facing California, including "urban sprawl, mindless development spawned and exploited by speculators, the near certainty of catastrophic earthquakes, bumper-to-bumper mobility, pollution, private seizure of public wealth, and the complicity of government and land interests." As before, the problems Nader's Raiders had identified were very real. California's fractured system of government was approving patterns of development that were environmentally unsustainable. Many local officials really were uncomfortably cozy with developers. Speculators were promoting fraudulent land sales. But at the report's core was a deep skepticism of growth, a hostility to mobility, and a conviction that by converting public goods into private assets, the real estate industry was devouring the state.

Above all, Fellmeth and his colleagues wanted to halt the development of open land. And since they blamed big government's collusion with big business for sprawl, they turned to ordinary people to stop it. The first step would be ending competition among localities to attract new development, by sharing tax revenue evenly throughout the state. But they also wanted to change the tax structure to make development unprofitable, add new layers of community review and approval, and bar the state from upzoning—making zoning less restrictive to allow more development—open land. Plans passed by each community could target objectionable uses of the land and then phase them out over fixed periods of time. If growth was the problem, then local sovereignty was the solution.

The Raiders had spent enough time studying California to appreciate how much damage restrictive zoning was already inflicting on the state. The report traced concentrated poverty and racial segregation to the "snob zoning" of wealthy communities. "Land policies play perhaps the major role in the various kinds of discrimination which inhibit fluid movement in our society and belie the Horatio Alger myth," it declared. But the closest it came to a remedy was a tossed-off suggestion that all communities be required to provide at least 15 percent of their housing for low-income residents. Who would construct this housing, where they would put it, how towns could be persuaded to allow it, what would maintain its affordability, and how they would pay for it (beyond a vague reference to "state incentives") were of no apparent interest to the authors.

Half a century earlier, Charles Cheney had introduced single-family zoning to allow local communities to exclude unwanted populations. Fellmeth and his team had little in common with Cheney, beyond a deep hostility to new development and a faith in the ability of reformers to impose rational solutions on complicated problems. But they looked out at the world that Cheney had created—in which density had been largely outlawed, forcing new construction ever farther from urban centers, creating ever more sprawl—and, without any apparent awareness of the irony, decided to double down on Cheney's prescriptions, which had produced the problem in the first place. In their outrage over developers getting rich by turning land into housing, they failed to consider what would happen to ordinary Californians if housing became scarce. Ralph Nader promised to defend ordinary Americans against the depredations of business, but he seemed unable to grasp that he might need to defend them against the depredations of other Americans.

For more than a century, Americans like Frank Duncan had been moving to California seeking opportunity. And for just as long, many of those already in California had been trying to hoard the state's opportunities and exclude them. California's endlessly inventive legislators had, through the years, found a wide variety of ways to keep people out, always in the name of preserving their Eden. But now they found their most effective means of all.

At a California Assembly hearing shortly after the report's release, one of its authors warned of the dangers of both "overdevelopment of the central cities" and "the sprawl around the cities"—which, together with the report's warnings not to build on open land, effectively ruled out building anything, anywhere. The committee then heard from Kingsley Davis, a Berkeley professor and leading Malthusian prophet of doom, who pushed that thought to its logical conclusion, telling the committee that it should actively discourage workers seeking higher wages from migrating into the state, perhaps by constricting the supply of electricity to eliminate new jobs. The common theme was the idea that California should hang a NO VACANCIES sign on its door, preserving the state for those fortunate enough to already reside there.

Concern about the pace of California's growth had been increasing for decades. Planners had the chance to funnel growth into built-up areas, allowing California to keep expanding its population and economy while preserving the natural beauty and ecological functions of undeveloped areas. But as in New York, in Bassett's day, many felt that growth itself was the problem. In 1965, the ecologist Raymond Dasmann's jeremiad, *The Destruction of California*, warned that the state was passing the point of sustainability "unless the rate of population increase can be checked and slowed to a point where planning can overtake it," and proposed that any new arrivals be forced to compete for the existing supply of housing and jobs. In 1970, the president of the Los Angeles chapter of Zero Population Growth told the City Planning Commission, "We need fewer people here—a quality of life, not a quantity of life." A representative from the Sierra Club concurred, suggesting that the city rezone residential parcels to prohibit replacing the current structures with anything larger, as a means of lowering the birthrate. They saw other people—including children—as the greatest threat to their environment and their happiness, and zoning as the most powerful tool they had for keeping them out.

The first Earth Day arrived in 1970, and with it the blossoming of the environmental movement Rachel Carson had seeded a decade before. "The 1970s absolutely must be the years when America pays its debt to the past by reclaiming the purity of its air, its waters, and our living environment. It is literally now or never," President Richard Nixon declared as he signed the National Environmental Policy Act into law. Later that year, another California politician who would head to the White House—the then governor, Ronald Reagan—signed the California Environmental Quality Act (CEQA). The two laws forced government agencies to consider the environmental impact of their decisions. No longer could bureaucrats single-mindedly pursue their agencies' agendas without factoring in the collateral damage.

This was the background against which the Nader report on California land use arrived. It didn't introduce the ideas it contained, but it helped consolidate three trends. First, it clothed opposition to new development in the respectable costume of environmentalism, making it freshly appealing to liberals. Turning away new arrivals could be defended as a means of controlling a dangerously expanding population and preserving threatened natural treasures, not just a means of discrimination. "I happen to have a philosophical view that we should stop increasing the goddamn population," Fellmeth told me. Second, it gave opposition to new housing populist credibility, promoting local control as the remedy to unchecked growth and framing it as a means of opposing corporate greed and government corruption. And third, it closed off the last outlet for development in the state, by targeting construction on open land. Built-up areas—where development was most environmentally sustainable—had already spent a century fighting against admitting new arrivals, but as long as there were new fields to be plowed under, housing remained affordable. Now that changed.

Governor Jerry Brown, delivering his first State of the State address in 1976, proclaimed that California had entered an "era of limits." The Golden State had long been a land of abundance; now

Brown encouraged Californians to think in terms of scarcity and trade-offs. His message found a receptive audience and not just in California. Battered by an oil embargo, high unemployment, and runaway inflation, Americans began to think less about what they could gain from attracting new businesses and neighbors and more about what they stood to lose by sharing what they had. Instead of seeking to continue welcoming new arrivals while also protecting the environment, they came to see the two goals in oppositional terms. CEQA and other statutes gave individuals and advocacy groups powerful tools to defend the environment, allowing them to sue to stop destructive plans for freeways, ill-advised developments on fragile wetlands, or logging permits that put vulnerable species at risk. Citizens could at last challenge bureaucratic myopia. But what many Californians most wanted to defend, it turned out, weren't the last unspoiled places. They wanted to protect their own neighborhoods from any new construction and to stop new people from moving in.

Two years after CEQA was passed, a collection of landowners and residents of Mono County sued to block a condominium development that had been approved by the county board of supervisors, their own elected officials. In a landmark 1972 ruling, the California Supreme Court found in their favor. Henceforth, all private projects in the state that required government approval would have to pass through the gauntlet of environmental review, leaving them open to lawsuits. And California's zoning laws already subjected almost every conceivable housing development to government approval. Years of amendments and court rulings have periodically reshaped the precise requirements, but that basic principle has stood. Anyone with the time and resources to go to court can file an anonymous lawsuit to block or delay any project, or at the very least threaten to hold it up to extract concessions.

And since 1972, that's precisely what they've done. In 2008, a developer won approval for a twenty-two-story tower in Hollywood, on the site of an auto showroom turned Old Spaghetti Factory restaurant. Local residents sued over the zoning variances the city had granted, losing, but delaying the project for long enough to force the construction loan into default. The project eventually went forward with a new developer, who determined that the old structure on the site could not safely be preserved and demolished it, salvaging its most distinctive elements to construct a replica. Residents sued over the demolition. By 2015, the new tower on Sunset Boulevard was ready for its close-up, and forty tenants moved in. But a California court agreed with the local residents that the project had broken the rules, by, among other things, not filing a new environmental impact statement under CEQA that took into consideration that the historic structure would now be a *replica* of a historic structure. Some forty tenants were forced to move out of the completed building, and along with the adjacent park it sat unused for the next three years. In the end, the 299-unit building was occupied, but the lawsuits had taken a decade to resolve, driven up costs, and served as a warning to other builders. It's an extreme story, perhaps, but by 2018, 60 percent of CEQA lawsuits over private developments targeted housing, overwhelmingly multifamily developments proposed for affluent areas.

CEQA delays are used by labor unions to extract higher wages, by local residents to force developers to provide amenities, and by NIMBYs to make construction prohibitively expensive. Often, the results are perverse, doing more to harm the environment than to protect it. Far from preventing sprawl, as Fellmeth had hoped, the empowerment of local communities accelerated it by making the production of new housing in dense urban areas incredibly difficult and forcing construction out to the exurban periphery. A rational city would leap at the chance to turn a parking lot into an apartment building. But as of 2024, the site of a proposed 495-unit building in San Francisco that spent years trying to overcome CEQA challenges remained a parking lot. Even when there are no legal challenges, the costs of CEQA are real. Local agencies take an average of two and a half years to approve housing projects that require environmental impact statements, and the projects are frequently reduced in size or scope as a result. The expense and uncertainty have squeezed out many small-scale redevelopment projects; builders are more likely to buy up several lots and consolidate them, erecting a larger building that can cover the costs of navigating the process.

By 2023, California's era of limits had so constricted the supply of housing that the median price of a single-family home in the state topped $900,000, more than ten times the median household income. The money that purchased an entire house in 1970, adjusted for inflation, would now barely suffice to buy a pair of parking spots in the garage of a San Francisco condominium. Over the last half century, instead of quintupling, California's population has not quite doubled. But even as its growth has slowed dramatically, the production of housing has slowed even more. Thirty-seven percent of state residents say they have seriously considered leaving because of housing prices. Every year since 2000, the number of Californians moving out of the state has outstripped the number of Americans moving in, by a cumulative total of millions, and the lowest-income residents were likeliest to leave. More than 170,000 Californians now lack any housing at all, living out on the streets.

Fifty years after the Nader report on land use in California, Fellmeth himself has no regrets. Development imposes costs on existing residents and on the environment, he says, and California needs a planning process that weighs those costs against the benefits. Like most Californians, he can see that housing has become unaffordable. He bought a home for $90,000, he tells me, and sold it forty years later for more than $1 million: "There's something wrong with a situation where the price of a house goes up that much." But he blames an increasing population, lack of competition, inflation, and the finance sector for high prices and the lack of supply, not the laws he's long supported.

Environmental laws have had a major impact on the production of housing, but they were just one element of a much broader shift. Americans were losing faith in democracy; they no longer believed it could produce a government that acted on their behalf. In 1964, for example, 77 percent of Americans said they trusted the federal government; a decade later, just 36 percent said the same. Since they no longer trusted the government, local activists pressed for the right to second-guess its conclusions. The theory was that public-spirited citizens and public-interest groups would serve as watchdogs, holding bureaucrats to account and ensuring their decisions benefited the public and not special interests.

The same shift took hold in the world of zoning, where activists like Jane Jacobs pushed for participatory planning. A set of legal changes bolstered their efforts, promising to level the playing field, allowing disadvantaged communities to defend their interests against bureaucratic indifference and malice. Some nonprofits worked diligently to put that vision into practice. In general, though, the more educated and more affluent a neighborhood, the better able its residents were to challenge government decisions they disliked—even when the changes they opposed, like erecting a new apartment building, did them no material harm. As a result, new construction concentrated in less affluent areas, where challenges were less likely. In Los Angeles, areas with active community associations succeeded in "downzoning" their neighborhoods for lower density, even as neighborhoods that lacked such groups were "upzoned" for more intense use. Because the social capital necessary to organize such groups—connections to politicians, ties to professionals with relevant expertise, links to nonprofit workers—was tightly concentrated in affluent white areas, L.A.'s minority neighborhoods bore the brunt of development. Much of the new housing created in large cities today is thus funneled into areas of concentrated poverty, sometimes displacing existing residents, while large, affluent swaths of these cities are restricted to low-density homes.

The authors of zoning thought it would create simple categories that would offer property owners clear guidance and predictability, with zoning boards of appeal included as a safety valve for exceptional circumstances. Over the last half century, though, as categories of zoning designations have proliferated and new restrictions have been layered on, the system has reversed this design. New projects that are commercially viable under existing rules are now the exceptional circumstance; requests for variances have become the standard procedure. The new rules are so restrictive they would largely have prevented the cities they claim to protect from ever having been built in the first place. Out of every ten buildings in Manhattan, four could not have been built under current zoning codes.

In San Francisco, a third of all the buildings—containing more than half of the city's housing units—are out of compliance with the codes.

If you want to build a new structure almost anywhere in America, you would be well advised to start not with an architect but by retaining an attorney to guide you through the thicket of regulations. A visit to the zoning board will likely follow, with an extensive negotiation. Often, this results in scaling back the initial proposal, using more expensive materials, or otherwise altering the project. Always, it entails delays. And too often, it results in a form of civic blackmail, as boards and commissions use the review process to extract dollars from private parties, asking developers to build parks, construct infrastructure, or add affordable housing units in exchange for their approval.

The tax revolt of the 1970s, when voters put a cap on property taxes in California and backed tax cuts in many other states, left many towns and cities unable to raise the funds required to fulfill their ambitions, or even their obligations. By downzoning their land and then using the approval process to negotiate community benefits packages from developers, local governments figured out how to provide amenities to their current residents without charging them a dime. But there was still a bill to be paid. The costs are now passed on to the purchasers and renters of the new developments, driving up the price of residential and commercial space. Developers have learned that it's cheaper to target lower-income districts without active civic groups. But it's the areas where affluent professionals tend to cluster—where the schools are strong, amenities abundant, and jobs plentiful—that offer the greatest opportunities for Americans who are looking to build better futures for themselves and their children. And it's in those specific areas where activists have learned to leverage land-use rules to keep newcomers out.

When state legislatures delegated the power to regulate land use to local governments, they were putting decision-making authority in the hands of a group of voters who are remarkably unrepresentative of the broader public. The quarter of eligible voters who cast ballots in municipal elections are not just older but also better educated, whiter, wealthier, and more likely to be homeowners. The median voter in municipal elections in the thirty largest cities in the United States is fifty-seven, fifteen years older than the median resident eligible to vote. Voters under the age of thirty-five—those most likely to switch jobs, to rent, to move from one place to another—are outnumbered seven to one by the voters at the most sedentary stage of their lives, past the age of sixty-five. Local officials are painfully aware of these numbers and generally prioritize the interests of older homeowners above the needs of young renters, and of affluent and well-educated white voters above working-class voters of color.

But as unrepresentative as municipal elections might be, community hearings are far worse. One team of researchers examined thousands of public comments submitted at hearings on housing developments that included more than one unit. They found that homeowners were 46 percent of local voters, but an astonishing 73 percent of commenters, and that they were disproportionately likely to oppose new developments. The commenters were also more likely to be white, male, and over the age of fifty. As my colleague Jerusalem Demsas has argued, "Making it easier for people to lodge their disagreements doesn't change the distribution of power; it only amplifies the voices of people who already have it." If renters are outnumbered at public hearings, the people who would like to move into the proposed housing are often absent entirely. I listened to a parade of witnesses at one hearing in Cambridge testify against converting an old church building into condominiums. Then one more retiree stood up. She was there that night, she explained, because when a nearby building had undergone a condo conversion, she had come to testify against it on all the usual grounds: it would add traffic, change the character of the neighborhood, trample its history, alter its demographics. Afterward, she had been approached by a woman who intended to purchase one of the new apartments and who asked to buy her a cup of coffee. They talked and became friends. The project had gone ahead, and she'd made other friends in the new building. So, she'd come back that night to testify on behalf of the future residents of this new development, who weren't there to speak for themselves, and to ask her current neighbors to think about the new friends they might gain and not just what they stood to lose. I wish I could say that the opponents were shamed into supporting the project. She was met, instead, mostly with stares and grumbles. Watching the exchange made it clear that public hearings are intended to privilege the desires of existing residents above the needs of those who might take advantage of a neighborhood's opportunities. Participatory planning, in practice, narrows the range of interests and voices that can participate in planning.

The localist revolt of the 1960s was supposed to create a shift in power—away from big government and back to the people—that would restore democracy. But it created a far less democratic system, arming the educated, the wealthy, and the well connected with an effective veto over elected officials. Instead of winning elections, opponents of new projects had only to win their lawsuits, or at least spend long enough losing them to deter development. A movement that had promised to protect the public interest had instead empowered private individuals to obstruct it.

CHAPTER TEN

BUILDING A WAY OUT

Coming in out of a chill fog on a Tuesday evening in January 2023, a small crowd files into an elementary school auditorium in Washington, D.C. They're here for a strange sort of public hearing, a set piece of political Kabuki performed before blue-velvet drapes that more usually rise on first-grade recitals. WMATA, the capital's transit authority, has invited public comment on a plan to replace 160 parking spots next to the Takoma Metro Station with 16 Kiss & Ride spaces for drop-offs, add one additional bus bay, and alter the flow of traffic through the site. Or, at least, that's what the hearing notice says. What's actually at stake is a developer's plan to construct a 435-unit mixed-use development on the land the parking lot now occupies.

As the officials read through their scripted remarks, a compact, intense woman with close-cropped gray hair sitting in front of me audibly scoffs at some of their claims. When she stands to testify, she introduces herself as Sara Green, a forty-seven-year resident who's been involved in the battle over this site from the very beginning. "I was in the room, the first public hearing we had . . . in 1998," Green says. It turns out that I've shown up for one of the concluding skirmishes in a quarter-century struggle.

Green complains about the process and about the lack of a traffic study. But what really has her riled is that an earlier speaker called

Takoma "urban." "We are a suburban area, we are a historic district, we've always been proud of that," she insists. For most of those testifying, this is clearly the core of the dispute, even if the rules of the hearing require them to couch their objections in terms of parking spots and environmental impacts.

The hearing breaks up, and I ask Green to tell me more about her concerns. Although 15 percent of the units will be set aside for affordable housing, she says she's worried that the rest will be market rate. If the development were the same size, I ask, and all its units affordable, would that allay her concerns? Well, it wouldn't fix the height. "Look across the street at the houses, look at the width," she tells me. "We're not Dupont Circle . . . this is a lower-scale community."

Takoma Park, Maryland, is one of the most progressive places in the country. Founded in 1890 as a sylvan retreat from the bustle of the capital, it later became the headquarters of the Seventh-Day Adventist Church. By the 1960s, its aging housing stock— bungalows sheathed in asbestos siding and illegal wartime apartment conversions—attracted a vibrant and eclectic crowd of residents. "Takoma Park is the suburb for people who don't like suburbs," full of character and characters, a longtime resident would later explain. When the federal government proposed bulldozing a freeway through the neighborhood, Sammie Abbott, an irascible former CIO organizer, rallied the opposition with the slogan "No white men's roads through Black men's homes." It took thirteen years, but like Jane Jacobs he prevailed. In 1980, the triumphant Abbott became mayor and opened city government to participatory democracy. Three years later, he pushed through an ordinance designating Takoma Park a nuclear-free zone. And like other activists of his era, Abbott was determined to "prevent the reckless development and destruction of the residential quality of the community," as one friend later recalled. A commemorative plaque in the community center that bears his name lauds his fight "against high-density development." Today, the city's bungalows, Victorians, and colonial homes have been lovingly restored, and their prices have shot up. Although Takoma Park is trying hard to hang on to its reputation for eccentricity, it largely resembles the affluent streetcar suburbs you can find on the outskirts of every major city, complete with the requisite cafés serving artisan sandwiches and handcrafted espressos. It has become a suburb for people who like to say they hate suburbs.

The Metro station sits just across the D.C. border, within D.C.'s Takoma neighborhood—two jurisdictions sharing a single name. When WMATA acquired the land, it thought Takoma would be the last station on a line that now extends far out into suburbia. In 1999, it agreed to sell the developer EYA the space once allocated for terminus parking that it no longer needed. Outraged residents slowed the process to a glacial crawl. When WMATA held a hearing in 2005, Green was serving on the Advisory Neighborhood Commission in Takoma, D.C., representing the district that contained the parking lot. She came bearing nine hundred signatures on a petition opposing the plan, which then centered on town houses. Stuck without the requisite approvals, that proposal died in the 2008 financial crisis. By 2014, EYA was back with a new plan, this one featuring a mixed-use building. "This is a very large project, it is way too big," Green complained at a WMATA hearing that year, adding, "What people are asking for is something that fits this neighborhood, that respects the Takoma Historic Districts both in D.C. and in Maryland."

But if Green remains steadfast in her opposition today, the neighborhood is changing around her. At the 2023 hearing, there is a striking generational divide. Although some longtime opponents are back for this latest round, their ranks have thinned. Most of the younger people who stand to testify have come to support the proposal. Evan Yeats, the new ANC commissioner from Green's district, delivers a ringing endorsement of affordable housing, density, and transit-oriented development. A newly elected city councillor from Takoma Park reluctantly relays the objections of his constituents, before hastening to add that while he worries about the loss of long-term parking, he does not share any reservations about density. "We are well aware of the need for affordable housing all over, and we are well aware of the prospects for density in increasing opportunity, as opposed to disquiet, among immediately adjacent neighborhoods." The latest plan for the site features sixty units of affordable housing.

Green is still bravely fighting against the greed of profit-driven developers; she lights up as she recounts how Sammie Abbott killed the freeway. But while the 2005 hearing ran four hours, tonight the speakers' list is exhausted in forty minutes. A WMATA official asks if anyone else would like to speak, and a few hands are raised. A bespectacled young man approaches the microphone and looks up nervously. "Hi, I wasn't planning to speak," he begins. He says he's never been to a hearing like this before and is pleasantly surprised by how much support the plan enjoys. "I have a two-year-old son," he says, "and I would love for him to grow up in a world where parking wasn't the biggest concern." Increasing the amount of housing, he explains—all housing, not just affordable housing—is the best way to address the city's homelessness crisis. And he adds that he was struck by Green's testimony that she was present at a hearing in 1998. "To me, that is really telling," he says, "that this has been going on for twenty-five years, and we still have a parking lot there."

Across the country, there's a dawning awareness that something has gone very wrong and a growing willingness to do what it takes to make it right. Younger Americans can see that their generation doesn't have the same opportunities their parents enjoyed. Two centuries after Americans secured their freedom of movement, mobility has largely become the privilege of an educated elite. Over the past hundred years, local jurisdictions have gradually reasserted their right to regulate who will inhabit them, operating as private clubs for the benefit of their existing members and driving the cost of moving toward opportunity above the level most can afford to pay. In the Progressive Era, reformers deployed building codes, restrictive covenants, and zoning ordinances as mechanisms of stability and exclusion. During the New Deal, the federal government insisted that jurisdictions apply these measures to segregate their communities by land use, social class, and race. And in the 1960s, reformers skeptical of government bureaucracy gave small, well-organized groups of activists legal tools to overturn the decisions of elected governments. Together, these changes allowed the places in

America where opportunity is concentrated—places like Takoma Park—to sharply limit the supply of new housing. They have enriched existing homeowners while closing off the best-trod path to prosperity for millions of others.

American mobility began to decline around 1970, a fifty-year slide that has not yet ended. Increasingly restrictive zoning rules have played a key role in that decline. Research by the economists Peter Ganong and Daniel Shoag helps define the problem. As land-use regulation increases, they found, states issue fewer building permits and housing prices rise. As a result, fewer people at the bottom of the income spectrum move toward opportunity. They offer this example to illustrate the point: If a lawyer moved from the Deep South to New York City, he'd see his net income go up by about 39 percent, after adjusting for housing costs—the same as it would have done back in 1960. If a janitor made the same move in 1960, he'd have done even better, gaining 70 percent. But by 2017, his gains in pay would have been outstripped by housing costs, leaving him 7 percent worse off. Working-class Americans once had the most to gain by moving. Today, it's a privilege largely exercised by the affluent.

Among economists, the claim that housing regulations have diminished mobility and widened inequality is no longer novel, or even particularly controversial. Policy makers are now taking note, too. "For decades, exclusionary zoning laws—like minimum lot sizes, mandatory parking requirements, and prohibitions on multi-family housing—have inflated housing and construction costs and locked families out of areas with more opportunities," the Biden White House recently declared. But restoring American mobility won't be simple, and the challenge is far broader than zoning alone.

Location, location, location! The three most important rules of real estate are also the three most important rules for getting ahead in life. If you're lucky enough to grow to adulthood in a place that's booming—where employers are desperately searching for workers and new businesses are sprouting left and right, where families are stable and people are invested in their communities—the odds are overwhelmingly in your favor. And if you're not? For most of world history, you'd have been out of luck. You lived where you happened to be born, your prospects were tied to that specific place, and your identity was defined by it. But for two centuries, this was the magic of America: If you drew a losing ticket, you could trade it in for the location of your choice, and reinvent yourself there. And if that turned out to be a bad bet, too, you could try again. And again.

It wasn't that simple, of course. Moving required resources, entailed risk, and imposed the pain of dislocation. Migrants often faced exclusion and discrimination. In the places that conferred the greatest advantages, not everyone was equally welcome. Staying put was always the simpler, more comfortable option, but growth usually requires doing uncomfortable things. I don't like going to the gym, even though I know that I need exercise to stay healthy. And I don't like moving, even though I know that my serial relocations have given my family a better life. Choosing where to live is likely the single most consequential decision you'll make while bringing up your kids—more than what they eat or what they wear or how much screen time they get. And in America, despite all sorts of constraints, parents have generally been able to decide where they want to reside. Those who have actively exercised that choice have given their children enormous advantages, making it much likelier that their kids will enjoy success that outstrips their own.

Think of it this way. We've all heard that America is a nation of immigrants, a golden land where children can build futures beyond their parents' dreams. But the biggest advantage enjoyed by the children of immigrants turns out to be that 100 percent of their parents are *migrants*. Even after they landed in the United States, they traded in their tickets and chose new locations. One study, for example, looked at immigration over the past century and a half, focusing on fathers at the twenty-fifth percentile for income—that is, out of every four men in the country, three were earning more than this group. Over those years, the sons of immigrants consistently climbed higher up the income rankings than the sons of the native-born. That was true of immigrants who arrived here in different eras and from an array of different lands and backgrounds. But why were their children climbing higher? It wasn't an emphasis on achievement; education, the researchers found, didn't seem to make a big difference. The answer, instead, was location. When people who are born in America trade in their own tickets and select the same locations as immigrant parents, their kids do just as well. Americans—whether born here or abroad—succeed when they move toward opportunity. The real story of America is of *migrant* success, of a whole nation tuned to enable mobility.

In fact, our entire narrative of American immigration tends to obscure the degree of mobility it entailed. The typical immigrant arriving during the late nineteenth or early twentieth century was a young man, here to labor for wages and save enough to return home. The grandchildren of the immigrants who stayed would write the history books; those who helped build this country and then left have been erased from our collective memory. Overall, perhaps one in three immigrants went home, but from some countries in some decades most who came returned. That was less a mark of failure, though, than evidence of how immigrants used the greater possibilities of mobility within the United States to their own advantage. Even those who headed back after spending a few years in the United States landed better-paying jobs on their return than did their neighbors, despite having started off poorer and less skilled. But that simply underlines the key point; immigration was less a directed flow than a continual churn as people leveraged mobility to improve their lot in life.

But moving alone has never been enough. When you move, you cut yourself off from family, from networks of support, from the culture that has shaped you, and from familiar routines. Families that bounce around within impoverished regions, or that are displaced from one struggling community, only to land somewhere else equally bleak, are rarely better off for it. The key is to move someplace where the economy is growing. The prolific bank robber Willie Sutton reputedly said he robbed banks because "that's where the money is"; Americans have moved toward prosperous, growing places for much the same reason. But over the past few decades, the rivers of migrants have started to run backward. Americans are moving away from the richest parts of this country and out toward poorer regions, away from thriving neighborhoods and out toward struggling ones. As a strategy for getting ahead, it's like Sutton sticking up a lemonade stand: you're in the wrong place for a big haul. As I've talked to people around the country, I keep hearing a common theme. Instead of going to where the money is, they're moving to places where the housing is affordable.

College graduates continue to move to wealthy neighborhoods, even though the cost of housing bites deep. But, unlike their parents or grandparents, they can't move to a thriving place in the expectation that they'll be better off. Artificial constraints on housing have driven prices up so high that they effectively erase anything people might have gained by moving to a wealthier area, or even leave them marginally behind. They may not end up with more disposable cash, but by settling in a prosperous place, they can still offer their families a host of other amenities and improve their prospects in life.

For those without college degrees it's a very different picture. Someone without a high school degree moving from the most affordable community in America to the least would earn much more, but real estate costs would force them to reduce their consumption by 27 percent. So instead, many stay put, all too often in places sinking into concentrated, intergenerational poverty.

And that reduced mobility is costing everyone. In comparative terms, the United States remains unusual, with Americans relocating more often and over longer distances than residents of the average developed country. Americans, for example, still move between states about twice as often as Europeans move between regions of their own nations. But the relative dynamism of the U.S. economy was largely a function of the extreme mobility of the labor force, and as American mobility has declined, its rate of GDP growth has slowed to European levels. How much economic growth have we lost by keeping people from moving to places where they can be more productive? A pair of economists recently took a stab at an answer. They imagined a world of perfect mobility in which the three most productive U.S. metropolitan areas—New York, San

Francisco, and San Jose—constructed enough homes to accommodate everyone who wanted to move there. That alone, they calculated, would have boosted GDP by about $2 trillion by 2009, or enough to put an extra $8,775 into your pocket, and the pockets of every other American worker, each year. And slightly more than half of Americans, in this scenario, would be living someplace other than where they are today. It's a rough estimate, but it gives a sense of the scale of the distortions we have introduced, and the price we are each paying for them.

When Americans move to places where the economy is growing quickly, jobs are abundant, and wages are high, their migration also boosts the places they've left behind, by tightening the labor supply and lowering the demand for and therefore the cost of farms or houses. Mobility narrows the gap between the richest and the poorest states in America, making our society more equal. Between 1880 and 1980, what people earned in the most prosperous parts of the country and the least prosperous converged at a steady rate. After 1980, though, the convergence slowed and then stopped. And over the last two decades, it has actually reversed, with the gap between what Americans earn in the richest and poorest states widening. A nation that was becoming more equal is now growing more unequal, and Americans in the places left behind are frustrated and angry.

As immobility widens our economic divides, it is doing the same for racial inequality. One study looked at thousands of Americans born from the 1950s to the 1980s. Black Americans growing up today have become strikingly less mobile, with 69 percent remaining in the county in which they were born, as opposed to just 45 percent of white Americans tracked by the study. Adjusting for a host of factors, from education to homeownership to family structure, still leaves a fifteen-point mobility gap between Black and white Americans. Another team of researchers recently found a different way to quantify the same trend. They showed that by age twenty-six white young adults had moved an average of 194 miles from home, while Black young adults had moved just 133 miles by the same age. The huge racial gap in American mobility is new—even in the days of

Jim Crow or the era of redlining, it was a fraction of its current size—and given mobility's effect on economic opportunity it is a crisis within a crisis.

So, the land-use restrictions that constrain American mobility are costing us trillions, putting states on divergent paths, increasing inequality, and worsening the effects of racism. But that's just a taste of the damage. They might also, for example, be leading families to wait longer to have children and to have fewer than they want. Spatial segregation has entrenched educational inequality, because access to schools is based largely on access to housing within specific geographic boundaries. The sprawling patterns land-use restrictions have produced in new developments appear to be worsening obesity, because Americans walk less and drive more. And those same patterns are also worsening global warming. Every day, it seems, researchers add more entries to the dismal list of harms caused by restrictive zoning.

The freedom to move promised Americans the right to choose a community, and to stay there, but it also promised the right to leave, to go in search of something better. And each year, fewer Americans find themselves in a position to do that. If zoning's role in this crisis is now widely accepted, though, there is less attention being paid to other systems of land-use regulation that are still expanding their influence.

In the American metropolitan areas that are experiencing the greatest economic growth, huge numbers of structures and neighborhoods are now bound by historic preservation rules. And nearly a quarter of Americans live in housing governed by some form of private, collective entity—a condominium, cooperative, or homeowners' association. Efforts to fix mobility that focus on zoning while ignoring these other restrictions, like California's SB 9, are bound to disappoint.

The earliest efforts at historic preservation, in the nineteenth century, involved private individuals and voluntary associations purchasing and renovating buildings with sentimental value. In 1853,

Ann Pamela Cunningham formed the Mount Vernon Ladies' Association to save George Washington's home from "the grasp of the speculator and the worldling." Despite her pleas, Congress declined to help. If there was something worth saving, she and other Americans decided, they would have to save it themselves, raising the funds to purchase the property. That was one vision of historic preservation.

In Charleston, South Carolina, city leaders found a very different way to preserve the past. The city's rigid conservatism turned a once-thriving port city and commercial capital into a decaying backwater, abandoned by its most ambitious sons and daughters who left in search of opportunity. Charleston had refused, in the 1830s, to allow the railroads to run through the city down to its docks, rendering its port uncompetitive. The fourth-largest city in the nation when the Constitution was ratified, it had, by the outbreak of the Civil War, slipped to twenty-second. Defeat only made its leaders cling more tightly to the past, opposing growth or development. By 1920, it fell off the list of the top hundred largest cities entirely. Like Cunningham, the women of Charleston who led the city's preservation movement in the 1920s sought to preserve the glories of the antebellum South—although by now long faded—against the corruption of northern industry and Yankee commercialism. They argued that preservation could enhance tourism, if only new development could be excluded from the city's more scenic precincts. Not everyone agreed. "If it suits them to mummify Charleston and to make of our city only a museum, let them revel in it," John Patrick Grace, a former mayor, fumed. Grace, of Irish extraction, had drawn his political support from the city's working classes, not from its old elite. "Instead of selling the ruins of what they built," he asked, "why not build something ourselves?"

The old guard preferred mummification. South Carolina had already incorporated the standard zoning enabling act, written by Bassett for Hoover's commission, into its statutes. Then, in 1931, Charleston adopted a zoning ordinance that included a novel type of designation for the most ancient part of the city, creating an Old and Historic District. No new building could be erected there, nor any existing structure altered, without the approval of the five-member Board of Architectural Review. This was zoning pushed to its limit, placing any visible change to private property under the purview of appointed officials. Instead of purchasing the properties they wanted to preserve, they would simply place restrictions on what the people who owned them could do with them, externalizing the costs. The plan would maintain within the city, as one newspaper put it, "a place of charm for residence by substantial and cultured people." City planners were ecstatic. Charles Cheney weighed in from the West Coast, hailing it as "one of the most forward advances in city planning work and architectural control that we have ever yet had in the country."

But it was a very particular vision of the past that Charleston chose to preserve. The Board of Architectural Review's resident expert aimed to restore the district to its appearance in 1860, a loaded date in a city that built its wealth through slavery. The historic district had long been integrated, after a fashion, with white families residing in its stately mansions and Black families consigned to shacks and huts along the alleys. The city and the preservationists spent the next several decades squeezing Black residents out of the area, including seizing their modest homes by eminent domain and clearing them away, as the historian Stephanie Yuhl has documented. The imposition of a segregated landscape, they made clear, was a feature of their design, not a bug. What remained was not the city as it ever was, but the city as its white elites clearly wished it had always been.

The idea of historic preservation districts spread slowly at first, but gained momentum during the broad backlash against urban renewal in the 1960s. As it did so, the locus of concern shifted away from the preservation of sites like Mount Vernon, nationally recognized for their historic significance, or historic Charleston, an embalmed relic of a bygone era. "The United States is a nation and a people on the move," a 1966 report by the U.S. Conference of Mayors said, noting that 20 percent of Americans moved each year. "The result is a feeling of rootlessness combined with a longing for those landmarks of the past which give us a sense of stability and belonging." Preservation, the report argued, could be the antidote to the corrosive effects of mobility, addressing the anomie of urban life and maintaining the distinctiveness of local communities. Congress took up its call, passing the National Historic Preservation Act into law later that year. The federal law offered new recognition for historic areas, if not much in the way of actual protection, but state and local governments swiftly enacted their own measures, and historic districts grew quickly. They proved particularly popular in residential neighborhoods where professional-class families were seeking stability, whether by accelerating gentrification or warding off new development.

That historic districts were born of hostility to mobility is both telling and tragic. The American longing for the landmarks of the past has indeed been bolstered by our mobility, but that is reason to regard mobility and preservation as twinned impulses, not oppositional forces. Our nostalgia is fueled by our wanderlust; we most venerate the past when we are moving toward the future. Wiser policies would have sought to preserve landmarks in ways that opened the door for new arrivals to appreciate them. Instead, by allowing communities to designate entire districts as historic, policy makers enabled local residents to wield the past as a weapon against the future. Moreover, in the name of equity, advocates of preservation quickly broadened the range of structures that could be recognized. Why should only the mansions of the wealthy be eligible? Why not neighborhoods of vernacular architecture, or buildings that reflect the day-to-day lives of most Americans? The professional classes soon began using preservation as a new tool of exclusion. The key criteria of significance turned out to be not what a structure had once held or how it looked or who designed it but how well organized its neighbors were and how odious they found the plan to replace it.

In 1986, Washington, D.C., landmarked a parking lot. The affluent D.C. neighborhood of Cleveland Park, worried that a proposed mixed-use development above a Metro stop would bring greater density, suddenly discovered that the aging strip mall it was slated to replace was a pioneering example of the form and so deserved to be preserved, including the spots in which shoppers parked their cars. Once again, the sovereign village made its appearance as the president of the local historical association explained that she wanted to save "the neighborhood atmosphere of our little village," and that the question was whether an urban neighborhood could control what would happen to it. "If the Park and Shop goes, it's the first step," another resident declared. "This is my neighborhood, and I'm not going to let it look like Bethesda"—as if that affluent cluster of taller buildings slightly to the north were some sort of slum. She made good on that vow, scrolling through old newspapers on microfilm until she found the opening date of the strip mall—1930—to prove its antiquity. The entire neighborhood gained protection, with the strip mall and its parking lot singled out as contributing properties. With enough effort and a mastery of bureaucratic procedures, even something as banal as a strip-mall parking lot could be declared historic.

When I lived in Cambridge, Massachusetts, I used to walk past a small falafel shop each day, in a curious single-story hut sheathed in glossy white bricks and topped with a crenellated rectangular turret. It was built to look like a White Castle restaurant, the pioneering fast-food chain that used its distinctive architecture to advertise the consistency of its product. In fact, it was a White Tower, a knockoff chain exploiting the solid reputation of the larger business. In 1937, White Tower was sued for infringing the trademark of White Castle, and lost; as part of the settlement, the entire building was reclad with enameled steel panels. In 1999, the City of Cambridge designated it a landmark on the grounds that it was "the earliest example in Cambridge of fast-food architecture," a particularly remarkable claim in a progressive city that abhors national chains in general and fast-food restaurants in particular. The designation report recommended restoring the restaurant to its original, trademark-infringing appearance. The otherwise baffling decision to declare a fast-food franchise historic was explained by the fact that the property owner had been pursuing a plan to redevelop the site, which sits next to a major intersection and a subway station, as a multistory building. All sorts of structures become historically significant when the alternative is transit-oriented development—even the cookie-cutter architecture of failed, knockoff burger joints.

As American cities revived, bringing the professional classes back into urban areas, they brought with them their penchant for designating their residential neighborhoods as historic districts. In Manhattan, 27 percent of all lots are now located in historic districts or otherwise landmarked, predominantly in the borough's most affluent areas. Nearly 19 percent of Washington, D.C.'s, lots are similarly protected, including much of the D.C. neighborhood of Takoma. And in Baltimore, almost a third of the city is on the National Register of Historic Places. Not every city embraced the tool with equal enthusiasm, although those differences underscore how little relationship such designations share with any objective estimate of historical importance. In history-saturated Philadelphia, just 2.2 percent of the city's total lots receive local protection, and change-averse San Francisco has seen fit to designate only 1.4 percent. But where landmarking has become popular, it's been an effective means of warding off development. In Manhattan, when a neighborhood is designated historic, new construction within it drops by about 20 percent below the city's already grossly inadequate rate.

Government rules, though, have their limits—even those concerning historic preservation. You can't regulate how frequently your neighbor mows her lawn with zoning ordinances. Restrictions written into deeds can be remarkably broad but are often difficult to enforce in practice. So, developers and homeowners continued to experiment with other ways to defend the exclusivity of their communities. One popular solution in the first half of the twentieth century was the neighborhood improvement association. These groups, under a variety of names, collected dues from local residents in exchange for providing basic services like cleaning the streets and pressing government for an array of amenities, including better sewers, transportation, and parks. Their primary preoccupation, however, was using the power of collective action to enforce racial covenants and exclude minority groups. After *Shelley v. Kraemer* made racial covenants unenforceable in 1948, neighborhood associations adopted new tactics. In urban areas, many pushed their communities to adopt occupancy standards or conservation agreements—

binding rules limiting the number of residents in a unit or other uses of property. Unable to enforce restrictions on the basis of race, these groups instead turned to exclusion on the basis of class. Together with the "strict enforcement of building and zoning laws," as one researcher found in Chicago, they aimed begrudgingly to "allow wealthier Negroes to purchase homes in white communities" while still excluding working-class Black families.

But community associations were proliferating in suburbia, too. Rising real estate values on the urban fringe encouraged builders to build more single-family homes, packing them onto smaller lots with shared amenities. By adding community associations into their new subdivisions, developers could promise buyers greater control. The associations would maintain the new shared spaces and defend the developments against the intrusion of less affluent residents. Homeowners' associations began to function as local governments on steroids, restricting everything from the minimum age of residents to the height of the grass on the lawn. Towns and counties quickly discovered the attractions of these rules, encouraging, or even requiring, new subdivisions to adopt them.

If you're buying a new home today, it's probably in some sort of homeowners' association; these groups now govern two-thirds of all new units and more than three-quarters of those built for sale. But this is a stunningly new development. In 1970, community associations—cooperatives, condominiums, and planned communities—remained unusual, housing scarcely two million Americans. By 2021, they housed more than seventy-four million Americans and had become the dominant form of new housing in the country. Even if every zoning and building code in the country were repealed tomorrow, a third of the country would still reside in housing governed by community associations—living in literal members-only clubs, under sets of rules that can be far more restrictive than anything the government itself can legally impose.

Progressive reformers might have played a key role in choking off American mobility, but other strands of the progressive tradition contain the seeds of its renewal. All along, there have been progressives who have placed less emphasis on the top-down imposition of social order by impartial experts, and more on the importance of diversity, equality, and opportunity. Progressive Era activists like Bruno Lasker denounced zoning as class-based segregation. In 1917, the NAACP successfully challenged Louisville's racial zoning ordinance, and in 1941 the ACLU came to Fred Edwards's defense and secured the right to cross state lines. Today, a host of young activists have seized on this second strand of the progressive tradition to make the case for new housing.

The result, as I saw at the WMATA hearing, is something of a generational divide. Where left-wing baby boomers worried about overpopulation and the loss of green spaces, their children tend to worry more about carbon emissions and climate change. Opponents of the Takoma development stressed its negative impact on its immediate environment, while supporters framed the changes it would introduce as positive for the broader environment, bringing greater density and affordability to a transit hub. One opponent of the development had purchased her home in 1975 for $36,000; today it is worth more than $900,000. If her concern that new construction would alter the character of her community was not shared by the younger people in the room, it was perhaps because anyone who has tried to buy or rent in the neighborhood in the past twenty years is painfully aware that housing scarcity had already changed its character.

The Takoma project itself is still under review, but even its opponents now acknowledge it is likely to move forward. Any commercial property owner trying to develop the parcel would have cut their losses and pulled the plug a few years in. It survived a quarter century of delay only because the landowner is a public authority and its developer, EYA, has built its business around the dysfunction of the system, specializing in projects that scare off other firms. For McLean Quinn, who leads EYA, the work is personal. McLean grew up in Rochester, New York; his father had left the declining industrial city of High Point, North Carolina, for someplace with brighter prospects, landing at Kodak in northern New York State. By the time McLean was looking at college, Rochester was, itself, a declining industrial city, and his father pushed him to move elsewhere. The geography of American opportunity had changed by then, and he headed back to North Carolina, landing a job in Charlotte. A book on the concentration of economic success into a handful of megacities seized his imagination. He moved to Washington, where he's built a profitable development firm by tackling contentious projects—working to update the zoning of sites, changing plans to incorporate feedback from the community, and folding large numbers of affordable units into new developments. The fact that even EYA—a firm skilled at threading the needle of approval processes—has taken this long to move the Takoma project toward completion is not an encouraging sign. For housing advocates, Takoma may be a success, but it's hardly one that they can take to scale.

So how do we get America moving again? If we want a nation built on upward mobility, entrepreneurial innovation, increasing equality, vibrant community, democratic participation, and pluralistic diversity, then we need to build it. I mean that quite literally. We need to *build* it. We need to turn housing from a scarce asset back into an abundant resource, from an appreciating investment back into a consumer good. That won't be easy, and it won't happen overnight. But it starts with understanding how essential mobility has been to the United States, how much we're losing by restraining it, and how much we have to gain by restoring it. And it will require progressives, who constitute overwhelming political majorities in almost all of America's most prosperous and productive areas, to embrace the strain of their political tradition that emphasizes inclusion and equality.

The crisis of housing affordability has already attracted a host of experts advocating specific solutions. The urban planner M. Nolan Gray wants to abolish zoning, relying instead on comprehensive planning and nuisance regulation. The journalist Henry Grabar is concerned by the spread of parking and suggests reclaiming our cities for people instead of cars. The architect Daniel Parolek points to the missing middle, advocating construction of more duplexes and fourplexes and townhomes. Daniel Aldana Cohen and Mark Paul want to build social housing, mixed-income, publicly owned developments where market-rate renters subsidize the poorer households who live alongside them. The Brookings Institution's Jenny Schuetz, recognizing the complexity of the problem, has a seven-part plan; UCLA's Shane Phillips breaks it down even further, offering fifty policy recommendations. You can walk into a bookstore and find a dozen other solutions. All would do something to help, but not all would strike at the core of the issue.

America faces not an affordable housing crisis—houses remain remarkably cheap in economically depressed regions—but a mobility crisis. The loss of mobility is experienced as a loss of agency, a loss of opportunity, a loss of dignity, a loss of hope. Building subsidized housing in a place with few jobs will help solve the problem of affordability, but it will only worsen the loss of mobility. From the story these pages contain, I want to distill three principles that can help us address our desperate crisis of mobility.

The first principle is tolerance. Organic growth is messy and unpredictable. Most of the regulations that restrain mobility sprang from an attempt to impose order and rationality on the landscape and from the mistaken assumption that controlling the form that buildings take is an efficient means of reforming the people they contain. To approach a community in the belief that order can be imposed architecturally, as Jane Jacobs wrote, "is to make the mistake of attempting to substitute art for life." Like other natural processes, the evolution of the built environment will be full of false starts and dead ends, full of contradictory preferences and jarring contrasts and all the wasteful chaos that the first progressive planners hoped to banish forever. Contemporary zoning codes are stuffed full of special districts and overlays and exceptions, evidence of the failure of applying standardized solutions to the rich and varied lives of human communities. This is why zoning variances—intended as rare exceptions—have gradually become the rule. Respecting organic growth requires a degree of humility, an acknowledgment that we see the future only imperfectly and that there may be more than one viable way forward. Usually, the best response to the discovery that a land-use rule is blocking some desired outcome is not to split it into five more detailed and specific rules, but to ask whether it needed to be so prescriptive to begin with.

Our most iconic landscapes emerged not through rigorous central planning but from the aggregated decisions of individuals working within loose guidelines. Take the iconic New England village, centering on the town green, long held up as a model of community and stability—a built form that many earnest planners have since tried to replicate through highly prescriptive rules. In colonial New England, early attempts to form nucleated settlements by means of top-down planning failed spectacularly as farmers dispersed across the countryside. Not until the nineteenth century did the New England village emerge in recognizable form as a clustering of houses and commercial buildings in a market center, often built around a former meetinghouse lot turned into a town green by the disestablishment of the church. These were messy and chaotic spaces, mixing substantial homes with the smoke and din of a blacksmith's forge and the odors and cries of the market, commingling commercial, residential, and industrial uses. So quickly had they sprung up, it seemed obvious they would not last. "A village, with its scattered white houses, often reminds one of an encampment, with its white tents, that to-morrow morning, at the sound of the bugle, will be struck, and disappear," wrote Nathan Henry Chamberlain in 1858. And indeed, these local centers soon lost their economic rationale, and with it their shops and their bustle. Only then did they become orderly residential districts—particularly if they lay within striking distance of rising urban centers, where improving transportation transformed them into suburban retreats, whose residents exalted them as authentic relics of colonial life. To have frozen this evolving landscape at any of its varied stages by imposing rigid rules would have precluded it from adapting to meet emerging needs, as indeed such rules now keep New England's town centers from continuing to evolve and thrive.

To that tolerance for imperfection in the arrangement of buildings we must add a tolerance for imperfection in their form. A wide array of housing arrangements evolved organically to meet the demands of America's golden age of mobility, from the New England triple-decker to the New York tenement to the New Orleans shotgun house. Again and again, Americans have investigated the housing conditions of the poor, declared them unacceptable, and responded with laws banning certain classes of structure and tightening building standards—as if the problem were the buildings and not the poverty. We have slowly purged from our landscape most forms of genuinely affordable housing. Far from solving poverty, we have exacerbated it, by making it more difficult to obtain affordable housing in the places that offer real economic opportunity, physical security, and social connection. If we want to improve housing for the poor, the simplest solution is to transfer cash to Americans living below the poverty line, allowing them to decide for themselves what they value and where to procure it. Barring that, if we want to give every American a safe, decent place to live, we can allocate sufficient public funding to build the tens of millions of new housing units that restoring mobility requires. But if we are to continue to lean heavily on markets, then to ban most types of affordable housing while failing to alleviate poverty or to build alternatives is to compound malignant indifference with overt cruelty. We are now reaping the whirlwind, with growing inequality and a mounting homelessness crisis.

The short-term solution is to legalize a far wider variety of housing arrangements. Homelessness, as the scholars Gregg Colburn and Clayton Page Aldern have shown, is a housing problem. The wide variation between cities in the rates of homelessness, they found, can't be explained by differing rates of mental illness or substance abuse; cities with high rates of poverty and unemployment often have low rates of homelessness. But in booming cities that have made it inordinately difficult to build, where rents are high and vacancies are low, rates of housing insecurity and homelessness soar. As Edward Bassett moved around in his youth, he rented rooms in a residential hotel and a bachelor apartment building, boarded in a room in a private home, and rented an apartment in a subdivided house. The zoning codes he disseminated generally ban these forms of housing, leaving little in the way of low-cost options. The poor are then forced to stay in regions of the country with concentrated deprivation and limited prospects, to move to cities with illegally converted rental units with few protections, or to go unhoused entirely.

Some jurisdictions are now experimenting with what they call micro-apartments or tiny houses, and others with co-housing, but such arrangements are usually aimed at young college graduates and regulated in ways that make them even more expensive than most existing housing units. With my first paycheck as a municipal employee, I rented a 150-square-foot studio in an aging Manhattan apartment building. It had a tiny closet, a bathroom that was scarcely any larger, and along one wall a two-burner range, a sink, and a refrigerator. The window looked out on an air shaft. For this incomparable luxury, I paid 43 percent of my pretax income and considered it a steal. Most micro-apartments are required to be at least three times this size. But my nano-apartment allowed me to live close to a transit line, hold a job, cook my own meals, and enjoy a measure of privacy. Other New Yorkers bribe superintendents to turn a blind eye as they subdivide apartments or live in the illegally converted basement units that have proliferated in the outer boroughs, with sometimes deadly consequences. Instead of barring the construction of such units on the grounds that they are less than ideal, we'd do better to legalize and regulate a much broader array of housing options. Not every form of housing will be appropriate for every individual or for every stage of life—and that's fine. A young woman on a tight income might find a residential hotel useful, a retiree might appreciate a co-living space, a family might want a house. By approaching regulation with greater humility, though, and a commitment to allowing housing to evolve organically, we can help people find the forms of housing that work best for them at each stage of life.

The second principle that should guide our policy is consistency. Rules work best when they apply uniformly and predictably over the widest possible geographic areas. Zoning's original sin, in Modesto, was to announce that a specific use of the land was odious in most of the city but perfectly fine in one particular neighborhood. To say, like the Supreme Court, that putting some kinds of buildings into certain areas is like putting a pig in the parlor and not the barnyard is to designate some neighborhoods parlors and treat others like barnyards. Rules that apply uniformly across a city will tend to produce neighborhoods with diverse populations and diverse uses and provide equitable protections to residents and businesses. Rules that are tailored to the desires of specific neighborhoods or that prescribe certain uses in certain places will tend, over time, to concentrate less desirable uses in poorer areas. No one should be asked to live in a barnyard.

The clarity of these consistent rules is equally crucial. Builders should be able to read the rules, design a commercially viable development that complies with them, and file their plans with confidence that they will be swiftly approved. That will speed the construction of housing while keeping costs to a minimum. Too many zoning ordinances are designed, instead, to force every developer to come to the table for an extended period of review, hearings, public input, and negotiation. Not only does this slow the production of housing and drive up its costs; it also pushes the burden of all kinds of development into impoverished communities. Developers often choose to place projects where they will encounter less well-organized opposition; the less desirable the development, the likelier that outcome. "If you're in a wealthy neighborhood, and they're educated, they're going to be harder to deal with," one commercial developer active in Flint told me. "If you're in a poor neighborhood that's less educated, they're probably going to be easier to deal with." He paused, realizing what he'd just said. "I wish that wasn't on tape," he said, chuckling. But this is hardly news for residents of low-income neighborhoods packed with warehouses and gas stations and drive-through restaurants providing services to more affluent people who have banished these establishments from their own neck of the woods.

To see the difference that clear, simple, and consistent rules can make, consider this tale of two cities. In 1961, New York City comprehensively overhauled its zoning code for the first time since Bassett's 1916 plan had been put into effect. A 1950 study had warned that the city's zoning would allow for a theoretical population of more than 70 million. It projected, instead, a peak population of 8.6

million and recommended cutting back the permissible height, bulk, and density of buildings so as to achieve the optimal distribution of that population. A second report, in 1958, projected a plateau around 8.3 million and zoned for a theoretical capacity of roughly 11 million. Both reports warned of the dangers of congestion and overpopulation, which were presumed to be drivers of suburban flight. Zoning became a tool for managing the population, prescribing both what buildings should look like and where people should live, on the theory that left to their own devices, people were making the wrong choices. There were critics of rezoning, even at the time, who warned it would stifle the city's dynamism. One prominent architect warned the code would "triple rents on new buildings in Manhattan," but his concerns were dismissed by the Planning Commission as hysterical. In 1958, the city had 2.6 million housing units, and the new plans allowed for a zoned capacity of 3.6 million housing units—which, not coincidentally, is precisely what the city contains today. The presently constrained housing supply in New York, in other words, was not only foreseeable, and not only foreseen, but deliberately foreordained.

In 1958, on the other side of the globe, Tokyo had just 1.8 million housing units; by 2018, it could boast 7.7 million units. That, too, was the result of deliberate choices. Japan passed a raft of laws in the late 1960s and early 1970s tightening environmental review and delegating planning authority to local communities, just like the United States, and citizen activists turned to the courts to defend the public interest, winning significant victories. By the 1990s, rising demand to live in prosperous urban areas was inflating housing prices and rents. To that point, the two cities were on parallel trajectories. But zoning works differently in Japan. Although local jurisdictions decide which zoning designations to apply where, the 12 categories they can apply are defined by the national Building Standards Law (BSL). (New York City alone, by contrast, has 21 basic districts, 134 special-purpose districts, and 11 use rules that can also apply, all locally defined.) Japan's economic struggles convinced the national government that the lack of affordable housing needed to be addressed, even if that meant overriding local objections to development. It made a series of technical changes to the BSL categories, beginning in the mid-1990s, that loosened restrictions. Since 2000, the housing stock in Tokyo has expanded roughly four times as fast as in New York, even as new units have grown larger, slowing the rise of prices in the central city while limiting it even more sharply in the outlying areas.

There are lessons here for us if we care to learn them. Japan's small number of straightforward zoning categories allows for most construction to be done as of right—following clearly stated rules, without the need for time-consuming reviews or special permission. This policy decreases construction costs and allows for developers based in one city to easily navigate the rules in another, increasing competition. Not only is Tokyo's housing both abundant and comparatively affordable, but the ease of construction has kept prices low enough for workshops and light industry to be interspersed with the housing and stores. That shortens commutes and keeps streets livelier and safer at all hours. In our federal system, Bassett's standard enabling act delegated state-level authority over land use to local governments a century ago, but there is nothing to stop states from passing new enabling acts that define a limited number of categories for municipalities to apply as they see fit. Some legislatures are already edging in this direction, however tentatively, by banning single-family zoning or by overriding local regulations where municipalities don't allow for a bare minimum of multifamily units. Letting more Americans move to prospering areas isn't merely a local issue; it's both a vital state-level interest and a national priority. But at whatever level we set the rules, and whatever we want those rules to be, the emphasis should be on defining a limited number of clear and consistent categories that allow for as-of-right development.

Finally, the third principle we need to adopt is abundance. We need to provide so much housing that when the music stops, everyone can claim a seat. And it's not enough just to provide every American with decent housing. If it isn't located in the right places, that housing will become a millstone instead of a springboard, holding people back instead of launching them forward. The programs that aim to help Americans in lower income brackets, who would most benefit by moving toward opportunity, too often freeze people in place. Large-scale public housing projects enforce economic segregation through their eligibility criteria that limit income, concentrating poverty. But even alternatives like scatter-site development, spreading units over a broader geographic area; inclusionary-zoning programs, which add affordable units to new developments; and Section 8 rentals, which use federal funds for vouchers that can be used to rent market-rate units, almost invariably give local residents first claim on their extremely limited supply. Where opportunity is greatest, demand is typically highest, making it hard for anyone who doesn't already live in the jurisdiction to benefit. Waiting lists for these programs are often years long, and lotteries offer bad odds; none of these programs receive funding remotely commensurate with the need. If you're fortunate enough to secure a permanently affordable unit or a rent-controlled apartment in a city that isn't thriving, the decision to move toward a city with more opportunity entails surrendering a valuable prize for an uncertain return. Thelma Price's HUD-subsidized $198 monthly rent in Flint, with no similar prospects anywhere else, anchors her to the city as surely as her family does.

If these programs have often succeeded in tying residents to places where opportunities are diminishing, they have also done little to help people move to places where their chances are better. Since World War II, America has made it ever harder to build new housing, then tried to address the rising prices that result from this artificial shortage by setting aside some portion of the housing stock to aid those most in need. But without dramatically expanding the supply, reallocating the existing housing only exacerbates the problem of affordability. Rent control is nice for those who can obtain it, but it drives up the cost of the other rental units in a jurisdiction and disincentivizes new construction. At the extremes, it even deters landlords from leasing existing units. Inclusionary-zoning ordinances helpfully build income diversity into new developments by adding units designated as affordable. But inclusionary zoning inflates the price of the market-rate units in the same development, because their builders need larger profits to make up for their losses on the affordable units. Housing vouchers are theoretically portable, but particularly in competitive markets many landlords won't accept them. Where prices are highest, the rents exhaust the fixed pool of federal funds fastest, leaving fewer vouchers to go around. And all the while, the gap between the richest and the poorest places keeps widening, and cities that offer the greatest opportunities grow more expensive. Without addressing the constraints on supply, none of these approaches can ever meet the need.

The only solution is to build such an abundant supply of housing that it reverts to being a consumer good and not an investment asset. Most developers focus on the top end of the market, where margins are highest. Loosening regulations can help make other modes of housing viable for commercial developers, but even if much of the new supply is priced out of range of most Americans, as long as we add enough, many people are likely to benefit. When Americans still observed Moving Day, they intuitively understood that the construction of a fancy new apartment building would set off a long chain of moves as one family moved into a sparkling new unit and a chain of other families bumped up to the apartments each had vacated in turn. New housing, even luxury housing, could improve life for people all along the economic chain. That's no less true today. One recent study traced that chain for six links, then modeled the results. A new building with a hundred market-rate units, it concluded, would allow forty-five to seventy families to depart below-median-income neighborhoods for places with more opportunity, mostly within three years. And the people who don't move benefit, too, because the availability of new housing eases the supply crunch and holds down prices. Another study found that for every hundred existing rental units, introducing one additional market-rate unit lowers rents by 0.4 to 0.7 percent, and it lowers them across the board, even in the cheapest segment of the market. The more abundant housing becomes, the cheaper supplemental solutions like permanently affordable units and rental vouchers and mortgage subsidies and rent control will be to implement, and the fewer people who will need them. The best way to solve a supply crunch is to add supply—lots of it.

How much housing do we need? It's hard to say. For fifty years, we've been falling behind demand. Freddie Mac estimates it would take another 3.8 million units just to adequately house our current population, with the shortfall concentrated at the entry-level end of the market. Treat that as the lower bound. The trouble is, most of the existing units are located where regulation is loose and land is cheap, not in the places richest in opportunity, where industries are growing, jobs pay more, and schools are better. Producing genuinely abundant housing, sufficient to make our most prosperous metropolitan areas affordable for working-class residents once more, is a taller order. My colleague Annie Lowrey has estimated such a scenario would require some 75 million new units. That's the upper bound.

But even if housing were cheap and abundant, not everyone would move, so we don't actually need 75 million new units. As things stand, roughly 20 percent of American workers relocate from one metropolitan area to another over the course of a decade. If all those moves that will happen anyway were funneled into the most prosperous regions, where productivity is highest—places like New York and the Bay Area, but also Austin and northwest Arkansas—we'd have to add some 30 million new units over the next ten years, or 3 million new units per year—roughly double our current pace. It's an ambitious target, but it's also an attainable one. The right question isn't whether we can afford to do this but whether we can afford not to.

These three principles—tolerance, consistency, and abundance—can help us restore American mobility. The goal of policy makers shouldn't be to move Americans toward the coastal megalopolises, even if that's where opportunity is most concentrated today. It shouldn't be to move people into single-family homes or into town houses or into apartment towers. It shouldn't be to move people anywhere at all. Instead, they should aim to return to Americans their own agency, allowing them to pursue opportunity wherever they might find it and to choose the housing that works best for them. For some Americans, that might mean reviving faded towns; for others it might mean planting new ones. It might mean leaning into technologies that allow people to work remotely, from all over the country, or it might mean moving toward population centers that require and reward in-person labor. Individuals should be able to make their own choices. The genius of the American system was never that its leaders knew what was coming next but rather that they allowed people to decide things for themselves so that they might collectively produce the future.

And whatever policies we pursue, it's important to strive for balance while preserving a sense of humility. We can try to avoid allowing historic preservation and environmental review and participatory planning to choke off mobility while also aiming to safeguard cherished landmarks and preserving vulnerable ecologies and enhancing genuinely democratic decision making. We can try to free our markets to produce the housing that individual consumers want to buy while still regulating them to guard against abuses and supplementing them with housing for the people they exclude and harm. We can try to put public dollars to work expanding supply while guarding against having them used to segregate our neighborhoods. Public policy is not a realm that rewards ideological purity; the best outcomes require adjusting to empirical realities and entail constantly renegotiated compromises. The fatal hubris of zoning lay in the belief that any group of planners, no matter how clever or well intentioned, could sit in a room and prescribe for other citizens the best uses of their land. Any remedies will have to be grounded in humility, or risk producing a new set of harms that outstrips the old.

Perhaps American mobility was merely a life stage in the growth of the republic, an artifact of our restless youth. After two centuries of continual change, America might have matured into a society like any other, in which most significant aspects of our identity— where we live, how we pray, whom we know, what we earn—are less chosen than inherited. If what we've experienced this past half century isn't just a prolonged mobility recession, but a permanent change in the structure of American life, we'll need to develop a wide range of new tools and strategies for delivering opportunity, community, tolerance, and prosperity. We'll need to redesign public policy around an assumption of stasis. Many European nations already tailor their spending in this way, redistributing the fruits of growth in prosperous places to immobile populations in declining regions, prioritizing the retention of existing jobs over the acquisition of new ones, and accepting the high levels of unemployment—particularly among younger workers and historically disadvantaged populations—this entails. Historically, the United States has offered a somewhat threadbare social safety net, incentivizing people to move toward opportunity instead of seeking to sustain them where they live. Today, however, the United States combines increasingly European levels of geographic immobility with American-style parsimony, delivering the worst of both worlds. We neither help workers move toward opportunity nor do enough to provide for them when they can't. The United States has weathered many shifts in the distribution of opportunity, only to emerge more prosperous than ever, and most economists expected that workers who lost their jobs through the shocks of environmental regulation and of free trade with Mexico and China would find new and better opportunities. Their models, though, were validated against historical data and failed to account for new barriers to mobility. Instead of relocating, most of these workers were trapped in places with few prospects. Some politicians are now pushing for European-style redistribution to alleviate their suffering.

The other option is to tear down the barriers to mobility and return to the social and economic dynamism that long made America distinctive. The decrease in geographic mobility was produced over decades by a set of legal and political interventions, which suggests that it can be reversed. The question is whether those of us who have benefited from the changes of the last fifty years care enough about those we've abandoned to act.

In 1914, a journeyman baker named Bendyt Bressler moved into the three-story tenement on Suffolk Street on the Lower East Side of New York that I visited back in chapter 6. He had left his wife, his toddler, and his newborn daughter in Nadvorna in his native Galicia four years before and traveled to Hamburg. He crossed to New York in steerage class on the grand ocean liner *Kaiserin Auguste Victoria*.

Four years later, his family boarded the same ship to join him. Somewhere in the mid-Atlantic, his wife, Simeh, became Sadie; his elder daughter, Chane, Annie; and little Feige, Fannie. They needed a place to live together, and so Bendyt—by now, Benjamin—had rented an apartment in the redbrick tenement on Suffolk Street.

Bakeries studded the Lower East Side in those years like caraway seeds in a loaf of rye. A journeyman could do well for himself in the trade, with less experienced workers pulling down $16 to $24 each week, and a skilled hand earning as much as $28. The hours were long, the work labor-intensive, and the conditions trying, but at least in New York a baker could take hold of his own future. And even in hard times, a baker's children never went to bed hungry; there was always some stale bread to take home at the end of the day. Bressler had another child, and earned enough for his five-person family to live in an apartment of their own—the only family in their building without lodgers—and for his wife to stay home while his older children attended a parochial school. And soon enough, he moved to a larger apartment to accommodate his growing family, and then on to others that met their evolving needs.

Lawrence Veiller had warned that tenements would weaken morality and dissolve religious faith. The buildings, he believed, were inherently degrading, ruining their occupants. You can test that for yourself, though, if you're willing to take the risk. The Suffolk Street tenement house is still there, its redbrick facade freshly painted in house-flip gray and the window casements outlined in black. The first two floors have been combined into a single apartment, featuring cherrywood flooring and brushed-nickel hardware, renting for $7,500 a month. The nine-hundred-square-foot walk-up on the top floor, where the Bresslers once lived, now boasts stainless steel appliances and a marble bathroom, renting for a more modest $3,650. A pair of retro-chic lanterns flank the entryway. Marketing materials describe this structure as a "historic federal style building" and a "pre-war townhouse" on a quiet block "in Manhattan's trendy Lower East Side." The word "tenement" has been discreetly omitted.

Somehow, Bressler managed to spend most of his life in tenements without succumbing to moral turpitude. He had only a fifth-grade education, but his fourth child, Celia, was admitted to Hunter College. Instead of working seventy-eight-hour weeks in a hot, smoky bakery like her father, she moved out to Brooklyn and taught kindergarten in the New York City public schools. Her father's bet on mobility paid off for her, and for me. Celia was my grandmother.

The house I live in today is the fifteenth residence I've occupied in my life, already putting me a few moves above the American average. I have no particular desire to move again. I love my home, I love my neighbors, and I would be perfectly happy never to wrap another set of dishes in old newspapers. But then, I hadn't planned on moving here, either. I know that I've been luckier than I deserve in life, able to move in pursuit of opportunities when they've presented themselves, a freedom that fewer Americans enjoy with each passing year.

Out my window, they're putting the finishing touches on three large apartment buildings. The huge project they're part of includes a couple thousand new units, more than a fifth of them affordable. There will be assisted-living facilities for low-income seniors, dozens of apartments for homeless veterans, and affordable housing folded into luxury condo buildings. There will be offices and stores and parks. Like all new developments, it leaves a good deal to be desired. The architecture strikes me as blandly corporate. Local regulations, historic preservation, and participatory planning have combined to limit the development on the site to just a fraction of what it might have held. But I'm trying to practice my tolerance for imperfection. Although I have little affection for cookie-cutter six-story apartment buildings, I don't want to repeat Veiller's error of mistaking my own aesthetic judgments for the public good. (And familiarity breeds respect; in fifty years, when a new developer tries to build something taller on the site, local residents will probably try to landmark one of these buildings as an exemplary instance of an American vernacular.) Even if the development is smaller than it might have been, it will change the lives of my thousands of new neighbors. Each apartment will also set off a chain of moves, with families throughout the city and across the country bumping up to vacated housing. And by absorbing a portion of the local demand, it will ease the pressure on prices in the city's few remaining affordable neighborhoods. It won't make housing abundant here by itself, but it's a good start.

I sometimes find myself thinking of Bendyt, a man I never met, while I watch the workers erecting the buildings. He came to this country in search of opportunity, then kept moving when he got here, from one apartment to another, from one bakery to the next. He found steady work, but he found much more. He encountered strangers from across the country and around the world, and they mostly tolerated each other, in a land where the constant mixing of the population had made "stranger" a friendly salutation. That was not a small thing. He and the other immigrants from Nadvorna formed the First Nadworner Sick and Benefit Association and erected a monument to the slaughtered Jews of his native town. They'd been trapped in a land where identities were heritable and inescapable, a fate my great-grandfather's mobility had spared him from sharing. In America, he was free to fashion his own identity. He gave his name first as Beniy and then as Bennie and then as Benjamin, easing himself into his new culture like a swimmer entering a cold pool. In this imperfect land, he discovered, mobility sometimes allows you to alter your identity and your destiny. He left behind all he'd known to give his children a better life, and they kept moving, doing the same for children of their own. He was, in short, exactly the sort of man Veiller and Bassett and Cheney fought so hard to keep out of their own backyards.

I hope someone just like him moves into mine.

ACKNOWLEDGMENTS

This book began more than a decade ago, in a triple-decker in Cambridge, where I looked at my children and wondered whether the world I would pass on to them would offer the same opportunities as the one I had inherited. That question sent me pulling books off shelves, visiting archives, and stopping people on streetcorners to find out how the world looked to them. I hope that the result will surprise even those who have longed studied the many subjects within these pages, from land use in colonial New England to the architectural design of tenement houses. But it could never have been written without my ability to draw on the writing of countless scholars who came before me, and who deserve much more than terse references in the endnotes. To all of them, my thanks; I hope I have done right by your labors.

If one measure of the urgency of a subject is the quality of the writers and researchers who are drawn to explore it, then the mobility crisis is a five-alarm fire. A few bear special mention. Jesse Kanson-Benanav and the others who came together to found A Better Cambridge in 2012 showed me that change was possible. A conversation that same year with Peter Ganong about his research with Daniel Shoag into the role that zoning played in declining mobility seized my imagination and helped put me on the path that led to this book. Ed Glaeser's research on housing, as on so many other urban issues, was pathbreaking. Ryan Avent's *The Gated City* and Matt Ygle-sias's *The Rent Is Too Damn High* played a crucial early role in popular-izing the cause of zoning reform. David Schleicher's broad-ranging "Stuck! The Law and Economics of Residential Stagnation" followed in *The Yale Law Journal* in 2017. It not only prefigured the title I've cho-sen for this book, but also offers the most sophisticated blend of legal and macroeconomic analysis of the subject. And at *The Atlantic,* I've learned much from Derek Thompson, Annie Lowrey, and Jeru-salem Demsas. This is by no means a complete list; my debts on this score are nearly inexhaustible.

No record carefully stored in an archive can ever be described as lost, but without the aid of many skilled archivists I do not know how much I ever would have found. I am grateful to the librarians at Boston College; Cornell University; Columbia University; the Uni-versity of Michigan-Flint; Flint's Sloan Museum; and the McHenry Museum in Modesto, California, for their assistance. And I am thankful for every person who consented to talk with me and who gave so generously of their time. For each one quoted by name in the text, there were three others who deeply informed the work.

Some of my debts are more personal. At Columbia, Simon Schama convinced me that history should be a pleasure to read, Eric Foner that it could matter, and Matthew Jones that it could be fun. I was fortunate to train as a historian at Brandeis under the guidance of extraordinary scholars: Jacqueline Jones, who recruited me; my adviser, Michael Willrich; Jane Kamensky and Heather Cox Richard-son, the other members of my dissertation committee; and David Hackett Fischer, David Engerman, Alice Kelikian, and Jonathan Sarna, who taught me so well. I likewise learned much from former colleagues at Babson College and at Harvard University's History & Literature program.

I want to thank the people who brought me to *The Atlantic:* Ta-Nehisi Coates, who thought an anonymous commenter on his blog deserved a shot to write; John Gould, Bob Cohn, and James Bennet, who took a chance on me; and David Bradley, for his trust. And I owe enormous gratitude to the magazine's current leadership, not just for giving me the space to write this book, but for their constant support and encouragement: Adrienne LaFrance, for wisdom exceeded only by her kindness; Jeffrey Goldberg, for editing with a keen intelligence but always leading with his heart; Peter Lattman, for his steadying hand; and Laurene Powell Jobs, for her faithful stewardship. On their watch, the magazine has thrived, growing so swiftly that I now have too many colleagues to thank by name. But I am obliged to single out Juliet Lapidos, who, in addition to everything else, gave me confidence that my colleagues would be in the ablest of hands whenever I disappeared to research and write.

I hope this book will attract many thoughtful critics, and on that score, I've already been lucky. Marie-Amélie George and her colleagues at Wake Forest Law School allowed me to present a portion of the book at their faculty workshop. I'm also particularly grateful to Cullen Murphy, for his gentle yet pointed critique; to Jerusalem Demsas, for sharing her many insights; and to my parents, for reading many early drafts.

Books take a team, and I've had a great one. My agent, Elyse Cheney, not only believed in the book, but saw it through, and made it better at every step of the process. At Random House, Andy Ward took a gamble on a first-time author. Only my patient editor, Hilary Redmon, will ever know how far this manuscript has journeyed from its initial draft; whatever glaring flaws it still possesses are apparent only against the backdrop of her countless improvements. The cover was designed by the brilliant Oliver Munday. Hilary McClellen fact-checked the book on an impossibly tight timeline. And a whole team at Random House got behind the project including Craig Adams, London King, Ayelet Durantt, and Miriam Khanukaev.

It would, I suppose, betray the spirit of my argument to say that it takes a village to write a book—better, perhaps, to conceive of it as a voluntary community. And I've been blessed with an assemblage of friends who've chosen to support me through this process, serving as sounding boards and safety valves.

The greatest debts, of course, are those I owe to family. To my grandparents, who never stopped believing in the promise of this country even if it had not always believed in them. To my parents, who not only moved toward opportunity but brought me with them, kicking and screaming. They continue to set a standard of intellectual curiosity, open generosity, and moral purpose that I can only hope to emulate. To my sister Avigail, who strikes her own balance between past and present with her work every day, and has provided invaluable encouragement and also the occasional dinner. To my brother Binyamin, who shares my obsession with this topic, and remains my favorite sparring partner.

To my wife, Emily, I owe everything—including an apology for all the nights on the road, the missed occasions, the shifted obligations this book entailed. Thank you for seeing me through it; I never could have done it without you. And finally, to my children, Elisheva and Joshua. This book was inspired by you and grew up along with you. I hope that one day, you will understand why I wrote it and make your own attempts to leave the world a little better than you found it.

NOTES

CHAPTER ONE: A NATION OF MIGRANTS

4 **The crisis shows up:** Charlynn Burd, Michael Burrows, and Brian McKenzie, "Travel Time to Work in the United States: 2019," American Community Survey Reports, U.S. Census Bureau, March 2021.

4 **And it shows up in the record number:** "America's Rental Housing, 2024," Joint Center for Housing Studies of Harvard University, Jan. 2024.

4 **I thought about it when:** The population of Cambridge was 104,839 in 1910 and 105,162 in 2010. But the number of residents under the age of fifteen had dropped from about 30,000 in 1910 to 10,000 in 2010.

5 **"Foreigners are coming in increasing numbers":** *Annual Report of the Massachusetts Civic League* (Boston: A. T. Bliss, 1911), 15.

5 **A settlement house worker:** Robert A. Woods and Albert J. Kennedy, *The Zone of Emergence: Observations of the Lower Middle and Upper Working Class Communities of Boston, 1905–1914,* 2nd ed. (Cambridge, Mass.: MIT Press, 1969).

7 **"is devoured with a passion":** Michel Chevalier, *Society, Manners, and Politics in the United States: Being a Series of Letters on North America,* trans. Thomas Bradford (Carlisle, Mass.: Applewood Books, 2007), 286.

7 **"We are a migratory people":** "A Migratory People," *Atlanta Constitution,* Jan. 21, 1892, 4.

9 **"When the mobility of population":** Carl Lotus Becker, *The United States: An Experiment in Democracy* (New York: Harper, 1920), 168.

12 **The country may be older:** Patrick J. Purcell, "Geographic Mobility and Annual Earnings in the United States," *Social Security Bulletin* 80, no. 2 (2020).

12 **The spread of occupational licensing:** Janna E. Johnson and Morris M. Kleiner, "Is Occupational Licensing a Barrier to Interstate Migration?," *American Economic Journal: Economic Policy* 12, no. 3 (Aug. 2020): 347–73.

12 **Two-earner households may be:** Chandra Childers et al., "Geographic Mobility, Gender, and the Future of Work," Institute for Women's Policy Research, July 2020.

13   **Between 1985 and 2014:** Sergio Salgado, "Technical Change and Entrepreneur-
      ship," SSRN, June 2, 2020.

14   **Switching jobs frequently:** Raven Molloy, Christopher L. Smith, and Abigail K.
      Wozniak, "Declining Migration Within the U.S.: The Role of the Labor Market,"
      Working Paper 20065, NBER Working Paper Series, April 2014; Raven Molloy,
      Christopher L. Smith, and Abigail Wozniak, "Changing Stability in U.S. Employ-
      ment Relationships: A Tale of Two Tails," Working Paper 26694, NBER Working
      Paper Series, Jan. 2020, 46.

14   **In 1970, about eight:** Raj Chetty et al., "The Fading American Dream: Trends in
      Absolute Income Mobility Since 1940," *Science* 356, no. 6336 (2017): 398–406.

14   **Compared with Americans at the beginning:** Americans have also grown less
      likely to actually attend the groups to which they still belong, shifting toward pay-
      ing membership fees. Matthew A. Painter and Pamela Paxton, "Checkbooks in the
      Heartland: Change over Time in Voluntary Association Membership," *Sociological
      Forum* 29, no. 2 (2014): 408–28; Robert D. Putnam, "Tuning In, Tuning Out: The
      Strange Disappearance of Social Capital in America," *PS: Political Science and Politics*
      28, no. 4 (Dec. 1995): 664–83.

14   **A majority of Americans:** "The Loneliness Epidemic Persists: A Post-pandemic
      Look at the State of Loneliness Among U.S. Adults," Cigna / Morning Consult,
      Dec. 2021.

14   **And while half of Americans:** "What We Do Together: The State of Associa-
      tional Life in America," U.S. Senate, Joint Economic Committee, May 15, 2017.

15   **Trump spoke to the anger:** Yoni Appelbaum, "Why Donald Trump Supporters
      Are Voting Alone," *Atlantic*, April 7, 2016.

15   **And those who had never:** Robert P. Jones and Dan Cox, "Still Live Near Your
      Hometown? If You're White, You're More Likely to Support Trump," *PRRI* (blog),
      Oct. 2016.

16   **his voters were much likelier:** Emma Green, "It Was Cultural Anxiety That
      Drove White, Working-Class Voters to Trump," *Atlantic*, May 9, 2017.

16   **Partisan sorting within states:** Ethan Kaplan, Jörg L. Spenkuch, and Rebecca
      Sullivan, "Partisan Spatial Sorting in the United States: A Theoretical and Empiri-
      cal Overview," *Journal of Public Economics* 211 (2022).

16   **Democratic voters are now:** Jonathan Rodden, *Why Cities Lose: The Deep Roots of
      the Urban-Rural Political Divide* (New York: Basic Books, 2019).

16   **A study of California:** Matthew E. Kahn, "Do Liberal Cities Limit New Housing
      Development? Evidence from California," *Journal of Urban Economics* 69, no. 2
      (2011): 223–28.

16   **"We have built a country":** Bill Bishop, *The Big Sort: Why the Clustering of Like-
      Minded America Is Tearing Us Apart* (Boston: Houghton Mifflin Harcourt, 2009), 40.

17   **The problem isn't that:** Even though Democrats are marginally likelier to move
      to dense places and Republicans to more rural ones, the effect is far too small to
      explain much of our polarization. Instead, as the political scientists Gregory Mar-
      tin and Steven Webster have shown, when people move into a new neighbor-
      hood, they tend to adopt the views of those around them. Gregory J. Martin and
      Steven W. Webster, "Does Residential Sorting Explain Geographic Polarization?,"
      Political Science Research and Methods 8, no. 2 (2020): 215–31.

19   **if you ask them:** "Cato Institute 2022 Housing Affordability National Survey,"
      Cato Institute, Aug. 2022.

20   **The notion that a prospering:** *High Cost of Living in the District of Columbia* (Wash-
      ington, D.C.: Government Printing Office, 1919), 772–73.

20 **In the words of one:** "120 Ideal Homes in Shepherd Park," *Washington Post*, June 15, 1930, R1; Paul W. Valentine, "Neighbors Inc. Holds Fast for Integration," *Washington Post*, Jan. 5, 1969, 55.

21 **By the 1960s, according:** Marvin Caplan, "Shepherd Park: Creating an Integrated Community," in *Washington at Home: An Illustrated History of Neighborhoods in the Nation's Capital* (Northridge, Calif.: Windsor Publications, 1988), 265.

21 **Realtors used blockbusting tactics:** Contemporary accounts tell of realtors who would sell a home to a Black family, knock on doors up and down the street to induce white families to sell before property values plunged, then turn around and charge elevated prices to Black families moving into previously white neighborhoods. This "blockbusting" accelerated white flight.

21 **Today the neighborhood is:** "About the SPCA," Shepherd Park Citizens' Association, accessed Dec. 21, 2022, www.shepherdpark.org/about; Caplan, "Shepherd Park," 265; Clemmie Edward Gilpin, "Neighbors, Inc.: Goal Structure and Organizational Survival, an Exploratory Case Study" (PhD diss., Pennsylvania State University, 1988), 183; Sheryll Cashin, "In Shepherd Park, We're Working Toward a Racially Diverse Eden," *Washington Post*, August 25, 2017, C4; Marvin Caplan, "The Last White Family on the Block," *Atlantic*, July 1960, 54–56.

22 **The population has declined:** Valentine, "Neighbors Inc. Holds Fast for Integration"; Gilpin, "Neighbors, Inc.," 132–36.

CHAPTER TWO: THE DEATH OF GREAT AMERICAN CITIES

24 **Hechler left his occupation:** Rudolph Hechler, Thirteenth Census of the United States, 1910, Manhattan Ward 17, New York, 5B, NARA Micropublication T624, roll 1034; Rudolph Hechler, Fourteenth Census of the United States, 1920, Bronx Assembly District 1, Bronx, N.Y., 4A, NARA Micropublication T625, roll 1130; Rudolph Hechler, Fifteenth Census of the United States, 1930, Bronx Assembly District 1, Bronx, N.Y., 6B, NARA Micropublication T626; Rudolph Hechler, Sixteenth Census of the United States, 1940, Manhattan Assembly District 3, New York, 61A, NARA Micropublication T627, roll 2631.

24 **On his own block:** *Greenwich Village Historic District Designation Report* (New York: Landmarks Preservation Commission, 1969), Vol. 2, 399–400.

25 **A rack by the door:** "555 Hudson Street," ca. 1940, Department of Finance, Manhattan 1940s Tax Photos, Block 633, Lot 56, New York City Municipal Archive; David Hechler, interview by author, Aug. 15, 2022.

26 **The building was sold:** "Greenwich Village," *New York Times*, July 23, 1946, 25; "Six Buildings Sold on 7th Ave Corner," *New York Times*, Nov. 15, 1947, 25.

26 **On the first floor:** Anthony Flint, *Wrestling with Moses: How Jane Jacobs Took On New York's Master Builder and Transformed the American City* (New York: Random House, 2009), 14–15.

26 **"The front of No. 555":** *Greenwich Village Historic District Designation Report*, 2: 400.

27 **In 1956, in front:** Leticia Kent, "Oral History Interview of Jane Jacobs," Oct. 1997, 23, Greenwich Village Society for Historic Preservation Archives.

28 **She watched Samuel Halpert:** Jane Jacobs, *The Death and Life of Great American Cities* (New York: Vintage Books, 2016), 50.

28 **The small stores peppering:** Alex Krieger and William S. Saunders, *Urban Design* (Minneapolis: University of Minnesota Press, 2009), 9.

30 **"Nothing that was done":** Jacobs, interview by Roberto Chavez, Tia Duer, and Ke Fang for the World Bank, Feb. 4, 2002, 14.

30 **At an intellectual level:** Jacobs, *Death and Life of Great American Cities*, 253.

30 **A newspaper columnist visiting:** Brooks Atkinson, "Jane Jacobs, Author of Book on Cities, Makes the Most of Living in One," *New York Times*, Nov. 10, 1961, 32.

31 **Where civic boosters once sketched:** Mumford used the term in 1916, the same year he conducted an investigation of the garment industry, and recommended that it be decentralized and spread out over the region. In his hostility to density, he outstripped even Veiller. His notes are quoted in Donald L. Miller, *Lewis Mumford: A Life* (New York: Weidenfeld & Nicolson, 1989), 30, 72.

31 **They pressed for decentralization:** Jacob Anbinder, "'Power to the Neighborhoods!': New York City Growth Politics, Neighborhood Liberalism, and the Origins of the Modern Housing Crisis," Joint Center for Housing Studies of Harvard University, March 2024, 9.

32 **A sound engineer compared:** Kent, "Oral History Interview of Jane Jacobs," 28–31.

32 **"Responsiveness is what makes":** Jacobs, interview by Chavez, Duer, and Fang, 33.

32 **"The art of negating":** Jacobs, *Death and Life of Great American Cities*, 131.

33 **A government catering:** Jacobs, interview by Chavez, Duer, and Fang, 36.

33 **This represented, she argued:** Jacobs, *Death and Life of Great American Cities*, 281.

33 **"The key link in a perpetual":** Ibid., 271.

CHAPTER THREE: THE FREEDOM TO MOVE

39 **Settled populations saw them:** A. L. Beier, *Masterless Men: The Vagrancy Problem in England, 1560–1640* (London: Methuen, 1985), 29–31.

39 **"Vagrants, begone!":** Benjamin Long, *An Oration Spoken in the Grammar-School of Christ's-Hospital* (London: printed by William Godbid, 1675), 9.

39 **The authorities responded to:** Nandini Das et al., *Keywords of Identity, Race, and Human Mobility in Early Modern England* (Amsterdam: Amsterdam University Press, 2021), 284–90.

40 **English Protestants took a dim:** Elspeth Graham, "'Licencious Gaddyng Abroade': A Conflicted Imaginary of Mobility in Early Modern English Protestant Writings," *Études Épistémè*, no. 35 (2019).

40 **To answer those questions:** McDermott's remarkable account of this quiet intellectual revolution is worth reading in full: Scott McDermott, *The Puritan Ideology of Mobility: Corporatism, the Politics of Place, and the Founding of New England Towns Before 1650* (London: Anthem Press, 2022).

41 **"They ought not to departe":** John Winthrop, *The Journal of John Winthrop, 1630–1649* (Cambridge, Mass.: Harvard University Press, 2009), 126.

41 **"Solomon sent ships to Ophir":** Thomas Hooker, *A Survey of the Summe of Church-Discipline* (London: printed by A. M. for John Bellamy, 1648), 50.

41 **If people could depart:** Ibid.

42 **Hugo Grotius announced that:** Jane McAdam, "An Intellectual History of Freedom of Movement in International Law: The Right to Leave as a Personal Liberty," *Melbourne Journal of International Law* 12, no. 1 (June 2011): 8–9.

43 **During the seventeenth century:** Timothy H. Breen and Stephen Foster, "The Puritans' Greatest Achievement: A Study of Social Cohesion in Seventeenth-Century Massachusetts," *Journal of American History* 60, no. 1 (1973): 5–22.

44   **Sometimes, these proprietors gave:** Stephen Innes, *Creating the Commonwealth: The Economic Culture of Puritan New England* (New York: W. W. Norton, 1995); John Frederick Martin, *Profits in the Wilderness: Entrepreneurship and the Founding of New England Towns in the Seventeenth Century* (Chapel Hill: University of North Carolina Press, 2014).

44   **Those who were warned out:** Gabriel J. Loiacono, *How Welfare Worked in the Early United States: Five Microhistories* (New York: Oxford University Press, 2021), 14.

44   **By law, no one could:** B. Katherine Brown, "The Controversy over the Franchise in Puritan Massachusetts, 1954 to 1974," *William and Mary Quarterly* 33, no. 2 (1976): 230.

44   **In general, Black people:** Loiacono, *How Welfare Worked in the Early United States,* 8–10.

44   **Between 1690 and 1795:** Barry Levy, *Town Born: The Political Economy of New England from Its Founding to the Revolution* (Philadelphia: University of Pennsylvania Press, 2011), 286.

45   **They would be surrounded:** Ibid., 42–50.

45   **In the seventeenth century, chunks:** Kenneth A. Lockridge, *A New England Town: The First Hundred Years* (New York: W. W. Norton, 1985), 93–99.

45   **Dedham itself, though, remained stable:** Ibid., 139–40.

46   **The joint-stock corporation swiftly evolved:** Michael P. Winship, "Godly Republicanism and the Origins of the Massachusetts Polity," *William and Mary Quarterly* 63, no. 3 (2006): 444–47; Mark Peterson, *The City-State of Boston: The Rise and Fall of an Atlantic Power, 1630–1865* (Princeton, N.J.: Princeton University Press, 2019).

46   **The sovereign town:** Michael Zuckerman, *Peaceable Kingdoms: New England Towns in the Eighteenth Century* (New York: W. W. Norton, 1978), 27–45.

47   **The mandate was extended:** *Records of the Governor and Company of the Massachusetts Bay in New England* (Boston: W. White, 1853), 1:157, 205, 291.

47   **One early essayist quoted:** *Winthrop Papers* (Boston: Massachusetts Historical Society, 1929), 3:181.

48   **the land had been granted:** Massachusetts told landowners that if they failed to build or improve upon the land within three years, it could be seized. In other colonies, statutes allowed land to be seized if the owners failed to enclose it, drain it, mine it, or build gristmills or ironworks on it or if, after it had been put to some advantageous use, it had been effectively abandoned. John F. Hart, "Colonial Land Use Law and Its Significance for Modern Takings Doctrine," *Harvard Law Review* 109, no. 6 (1996): 1252–1300.

48   **So, for example, in 1692:** *The By-Laws and Town-Orders of the Town of Boston* (Boston: printed by Edmund Freeman, 1786), 10–11.

49   **"There is a great equality":** John C. Fitzpatrick, ed., *The Diaries of George Washington, 1748–1799* (Boston: Houghton Mifflin, 1925), 4:30.

50   **The great mobility:** Pekka Hämäläinen, *Indigenous Continent: The Epic Contest for North America* (New York: Liveright, 2022), 199.

50   **In response, the leaders:** Brent Tarter, *The Grandees of Government: The Origins and Persistence of Undemocratic Politics in Virginia* (Charlottesville: University of Virginia Press, 2013), 24.

50   **With little cash in circulation:** Edmund S. Morgan, *American Slavery, American Freedom: The Ordeal of Colonial Virginia* (New York: W. W. Norton, 2005), 141–42.

51   **Between 1650 and 1675:** Tarter, *Grandees of Government.*

51 **The justices of the peace:** The 215 justices of the peace in four Virginia counties from 1634 to 1676 each owned, on average, eleven hundred acres of land. Fifty of them served as burgesses and sixteen of them on the Council of State. Warren M. Billings, "The Growth of Political Institutions in Virginia, 1634 to 1676," *William and Mary Quarterly* 31, no. 2 (1974): 225–42.

53 **The Northwest Ordinance was:** Denis P. Duffey, "The Northwest Ordinance as a Constitutional Document," *Columbia Law Review* 95, no. 4 (1995): 929–68.

53 **The titles would be:** Peter S. Onuf, *Statehood and Union: A History of the Northwest Ordinance* (Notre Dame, Ind.: University of Notre Dame Press, 2019), 39; Robert Alexander, *The Northwest Ordinance: Constitutional Politics and the Theft of Native Land* (Jefferson, N.C.: McFarland, 2017), 81–82.

54 **"Taking their fortune":** *History of Shelby County, Ohio* (Philadelphia: R. Sutton, 1883), 282.

54 **They could remain as long:** Josiah Henry Benton, *Warning Out in New England, 1656–1817* (Boston: W. B. Clarke, 1911), 114–17.

55 **If you wanted to join:** Kenneth J. Winkle, *The Politics of Community* (New York: Cambridge University Press, 1988), 48–50.

56 **And over the next two:** Donald Ratcliffe, "The Right to Vote and the Rise of Democracy, 1787–1828," *Journal of the Early Republic* 33, no. 2 (2013): 219–54.

56 **In Ohio, elections were:** Winkle, *Politics of Community,* 48–70.

56 **Local communities strongly favored:** Winkle's study of Clinton Township helps illustrate the point. In 1850, there were 384 eligible voters in the township; scarcely a quarter of them were still there a decade later, though continued population growth brought the total to 585. Voters who stuck around were wealthier and older than those who moved on, likelier to be merchants or professionals than laborers, and much more likely to hold elective office. Over the course of the 1850s, 40 percent of municipal, township, and county offices would be held by the 105 voters who remained for the entire decade. There was another, much larger group in Clinton—some 800 voters arrived in Clinton after 1850, voted at least once, and were gone before 1860—but less than 1 percent of them ever held office. Ibid., 93, 125.

56 **"A poor American citizen":** "Tramps," *Portsmouth Daily Times,* Nov. 27, 1875, 2.

57 **Legislators piled on other:** James Oliver Horton, "Race and Region: Ohio, America's Middle Ground," in *Ohio and the World, 1753–2053: Essays Toward a New History of Ohio,* ed. Geoffrey Parker, Richard Sisson, and William Russell Coil (Columbus: Ohio State University Press, 2005), 46.

CHAPTER FOUR: **A MIGRATORY PEOPLE**

58 **So when he was two:** David S. Reynolds, *Abe: Abraham Lincoln in His Times* (New York: Penguin Press, 2020), 1–35.

58 **But when he was seven:** Ibid.

60 **The American, Michel Chevalier:** Chevalier, *Society, Manners, and Politics,* 286.

60 **"In the United States":** Alexis de Tocqueville, *Democracy in America* (New York: Colonial Press, 1899), 2:144–45.

61 **"A Yankee will start":** Henry Anthony Murray, *Lands of the Slave and the Free* (London: G. Routledge, 1857), 464.

61 **"Perhaps there is nothing":** Simon Ansley Ferrall, *A Ramble of Six Thousand Miles Through the United States of America* (London: Effingham Wilson, 1832), 167.

61 **"Migration has become almost":** John Mason Peck, *A New Guide for Emigrants to the West* (Boston: Gould, Kendall & Lincoln, 1836), 111.

61 **"All was motion and change":** Frederick Jackson Turner, *The Frontier in American History* (New York: H. Holt, 1920), 354–55.

62 **"Westward the course of empire":** Elizabeth Kiszonas, "Westward Empire: George Berkeley's 'Verses on the Prospect of Planting of Arts' in American Art and Cultural History" (PhD diss., University of Arkansas, 2019).

62 **But in the wake:** John Adams and Alice Kasakoff, "Wealth and Migration in Massachusetts and Maine, 1771–1798," *Journal of Economic History* 45, no. 2 (1985): 367–68.

63 **Even so, ordinary laborers:** Joseph P. Ferrie, "Migration to the Frontier in Mid-Nineteenth Century America: A Re-examination of Turner's 'Safety Valve,'" National Bureau of Economic Research, July 1997, 9, 13.

63 **It wasn't just the migrants:** Ellen von Nardroff, "The American Frontier as a Safety Valve: The Life, Death, Reincarnation, and Justification of a Theory," *Agricultural History* 36, no. 3 (1962): 138–39.

63 **The results were dramatic:** Joseph P. Ferrie, "The End of American Exceptionalism? Mobility in the United States Since 1850," *Journal of Economic Perspectives* 19, no. 3 (2005): 208.

64 **"There is land enough":** Edward Everett, *Orations and Speeches on Various Occasions* (Boston: Little, Brown, 1870), 107.

64 **Although he was thirty-one:** Ray Allen Billington, *The Genesis of the Frontier Thesis: A Study in Historical Creativity* (San Marino, Calif.: Huntington Library, 1971), 166–72.

65 **"The exhaustion of the public":** Worthington C. Ford, "Regulating Immigration," *Epoch*, April 15, 1887, 229–30, quoted in David Carl Shetler, "Immigration Restriction and the Closing of the Frontier: A Conjunction of Fears, 1882–1897" (master's thesis, University of Montana, 1974), 54.

65 **His claim that the frontier:** I am indebted to the historian Benjamin Schmidt for first pointing out to me the shifting color schemes of these maps, the mysterious reappearance of the frontier line, and Robert Porter's xenophobia. If indeed the 1890 map was a deliberate fraud, the credit for detecting it is properly his. Author discussion with Benjamin Schmidt and Benjamin Schmidt, "Historical Data Revisualization: Turner, Walker, and Envisioning the Frontier," Annual Meeting of the American Historical Association, New York, Jan. 3, 2015.

66 **The superintendent of the 1890 census:** Robert P. Porter, "The Problems of Immigration," *Independent*, Oct. 1, 1891, 1.

66 **Henry Gannett, who crafted:** Henry Gannett, *The Building of a Nation: The Growth, Present Condition, and Resources of the United States, with a Forecast of the Future* (New York: H. T. Thomas, 1895), 114–15.

66 **The best evidence suggests:** The shading trick was simple. In 1890, and 1890 alone, instead of leaving unpopulated areas blank, the map shaded them in, reducing the contrast. The reporting of unsettled areas as settled requires a more technical explanation, and zooming in on one example may help. The 1890 census reported that Colorado's Prowers County, part of the land forming an isthmus of settlement stretching out to Denver, had a population of 1,969 spread over 1,644 square miles. The 1,541 square miles of Bent County, next door, contained only 1,303 people. Neither came close to meeting the threshold of being settled land, yet both were shaded on the map as if they contained between 2 and 6 peo-

ple per square mile. On the 1900 map, they reverted to being shown as unsettled land. The booming population of Prowers County actually placed it just above the 2-per-square-mile threshold in 1900, but a quarter of its people lived in the county seat of Lamar, and the census habitually subtracted such towns in large western counties from the total, so as not to offer a distorted picture of the extent of settlement. Drought had led many counties in the West to lose population, so some areas really had dipped back below the threshold of settlement. But that wasn't the only explanation, or even the most important one. The populations along the Arkansas River nearly doubled between 1890 and 1900, boosted by their ability to tap the river for irrigation. The acreage of cultivated farmland in the state of Colorado also doubled, even as the area reported by the census as settled declined. The unsettled areas were increasing because by 1900 the map-makers were being honest again. *Statistical Abstract of the United States, 1900* (Washington, D.C.: Census Office, 1901), 36; David J. Wishart, *The Last Days of the Rainbelt* (Lincoln, Neb.: Bison Books, 2013), 66–67.

66   **In 1900, under a new:** *Twelfth Census of the United States: Population* (Washington, D.C.: Census Office, 1901), 1: xxxiv.

67   **In a series of essays:** Frederick Jackson Turner, "Studies of American Immigration," *Chicago Record-Herald*, Sept. 25 and Oct. 16, 1901, quoted in Edward N. Saveth, *American Historians and European Immigrants, 1875–1925* (New York: Columbia University Press, 1948), 128–33.

67   **Recent scholarship has put:** In just a single decade after Porter declared America had run out of unsettled territory, the amount of farmland under cultivation increased by a third, from 620 million to 840 million acres. *Report on the Statistics of Agriculture in the United States* (Washington, D.C.: Government Printing Office, 1895), 3; *Census Reports: Agriculture, Part I* (Washington, D.C.: Census Office, 1902), xviii; Samuel M. Otterstrom and Carville Earle, "The Settlement of the United States from 1790 to 1990: Divergent Rates of Growth and the End of the Frontier," *Journal of Interdisciplinary History* 33, no. 1 (2002): 59–85.

67   **In the early 1960s:** Adam Shatz, "The Thernstroms in Black and White," *American Prospect,* Dec. 10, 2001, prospect.org/api/content/abbd4625-5a02-523b-84f1-574db4519d25/.

68   **He looked at Newburyport:** Stephan Thernstrom, *Poverty and Progress: Social Mobility in a Nineteenth Century City* (Cambridge, Mass.: Harvard University Press, 1980), 168.

68   **And Newburyport, if anything:** A similar study in Rochester found that only one family in five remained after a decade. Stephan Thernstrom and Peter R. Knights, "Men in Motion: Some Data and Speculations About Urban Population Mobility in Nineteenth-Century America," *Journal of Interdisciplinary History* 1, no. 1 (1970): 12; Blake McKelvey, *Rochester, the Flower City, 1855–1890* (Cambridge, Mass.: Harvard University Press, 1949), 3.

68   **When Thernstrom looked at Boston:** Thernstrom and Knights, "Men in Motion," 22.

68   **When Thernstrom saw this pattern:** Some 80 percent of laborers who managed to acquire property in Newburyport by 1860 stayed; almost 70 percent of those who did not departed. It was, he concluded, "unlikely that large numbers of these workmen were more successful in their new places of residence than were their counterparts who remained." Stephan Thernstrom, *The Other Bostonians: Poverty and Progress in the American Metropolis, 1880–1970* (Cambridge, Mass.: Harvard University Press, 1973), 42; Thernstrom, *Poverty and Progress,* 89.

69   **In 1996, when the economist:** Steven Herscovici, "Progress amid Poverty: Economic Opportunity in Antebellum Newburyport," *Journal of Economic History* 57, no. 2 (1997): 484–88.

69   **"A log-house is still standing":** Ferrall, *Ramble of Six Thousand Miles Through the United States of America,* 66.

69   **Estimates of migration:** Among a cohort of young men examined in 1850 and again in 1880, for example, 26 percent were living in a different county and another 36 percent in a different state. But among a similar cohort examined in 1880 and 1910, 30 percent were in a new county and 31 percent in a new state. Patricia Kelly Hall and Steven Ruggles, "'Restless in the Midst of Their Prosperity': New Evidence on the Internal Migration of Americans, 1850–2000," *Journal of American History* 91, no. 3 (2004): 835–36; Joseph P. Ferrie, "Longitudinal Data for the Analysis of Mobility in the U.S., 1850–1910," National Bureau of Economic Research, April 21, 2014, 13.

70   **Josiah Bishop Andrews was born:** Alfred Andrews, *Genealogical History of John and Mary Andrews, Who Settled in Farmington, Conn., 1640* (Chicago: A. H. Andrews, 1872), 263–65; Thomas Day and James Murdock, *Brief Memoirs of the Class of 1797* (New Haven, Conn.: B. L. Hamlen, 1848), 7–9.

70   **His wife took seriously ill:** Andrews, *Genealogical History of John and Mary Andrews,* 263–65; Day and Murdock, *Brief Memoirs of the Class of 1797,* 7–9.

70   **He moved to New York City:** "The Scientific Institution," *Evening Post,* Sept. 22, 1812, 1.

70   **Next, he hopped across:** Andrews, *Genealogical History of John and Mary Andrews,* 263–65; Day and Murdock, *Brief Memoirs of the Class of 1797,* 7–9.

72   **"They want more room":** "Moving Day," *Topeka Capital,* May 2, 1883, 4.

72   **"Be out at 12 you must":** "Tabernacle Services: The Temptations and Exasperations of Moving Day," *Atchison Patriot,* May 12, 1888, 1.

72   **In St. Louis, the publisher:** "The Moving Habit in St. Louis," *St. Louis Daily Globe-Democrat,* May 20, 1906, 75.

72   **"Many private families make":** "Business Changes," *Daily Republican,* Jan. 9, 1882, 3.

72   **In some places, in fact:** Lydia Maria Child, *Letters from New-York* (Athens: University of Georgia Press, 1998), 176.

72   **Moving Day, the humorist:** "Doesticks 'Helps Move,'" *Placer Herald,* June 27, 1857, 1.

73   **In southern New Jersey:** W. L. Tiffany, "Sketches from the Country: Moving Time," *The Knickerbocker,* June 1855, 585.

73   **"an essentially American institution":** "On the 1st of May," wrote Frances Trollope in 1832, "the city of New York has the appearance of sending off a population flying from the plague, or of a town which had surrendered on condition of carrying away all their goods and chattels." A decade later, another English author described "carts, which go at a rate of speed astonishingly rapid, laden with furniture of every kind, racing up and down the city." "Moving Day," *Times-Democrat,* Oct. 1, 1882; Frances Milton Trollope, *Domestic Manners of the Americans* (London: Whittaker, Treacher, 1832), 278–79; Mrs. Felton, *American Life: A Narrative of Two Years' City and Country Residence in the United States* (London: Simpkin, Marshall, 1842), 54.

73   **For some, Moving Day meant:** Elizabeth Blackmar, *Manhattan for Rent, 1785–1850* (Ithaca, N.Y.: Cornell University Press, 1991), 213–15.

73   **You could spot the approach:** "Moving Day," *Milwaukee Press and News,* Feb. 26, 1861, 1.

74 **The habit of annual moves:** A detailed study of residential mobility among men in Omaha between 1880 and 1920 found that just 3 percent stayed in the same home for as long as twenty years. Omahans of all backgrounds and social classes moved repeatedly—to larger homes, to new neighborhoods, to new jobs, or out of the city entirely. Over an eleven-year span, half of those who stayed in the city occupied three or more dwellings. Howard P. Chudacoff, *Mobile Americans: Residential and Social Mobility in Omaha, 1880–1920* (New York: Oxford University Press, 1972), 150.

74 **In London, complained the tenement:** "Model Tenement Houses," *New York Tribune*, Aug. 24, 1904.

74 **A paper in West Virginia:** "Moving Day," *Wheeling Daily Intelligencer*, April 2, 1890, 2.

74 **"That people should move":** Child, *Letters from New-York*, 177.

74 **"We are a moving people":** "Moving Day," *Chicago Tribune*, May 5, 1865, 3.

75 **In 1890, the census asked:** J. A. Collins, "The Decadence of Home-Ownership in the United States," *American Magazine of Civics*, Jan. 1895, 57.

75 **"The ownership of a home":** George K. Holmes, "Tenancy in the United States," *Quarterly Journal of Economics* 10, no. 1 (1895): 34–53.

77 **The iconoclastic composer Charles Ives:** Ives's perspective was widely shared. As one young family prepared to buy a house in the Philadelphia suburbs in 1903, promising their nine-year-old daughter a settled existence, she looked up dolefully and said, "But, mamma, then would we have to live in the same house all the time?" "No Moving Day," *Muscatine Journal*, Aug. 11, 1903, 4; Paul Moor, "On Horseback to Heaven," *Harper's*, Sept. 1948, 65.

77 **"In the United States":** Tocqueville, *Democracy in America*, 2:243.

78 **"Associations are created":** James Bryce, *The American Commonwealth* (New York: Macmillan, 1891), 269.

78 **Take, for example, religious faith:** Lincoln A. Mullen, *The Chance of Salvation: A History of Conversion in America* (Cambridge, Mass.: Harvard University Press, 2017), 6.

78 **In Kentucky, he chose:** Thomas B. McGregor, "Some New Facts About Abraham Lincoln's Parents," *Register of Kentucky State Historical Society* 20, no. 59 (1922): 213–18.

79 **"A man may be":** James R. Carnahan, *Pythian Knighthood, Its History and Literature* (Cincinnati: Pettibone Manufacturing, 1888), 525.

79 **The surge in voluntary:** Most studies support this association, although the questions typically focus solely on length of residence and make no effort to distinguish those who expect to keep moving from those who intend to settle. One national survey in the 1950s found that migrants caught up to, and perhaps actually overtook, long-term residents within five years. ("Voluntary Association Memberships of American Adults: Evidence from National Sample Surveys," *American Sociological Review* 23, no. 3 [June 1958]: 284–94.) And a study of Spokane found that residential mobility actually made people more likely to belong to voluntary associations. (Howard E. Freeman, Edwin Novak, and Leo G. Reeder, "Correlates of Membership in Voluntary Associations," *American Sociological Review* 22, no. 5 [1957]: 528–33.)

80 **Early in the nineteenth century:** Gerald Gamm and Robert D. Putnam, "The Growth of Voluntary Associations in America, 1840–1940," *Journal of Interdisciplinary History* 29, no. 4 (Spring 1999): 542–43.

80 **The new members of most:** George Emery and Herbert Emery, *A Young Man's Benefit: The Independent Order of Odd Fellows and Sickness Insurance in the United States and Canada, 1860–1929* (Montreal: McGill-Queen's University Press, 1999).

80 **In Massachusetts, the typical new:** Yoni Appelbaum, "The Guilded Age: The American Ideal of Association, 1865–1900" (PhD diss., Brandeis University, 2014), 47.

81 **"They come not only":** "At 'Home Sweet Home': Back Among the Old Folks in New Hampshire," *Boston Daily Globe*, Aug. 29, 1899, 8; Dona Brown, *Inventing New England: Regional Tourism in the Nineteenth Century* (Washington, D.C.: Smithsonian Institution Press, 1995), 135–45.

82 **Looking out on "the harbour":** Israel Zangwill, *The Melting-Pot: Drama in Four Acts* (New York: Macmillan, 1909), 199.

82 **President Theodore Roosevelt was:** Israel Zangwill, *From the Ghetto to the Melting Pot: Israel Zangwill's Jewish Plays* (Detroit: Wayne State University Press, 2006), 242.

82 **"The family, the tribe, the caste":** Horace Meyer Kallen, *Culture and Democracy in the United States* (New York: Boni and Liveright, 1924), 84, 197–99.

83 **The anthropologist Natalia:** Natalia Khanenko-Friesen, *Ukrainian Otherlands: Diaspora, Homeland, and Folk Imagination in the Twentieth Century* (Madison: University of Wisconsin Press, 2015), 57.

84 **President John Adams, a popular:** *The Percy Anecdotes* (New York: J. & J. Harper, 1832), 92. When, some decades later, Gilbert & Sullivan wished to parody jingoism in *HMS Pinafore*, they had their cast sing, "In spite of all temptations, to belong to other nations, he remains an Englishman!" In America, the jokes were about the possibility of choosing your national identity; in England, the humor lay in the absurdity of the very idea that anyone could do such a thing.

CHAPTER FIVE: DIRTY LAUNDRY

87 **In World War I, my great-grandfather:** "Col. Whitman, 65, Dies; Was Hero of Two Wars," *Hartford Courant*, Dec. 14, 1961.

89 **The fierce competition, coupled:** Paul Ong, "An Ethnic Trade: The Chinese Laundries in Early California," *Journal of Ethnic Studies* 8, no. 4 (1981).

89 **At first, the arrangement:** Ibid.; David E. Bernstein, "*Lochner*, Parity, and the Chinese Laundry Cases," *William and Mary Law Review* 41 (1999): 85.

90 **White citizens of Modesto:** "Modesto Vigilantes," *San Francisco Chronicle*, March 28, 1884, 4.

90 **The violence failed to drive:** "The Town Re-regulated," *Stanislaus County Weekly News*, April 11, 1884, 3.

90 **In June 1885, a washhouse:** "Fire in Chinatown," *Modesto Bee*, June 15, 1885, 3.

90 **A week after the warehouse fire:** Modesto, Stanislaus County, California, Sanborn Fire Insurance Maps, Sanborn Map Company, Jan. 1885.

91 **It was the residents:** "Our City Fathers," *Modesto Bee*, June 20, 1885, 3.

92 **The ordinance went into effect:** "Town and County," *Stanislaus County Weekly News*, Aug. 21, 1885, 3.

92 **Hang Kie was the first:** "The Chinese Case," *Modesto Bee*, Aug. 8, 1885, 3.

92 **Before his case could be heard:** "Modesto to the Fore Again," *Mail*, Sept. 8, 1885, 1.

92 **Legally, Kie was on:** William J. Novak, *The People's Welfare: Law and Regulation in*

Nineteenth-Century America (Chapel Hill: University of North Carolina Press, 1996), 44–45.

93 **In 1880, a member:** "Board of Supervisors," *Daily Evening Bulletin,* Feb. 10, 1880, 1.

93 **The city attorney replied that:** "Chinese Laundries," *Daily Evening Bulletin,* Feb. 16, 1880, 1.

93 **"I am opposed to Chinese":** "The Anti-Chinese Action in Brooklyn," *Sacramento Daily Record-Union,* Dec. 29, 1880, 2.

94 **Other cities tried their own:** "Board of Supervisors," *Daily Evening Bulletin,* Feb. 17, 1880, 1.

94 **In May 1880, it tried:** Bernstein, "*Lochner,* Parity, and the Chinese Laundry Cases."

94 **The courts were generally skeptical:** *In re Quong Woo,* 13 F. 229 (9th Cir. 1882).

95 **But the maximum-hours ordinance:** *Barbier v. Connolly,* 113 U.S. 27 (1885).

96 **"No reason whatever, except":** *Yick Wo v. Hopkins,* 118 U.S. 356 (1886).

96 **But even a law equally:** "Passed over the Veto," *Mail,* Dec. 15, 1885, 3.

96 **A local newspaper reporter:** "A Word to the Council," *Mail,* Dec. 8, 1885, 3.

96 **Stockton's ordinance, as the federal district judge:** *In re Tie Loy,* 26 F. 611 (9th Cir. 1886).

97 **Citing his ruling in the Stockton:** *In re Sam Kee,* 31 F. 680 (9th Cir. 1887).

97 **Taken together, this pair:** *In re Hong Wah,* 82 F. 623 (N.D. Cal. 1897).

97 **In 1904, Los Angeles commenced:** *Los Angeles, California,* Sanborn Fire Insurance Maps, Sanborn Map Company, 1906.

98 **He was selected by:** *Ex Parte Quong Wo,* 161 Cal. 220 (Cal. 1911).

98 **"It has been held":** Ibid.

99 **"the first zoning ordinance":** Gordon Whitnall, "History of Zoning," *Annals of the American Academy of Political and Social Science* 155 (1931): 9.

99 **Without the "high feeling":** Ibid.

100 **Kie moved his laundry:** "High Toned Chinese Wedding," *Stanislaus County Weekly News,* Jan. 11, 1889, 2.

101 **"The first zoning was racially":** Elizabeth Leedom, "West Modesto," *Modesto Bee,* Oct. 14, 1984, 20.

101 **Cheney had moved to Berkeley:** Fukuo Akimoto, "Charles H. Cheney of California," *Planning Perspectives* 18, no. 3 (2003): 253–75.

102 **"Not only do we find":** Oliver Miles Washburn, "The Housing Code," *Berkeley Civic Bulletin,* Nov. 14, 1914, 54–67.

102 **Most of Berkeley's subdivisions:** Maureen E. Brady, "Turning Neighbors into Nuisances," *Harvard Law Review* 134, no. 5 (March 2021): 1609–82.

103 **"The artificial and sometimes":** Charles Henry Cheney, "How Districts or Zones Help a City," *California Outlook,* May 2, 1914, 8.

103 **Cheney had a specific example:** "Elmwood Park," *San Francisco Chronicle,* Feb. 11, 1906, 50.

103 **Despite the promises of the developer:** "Berkeley Real Estate," *San Francisco Call,* Feb. 16, 1913.

103 **"One or two property holders":** Cheney, "How Districts or Zones Help a City," 8.

103 **"City planning in Berkeley":** Duncan McDuffie, "City Planning in Berkeley," *Berkeley Civic Bulletin,* March 15, 1916.

104 **The city attorney, Frank Cornish:** Frank V. Cornish, "The Legal Status of Zone Ordinances," *Berkeley Civic Bulletin,* May 18, 1915, 174.

104 **In December 1914, the Commission:** "Fights Slums in California," *Madera Mercury*, Feb. 19, 1915, 1.

104 **To accomplish that, Cheney:** "Second Annual Report" (Commission of Immigration and Housing of California, 1916), 310–11.

105 **The commission recommended the adoption:** "Districting Ordinance of the City of Berkeley" (Civic Art Commission, 1916).

105 **"The police power," the government's:** "Residence 'Zones,'" *San Francisco Chronicle*, Nov. 29, 1916, 18.

106 **The ordinance was passed unanimously:** "'Zone' Ordinance Cause of Clash," *San Francisco Chronicle*, May 1, 1916, 4.

106 **Those who owned lots:** Duncan McDuffie, "A Practical Application of the Zone Ordinance," in *The City-Planning Movement in Berkeley* (1916), 10–16; Charles Henry Cheney, "Districting Progress and Procedure in California," in *Proceedings of the Ninth National Conference on City Planning* (New York, 1917), 183–94.

106 **"If a dairy, an undertaker's":** Charles Henry Cheney, "The Necessity for a Zone Ordinance in Berkeley," *Berkeley Civic Bulletin*, May 18, 1915, 163.

106 **For all his public speaking:** "Study Housing Problems; Confer with Experts," *Oakland Tribune*, Dec. 6, 1914, 31.

107 **His mother was born in Iowa:** Suzanne Riess and J. R. K. Kantor, "Conversations with Sheldon Cheney," Regional Oral History Office, Oct. 10, 1974, 44.

108 **"Evidently the job of the city":** Charles H. Cheney, "Zoning in Practice," in *Proceedings of the Eleventh National Conference on City Planning* (Boston, 1920), 171.

108 **Only single-family zoning:** Cheney, "Districting Progress and Procedure in California," 190.

108 **Cheney's fear of an *invasion:*** "Second Annual Report," 86–96.

109 **Cheney's zoning scheme succeeded:** "Housing of U.C. Students Gives Worry," *Madera Mercury*, Aug. 9, 1920, 1.

109 **The men who were central:** McDuffie, "City Planning in Berkeley," 115; Cornish, "Legal Status of Zone Ordinances," 175; Cheney, "Necessity for a Zone Ordinance in Berkeley," 165.

109 **And Berkeley's first zoning:** Cheney, "Districting Progress and Procedure in California," 183–94.

109 **These cases have frequently:** John Metcalfe, "Berkeley May Get Rid of Single Family Zoning as a Way to Correct the Arc of Its Ugly Housing History," *Berkeleyside*, Feb. 17, 2021.

110 **The resolution passed:** Henry Grabar, "You Can Kill Single-Family Zoning, but You Can't Kill the Suburbs," *Slate*, Sept. 17, 2021; "Governor Newsom Signs Historic Legislation to Boost California's Housing Supply and Fight the Housing Crisis," Office of Governor Gavin Newsom, Sept. 16, 2021.

110 **As it happens, neither:** One analysis of SB 9 found that it would make development of additional housing viable on scarcely 5 percent of single-family lots in the state; another that in the state's largest cities, fewer than a hundred applications were approved in its first year. Ben Metcalf et al., "Will Allowing Duplexes and Lot Splits on Parcels Zoned for Single-Family Create New Homes?," Terner Center for Housing Innovation, University of California, Berkeley, July 2021, 9; David Garcia and Muhammad Alameldin, "California's HOME Act Turns One: Data and Insights from the First Year of Senate Bill 9," Terner Center for Housing Innovation, Jan. 18, 2023.

111 **A few blocks farther down:** Teresa Watanabe, "UC Berkeley May Be Forced by Court to Cut 3,000 Undergraduate Seats, Freeze Enrollment," *Los Angeles Times*,

Feb. 14, 2022; Shawn Hubler, Conor Dougherty, and Sophie Kasakove, "Berkeley vs. Berkeley Is a Fight over the California Dream," *New York Times*, March 16, 2022; *Save Berkeley's Neighborhoods v. The Regents of the University of California* (Court of Appeal of the State of California, First Appellate Division, District 5, June 5, 2020).

111 **Bokovoy's core complaint, though:** Isaac Chotiner, "A Clash over Housing Pits U.C. Berkeley Against Its Neighbors," *New Yorker*, April 28, 2022; Annie Lowrey, "NIMBYism Reaches Its Apotheosis," *Atlantic*, Feb. 26, 2022; Henry Grabar, "In California, College Students Are Now Officially Considered an Environmental Menace," *Slate*, Aug. 31, 2021; Southside Neighborhood Consortium, "Comments on Southside Proposed Zoning Districts," Jan. 27, 2020, Planning Commission Agenda, City of Berkeley, Feb. 5, 2020.

112 **In a different lawsuit:** *Make UC a Good Neighbor v. Regents of University of California*, No. A165451 (Court of Appeal of the State of California, First Appellate District, Division Five, Dec. 22, 2022).

CHAPTER SIX: TENEMENTOPHOBIA

113 **Not so long ago, this building:** "169 Suffolk Street" (1901), box 10, folder 47, Committee of Fifteen Records, Manuscripts and Archives Division, New York Public Library.

114 **In 1910, roughly three-quarters:** Adna Ferrin Weber, *The Growth of Cities in the Nineteenth Century: A Study in Statistics* (Ithaca, N.Y.: Cornell University Press, 1963), 460–61.

115 **By 1910, the Lower East Side:** Shlomo Angel and Patrick Lamson-Hall, "The Rise and Fall of Manhattan's Densities, 1800–2010," Marron Institute Working Paper 18, Nov. 2014.

115 **The eastern European Jews:** Other researchers put the estimate at one returning for every three who arrived, but either way the outflows were substantial. Oriana Bandiera, Imran Rasul, and Martina Viarengo, "The Making of Modern America: Migratory Flows in the Age of Mass Migration," *Journal of Development Economics* 102 (May 2013): 23–47.

115 **Among eastern European Jews:** Jonathan Sarna, "The Myth of No Return: Jewish Return Migration to Eastern Europe, 1881–1914," *American Jewish History* 71, no. 2 (Dec. 1981): 257.

115 **Jews placed a particular value:** Jason Barr and Teddy Ort, "Population Density Across the City: The Case of 1900 Manhattan," March 2014, 29.

117 **Bassett's life was built:** *The Autobiography of Edward M. Bassett* (New York: Harbor Press, 1939).

117 **Bassett enrolled at Hamilton College:** "George P. Bassett," *Water Works Engineering*, 1955, 434.

118 **"The bright young men seem":** A. G. Hopkins, July 28, 1894, box 6, folder 1, Edward M. Bassett Papers, Cornell University.

119 **But if there was one:** Edward M. Bassett, "Transit Problem of New York," *New York Evening Post*, 1909, 16.

119 **One vision would lead:** Edward M. Bassett, "Address of the Hon. Edward M. Bassett," Sept. 16, 1911.

120 **In 1908, Bassett traveled:** *Autobiography of Edward M. Bassett*, 116.

120 **By the time the Brooklyn Committee:** Edward M. Bassett, "Brooklyn City Plan," Nov. 16, 1912, box 14, folder 34, Bassett Papers.

121 **"In the morning, and especially":** Edward M. Bassett, "How New York Was Saved by Zoning," *Chicago Commerce*, June 26, 1920, 513.

121 **So were the merchant princes:** *Statement on the Limitation of Building Heights* (Fifth Avenue Association, 1913), 2.

121 **Like the citizens of Modesto:** Alfred W. Waters, "Letters: Fifth Avenue Congestion," *New York Times*, July 24, 1909, 6.

121 **The noontime hour, though:** "Beautify Fifth Avenue and Handle Its Traffic," *New York Times*, Dec. 4, 1910, 3.

122 **The Fifth Avenue Association's formal statement:** *Statement on the Limitation of Building Heights*, 18, 36.

123 **"They want relief from your shops":** *Excerpts of Speeches Made at the Fourth Annual Dinner of the Fifth Avenue Association*, 1913, 9.

123 **What the city really needed:** *Report of the Heights of Buildings Commission* (New York, 1913).

125 **"The Commission as a whole":** *Abstracts of Reports of the Immigration Commission* (Washington, D.C.: Government Printing Office, 1911), 48.

125 **A month before the Board:** Arthur Nichols Young, *The Single Tax Movement in the United States* (Princeton, N.J.: Princeton University Press, 1916), 209–29.

125 **The scheme, its supporters:** *Final Report of the Committee on Taxation of the City of New York* (New York: O'Connell Press, 1916), 41.

127 **This, he told his audience:** *Housing Problems in America: Proceedings of the Third National Conference on Housing* (Cambridge, Mass.: Harvard University Press, 1913), 211–13.

128 **It was a remarkable confession:** Sandra Opdycke, "Veiller, Lawrence Turnure (1872–1959)," in *American National Biography*, 1999.

128 **Veiller's exhibition, and the statistics:** "Reminiscences of Lawrence Veiller" (1949), 16, Columbia Center for Oral History.

128 **Veiller compared the sights and sounds:** Lawrence Veiller, "The Housing Problem in American Cities," *Annals of the American Academy of Political and Social Science* 25 (1905): 54–55.

129 **An essay on immigration:** Kate Holladay Claghorn, "Foreign Immigration and the Tenement House in New York City," in *The Tenement House Problem*, ed. Robert W. De Forest and Lawrence Veiller (New York: Macmillan, 1903), 2:78.

129 **New York's governor, Theodore Roosevelt:** "Reminiscences of Lawrence Veiller," 16.

129 **"The tenement house is an impediment":** William B. Patterson, "The Religious Value of Proper Housing," *Annals of the American Academy of Political and Social Science* 51 (1914): 43; Zachary J. Violette, *The Decorated Tenement: How Immigrant Builders and Architects Transformed the Slum in the Gilded Age* (Minneapolis: University of Minnesota Press, 2019), 16.

130 **Veiller was particularly appalled:** Lawrence Veiller, "Room Overcrowding and the Lodger Evil," *American City*, Jan. 1913, 30.

130 **Noting that the practice:** Lawrence Veiller, *Housing Reform: A Hand-Book for Practical Use in American Cities* (New York: Charities Publication Committee, 1910), 33.

130 **"The fact is that the new-law":** Edith Elmer Wood, *The Housing of the Unskilled Wage Earner: America's Next Problem* (New York: Macmillan, 1919), 24.

131 **The Jews on the Lower East Side:** "The Anti-High-Rent Agitation," *Real Estate Record and Builder's Guide*, April 9, 1904, 782.

131 **For New York's most impoverished:** New York State Assembly, Tenement

House Committee, *Report of the Tenement House Committee* (Albany, N.Y.: J. B. Lyon, 1895), 434–35.

131 **For most tenement dwellers:** *Abstracts of Reports of the Immigration Commission,* 727–72; Eric E. Lampard, "The Urbanizing World," in *The Victorian City: Images and Realities,* ed. H. J. Dyos and Michael Wolff (London: Routledge & Kegan Paul, 1973), 26–27.

132 **While the report recommended:** *Abstracts of Reports of the Immigration Commission,* 727–72; Woods and Kennedy, *Zone of Emergence.*

132 **Even the much-ballyhooed:** Robert Coit Chapin, *The Standard of Living Among Workingmen's Families in New York City* (New York: Charities Publication Committee, 1909), 56–60.

132 **Both the families and their lodgers:** For more on lodgers, see David T. Beito and Linda Royster Beito, "The 'Lodger Evil' and the Transformation of Progressive Housing Reform, 1890–1930," *Independent Review* 20, no. 4 (2016): 485–509; Martin J. Daunton, *Housing the Workers, 1850–1914: A Comparative Perspective* (London: Bloomsbury, 2015); Roy Lubove, *The Progressives and the Slums: Tenement House Reform in New York City, 1890–1917* (Pittsburgh: University of Pittsburgh Press, 1963).

133 **In fact, before Veiller ever:** Violette, *Decorated Tenement,* 26, 62–86, 202–5.

134 **Instead, Veiller had written:** "New York's Famous Model Tenements Are Failures," *New York Times,* Oct. 27, 1912, 1.

135 **The only way to make sense:** Violette, *Decorated Tenement,* 16–18.

135 **A real estate man, Mortimer:** C. A. Patterson, "National Convention of Building Managers and Owners," *Building Management,* June 1911, 30.

136 **"They stole my light":** *Final Report of the Committee on Taxation of the City of New York,* 327.

136 **But most property owners quickly grasped:** "Mortimer Favors Zoning," *New York Times,* July 9, 1916, E3.

137 **"Whence, to ask a very":** Bruno Lasker, "Unwalled Towns," *Survey,* March 1920.

137 **The apostles of zoning:** Charles H. Cheney, "Removing Social Barriers by Zoning," *Survey,* May 22, 1920.

138 **But Lasker's charge stung:** W. A. Evans, "Zoning and Health," *Progress,* April 1924, 5.

138 **The new law helped price:** Bassett, "How New York Was Saved by Zoning," 523.

138 **But Bassett, ever the careful:** One legal test for exercises of the police power was whether they were already in wide use. Zoning, an innovation, would fail that test. So Bassett set out to ensure that by the time a challenge came before a judge, it would be widespread enough to pass muster. *Autobiography of Edward M. Bassett,* 122.

139 **He spent the spring of 1921:** Jefferson Cleveland Grinnalds, "To the Secretary, Weston, WV," May 16, 1921, box 1, folder 2, Jefferson Cleveland Grinnalds Papers, Cornell University.

139 **The consummate technocrat, Hoover:** The committee concluded that softwood lumber sliced when it was raw to an inch of thickness would air dry to a maximum of $^{25}/_{32}$ of an inch. But the decision was also a deliberate compromise among a dozen competing standards, carefully balancing the needs of different interest groups. That the result was absurd—how could an inch board be less than an inch?—but nevertheless adopted simply underscores the efficacy of Hoover's approach. Rexmond C. Cochrane, *Measures for Progress: A History of the National Bureau of Standards* (U.S. Department of Commerce, 1966), 257.

140 **Hoover wasn't just concerned:** Paul U. Kellogg, "The City Gate of the New World," *Survey*, May 20, 1922, 271.

140 **His loathing of apartment buildings:** Herbert Hoover, foreword to *How to Own Your Home* (Washington, D.C.: Government Printing Office, 1923), v.

140 **The trouble was, in much:** Ruth Knack, Stuart Meck, and Israel Stollman, "The Real Story Behind the Standard Planning and Zoning Acts of the 1920s," *Land Use Law and Zoning Digest* 48, no. 2 (1996): 3–9.

140 **The committee managed to produce:** Advisory Committee on Zoning, *A Standard State Zoning Enabling Act* (Washington, D.C.: Government Printing Office, 1924), iii.

141 **"I prefer to think of Iowa":** Herbert Hoover, *The Memoirs of Herbert Hoover: Years of Adventure, 1874–1920* (New York: Macmillan, 1951), 1.

141 **Hoover was born in 1874:** Ibid., 1–5; Edwin C. Bears, "The Hoover Houses and Community Structures: Historic Structures Report," Herbert Hoover National Historic Site, West Branch, Iowa, Nov. 30, 1971.

142 **But when Hoover returned:** Lillian W. Kay, *The Ground on Which We Stand: Basic Documents of American History* (New York: Grolier, 1978), 276.

142 **"an exclusive and luxurious":** "The Madison Square (Advertisement)," *New-York Tribune*, Oct. 10, 1915, 44.

143 **But homeownership came at a steep:** Horace Frisby Clark and Frank A. Chase, *Elements of the Modern Building and Loan Associations* (New York: Macmillan, 1925), 443–44.

144 **That's why, when Hoover solemnly:** Hoover, foreword, v.

145 **The Village of Euclid sat just:** "Euclid Pays 'Em Real Money," *Cincinnati Post*, June 25, 1925, 9; *Official Illustrated History and Directory of Euclid, Ohio* ([Cleveland]: Review Publishing Co., 1928), 5–12; *Transcript of Record: Euclid v. Ambler* (Supreme Court of the United States, n.d.), 167–79.

146 **Over the next three years:** Christopher, who was entitled to bill for his time in addition to drawing a salary, pocketed more than $35,000 by the end of 1924—the equivalent of more than $600,000 in contemporary dollars.

146 **The engineer, Fred Pease:** Not content with double-dipping, Pease also told the federal government that as a public official of these jurisdictions he should be exempt from the income tax; the commissioner of revenue was not amused, and Pease lost his case. *Pease v. Commissioner*, No. 50283, 50889, 65238, 66847 (U.S. Board of Tax Appeals, March 6, 1934); "Euclid Pays 'Em Real Money," 9.

146 **And while Shaker Heights:** Virginia P. Dawson, "Protection from Undesirable Neighbors: The Use of Deed Restrictions in Shaker Heights, Ohio," *Journal of Planning History* 18, no. 2 (2019): 116–36.

147 **By May, it was holding:** *Transcript of Record: Euclid v. Ambler*, 167–68, 208.

147 **Much of the Euclid map:** *Official History of Euclid*, 5.

148 **So, the ordinance established:** *Transcript of Record: Euclid v. Ambler*, 41–42.

148 **The Ambler Realty Company:** Michael Allan Wolf, *The Zoning of America: Euclid v. Ambler* (Lawrence: University Press of Kansas, 2008), 41–43.

148 **In 1920, the Massachusetts Supreme:** *Brett v. Building Commissioner of Brookline*, 250 Mass. 73, 145 N.E. 269 (1924).

148 **A delighted Bassett:** Edward M. Bassett, "New Court Decisions on Zoning," *National Municipal Review*, June 1925, 346.

149 **Despite the village's protests:** *Transcript of Record: Euclid v. Ambler*, 100, 158.

149 **Euclid called Robert Whitten:** Ibid., 118–22.

151 **The case went up:** "Faith of Zoning Experts," *Kansas City Star*, May 12, 1925, 8.

151 **The court was dominated:** The best general discussion of this case may be found in Wolf, *Zoning of America*. But see also Seymour I. Toll, *Zoned American* (New York: Grossman, 1969); Garrett Power, "Advocates at Cross-Purposes: The Briefs on Behalf of Zoning in the Supreme Court," *Journal of Supreme Court History* 22, no. 2 (1997): 79–87; Richard H. Chused, "*Euclid*'s Historical Imagery," *Case Western Reserve Law Review* 51, no. 4 (2001).

151 **In framing Euclid's case:** *Transcript of Record: Euclid v. Ambler*.

153 **Even the nation's leading expert:** Ibid.

CHAPTER SEVEN: **AUTO EMANCIPATION**

158 **When GM began to close:** Andrew R. Highsmith, *Demolition Means Progress: Flint, Michigan, and the Fate of the American Metropolis* (Chicago: University of Chicago Press, 2015), 246.

159 **Wealth, he tells me:** Donald O. Cowgill and Mary S. Cowgill, "An Index of Segregation Based on Block Statistics," *American Sociological Review* 16, no. 6 (1951): 828.

160 **One recent study of segregation:** Stephen Menendian, Samir Gambhir, and Arthur Gailes, "The Roots of Structural Racism Project," Othering & Belonging Institute, University of California at Berkeley, June 2021.

161 **Some 225,000 whites:** Alan Taylor, *The Internal Enemy: Slavery and War in Virginia, 1772–1832* (New York: W. W. Norton, 2013), 48–49.

161 **Of 300,000 white people:** *Census of 1860: Recapitulation of the Tables of Population, Nativity, and Occupation* (Washington, D.C.: Government Printing Office, 1864).

162 **"Throughout the South":** Frederick Law Olmsted, *A Journey in the Back Country: Our Slave States* (New York: Mason Brothers, 1860), 476.

162 **By the eve of the Civil War:** John Hope Franklin and Loren Schweninger, *Runaway Slaves: Rebels on the Plantation* (New York: Oxford University Press, 2000), 281–82.

162 **"We went to bed one night":** Andrew Delbanco, *The War Before the War: Fugitive Slaves and the Struggle for America's Soul from the Revolution to the Civil War* (New York: Penguin Press, 2018).

163 **The North had one other:** Jim Downs, *Sick from Freedom: African-American Illness and Suffering During the Civil War and Reconstruction* (New York: Oxford University Press, 2012).

163 **The Yankee writer John Townsend:** John Townsend Trowbridge, *The South: A Tour of Its Battlefields and Ruined Cities* (Hartford: L. Stebbins, 1866), 537.

164 **Trowbridge recounted the story:** Richard Brandon Morris, *Government and Labor in Early America* (New York: Octagon Books, 1965), 416–19.

165 **The South's Black Codes:** William Cohen, *At Freedom's Edge: Black Mobility and the Southern White Quest for Racial Control, 1861–1915* (Baton Rouge: Louisiana State University Press, 1991).

166 **When the Civil War ended:** Ibid., 78–108, 274–98.

166 **"Cast down your bucket":** Alice Mabel Bacon, *The Negro and the Atlanta Exposition* (Baltimore: Trustees of the John F. Slater Fund, 1896), 13.

167 **Nearly 400,000 Black soldiers:** Chad L. Williams, *Torchbearers of Democracy: African American Soldiers in the World War I Era* (Chapel Hill: University of North Carolina Press, 2013).

167 **Over the course of the twentieth:** James N. Gregory, *The Southern Diaspora: How*

the Great Migrations of Black and White Southerners Transformed America (Chapel Hill: University of North Carolina Press, 2006), 14–22.

167 **The largest portion of the migrants:** Isabel Wilkerson, *The Warmth of Other Suns: The Epic Story of America's Great Migration* (New York: Vintage, 2010); Leah Platt Boustan, *Competition in the Promised Land: Black Migrants in Northern Cities and Labor Markets* (Princeton, N.J.: Princeton University Press, 2016), 51–61; Gregory, *Southern Diaspora*, 14–15; Chad Berry, *Southern Migrants, Northern Exiles* (Urbana: University of Illinois Press, 2000); Erdmann Doane Beynon, "The Southern White Laborer Migrates to Michigan," *American Sociological Review* 3, no. 3 (1938): 333–43; James R. Grossman, *Land of Hope: Chicago, Black Southerners, and the Great Migration* (Chicago: University of Chicago Press, 1991), 36–37.

169 **It was a perilous time:** Jeannie M. Whayne, "Low Villains and Wickedness in High Places: Race and Class in the Elaine Riots," *Arkansas Historical Quarterly* 58, no. 3 (1999): 297.

169 **Near the town of Elaine:** Marlisa Goldsmith, "Newly Discovered Documents Reveal What May Have Started Elaine Massacre 100 Years Ago," THV11 Digital, Feb. 21, 2020; Grif Stockley, "Elaine Massacre of 1919," in *Encyclopedia of Arkansas* (2020); Grif Stockley, *Blood in Their Eyes: The Elaine Massacre of 1919* (Fayetteville: University of Arkansas Press, 2020), 23.

169 **One of the Black men:** Ida B. Wells-Barnett, *The Arkansas Race Riot* (Chicago: Hume Job Print, 1920).

169 **Whether the Dotsons themselves:** *Congressional Record*, June 17, 1994.

169 **At some point, perhaps radicalized:** Dotson told an interviewer that he had come to Flint when he was three, attended school, then moved to Toledo with his father, who cooked at the Waldorf Astoria, and graduated from a Catholic school on Cherry Street, moving back to Flint for good at age eighteen. On every government document, Dotson listed his birthday as December 3, 1901. Toledo's Waldorf hotel opened its doors in 1916; Cathedral High School on Cherry Street opened its doors in 1919. The 1910 census shows the Dotsons in Mississippi; the 1920 census lists Dotson, then eighteen, as living in Arkansas. The Dotsons might have come north several times, living in Flint and Toledo between census enumerations. They might have moved to Toledo after 1920, allowing Dotson to attend high school there, before relocating to Flint. A more likely possibility is that Dotson, who was an unreliable narrator, invented a new past for himself that concealed his actual origins; by his own account, he episodically left Flint as an adult to work as a cook and might well have spent time in Toledo as a young man encountering the places he named. The congressional tribute to Dotson made no mention of Toledo, instead listing three other northern cities where he might or might not have lived. The 1930 census shows him living in Flint with a wife named Sarah, also from Mississippi; when he married in 1935, he listed himself as coming from Nashville and never having married before. J. D. Dotson, interview by Neil Leighton, Jan. 23, 1981, First Series, University of Michigan-Flint Labor History Project; "Marriage License No. 42366," Saginaw County, Mich., Aug. 7, 1935.

170 **As industrial jobs were finally opened:** Boustan, *Competition in the Promised Land*, 46–61; J. Trent Alexander et al., "Second-Generation Outcomes of the Great Migration," *Demography* 54, no. 6 (2017): 2249–71.

170 **The Dotsons landed in Flint:** Robert H. Campbell and Tom Wickham, "Blacks, Flint, and GM," *Flint Journal*, Feb. 7, 1993, A12.

171 **"They had one man who would":** Frank Hammer, "Exclusive Interview with Flint Sit-Downer," *Straight Talk*, June 17, 1982, 7.

171 **"When there wouldn't be no work":** Ibid.

172 **That was exactly what Dotson:** Dotson, interview by Leighton, 20; "AFL Decides Green Needs No Police Help," *Detroit Free Press*, April 12, 1940, 5; "Lewis Condemns War, Want in Midst of Plenty, at Flint 'CIO Day' Rally," *Daily Worker*, April 8, 1940, 6; "Lewis, Confident of CIO Victory, Urges Stand for Peace," *Flint Journal*, April 8, 1940, 13.

172 **If Flint was not:** E. S. Guckert, "The Housing Status in Flint, Michigan," Community Fund, n.d., 13–14, 26, box 1, folder 3, Alexander C. Findlay Papers, Genesee Historical Collections Center, University of Michigan-Flint.

173 **A new single-family:** *Building Permit Survey, 1929 to 1935* (U.S. Bureau of Labor Statistics, 1937), 70.

173 **As the auto industry boomed:** All population and demographic figures from the U.S. census, unless otherwise noted.

173 **In 1917, Flint's wealthy citizens:** Genora Johnson Dollinger, interview, Sept. 22, 1978, 11, First Series, University of Michigan-Flint Labor History Project.

174 **Those who couldn't stand:** *The City Plan of Flint, Michigan* (City Planning Board, 1920), 22.

174 **"Flint is now practically free":** Ibid., 26.

174 **In an unusually bald statement:** "John Nolen, City Planner, Explains New Zoning System and Its Value to Akron," *Akron Evening Times*, March 7, 1919.

175 **"It is in most respects":** John Nolen, "The Asheville City Plan," 1921, 44, box 18, John Nolen Papers, Cornell University.

175 **Flint was primed to buy:** Stephen M. Laux, "Political Culture and the Second Industrial Revolution: Flint Politics, 1900–1929" (master's thesis, University of Michigan-Flint, 1995), 91.

175 **Attached to the property deeds:** The outstanding account of the history of residential segregation and redevelopment in Flint is Andrew R. Highsmith's superb book on the subject. Highsmith, *Demolition Means Progress*, 32.

175 **The city did not immediately:** "Zoning Law Adopted," *Flint Journal*, June 3, 1927, 8; "City Zoning Law Adopted by Aldermen," *Flint Journal*, Oct. 5, 1926, 1; "Council Orders Public Hearings on Zoning Law," *Flint Journal*, Aug. 11, 1925, 1; "Planning Board Satisfied with Hearing Result," *Flint Journal*, Sept. 6, 1925, 1.

176 **In 1937, Genesee County:** "County Building Code Is Rejected," *Flint Journal*, Jan. 8, 1937.

176 **"Well, we don't know":** Walter Firey, *Social Aspects to Land Use Planning in the Country-City Fringe: The Case of Flint, Michigan* (East Lansing: Michigan State College, Agricultural Experiment Station, 1946), 52–56; Tom Dinell, *The Influences of Federal, State, and Local Legislation on Residential Building in the Flint Metropolitan Area* (Ann Arbor: Social Science Research Project, Institute for Human Advancement, University of Michigan, 1951), 38.

176 **In the city itself:** Samuel Simmons and Robert Greene, "Flint Community Survey" (Michigan Fair Employment Practices Commission, 1956), 3, box 11, folder 3, Olive Beasley Papers, Genesee Historical Collections Center.

177 **But white southerners were hired:** Beynon, "Southern White Laborer Migrates to Michigan."

CHAPTER EIGHT: **THE HOUSING TRAP**

178   **The Great Depression hit Flint:** Ronald Freedman and Amos H. Hawley, "Migration and Occupational Mobility in the Depression," *American Journal of Sociology* 55, no. 2 (1949): 175–76.

179   **The HOLC aimed to solve:** C. Lowell Harriss, *History and Policies of the Home Owners' Loan Corporation* (New York: National Bureau of Economic Research, 1951).

180   **The agency refinanced loans:** Price V. Fishback et al., "New Evidence on Redlining by Federal Housing Programs in the 1930s," Working Paper 29244, NBER Working Paper Series, Sept. 2021, 3.

180   **Nor did it confine itself:** Harriss, *History and Policies of the Home Owners' Loan Corporation*, 53.

181   **But dynamic communities were:** Federal Housing Administration, *Underwriting Manual* (Washington, D.C.: Government Printing Office, 1938), 935, 980.

182   **At one level, the FHA:** Amanda Tillotson, "Race, Risk, and Real Estate: The Federal Housing Administration and Black Homeownership in the Post World War II Home Ownership State," *DePaul Journal for Social Justice* 8, no. 1 (2014): 25.

182   **The third prong of FDR's approach:** Franklin D. Roosevelt, *The Public Papers and Addresses of Franklin D. Roosevelt, 1934* (New York: Macmillan, 1941), 480.

183   **The answer he landed on:** Nathan Straus, "Bulletin No. 18 on Policy and Procedure: Site Selection," U.S. Housing Authority, Feb. 13, 1939, 6.

183   **Taken together, these federal programs:** Andrew Whittemore, "How the Federal Government Zoned America: The Federal Housing Administration and Zoning," *Journal of Urban History* 39 (2012): 627.

183   **Where Hoover had simply:** Highsmith, *Demolition Means Progress*, 104–9.

184   **White southerners who had migrated:** *War Housing Program: Hearings Before the Committee on Public Buildings and Grounds* (U.S. Government Printing Office, 1943), 228–29.

184   **The FHA, however, had made loans:** Dinell, *Influences of Federal, State, and Local Legislation on Residential Building in the Flint Metropolitan Area*, 70.

184   **Frank Williams, for example:** Frank Williams, interview by Mark R. Depue, July 13, 2018, African-American Chronicles–Civil Rights Oral History Project, Abraham Lincoln Presidential Library.

185   **As bad as the wartime:** "Revolution in Cotton," *Recorder*, Aug. 1947, 3, box 1, folder 3, Urban League of Flint Papers, Genesee Historical Collections Center.

185   **In 1947, Frank's mother:** Michael J. Bennett, *When Dreams Came True: The GI Bill and the Making of Modern America* (Washington, D.C.: Brassey's, 1996), 287.

185   **But the GI Bill:** Fishback et al., "New Evidence on Redlining by Federal Housing Programs in the 1930s."

186   **Many sellers, in fact:** I owe a particular debt to my colleague Ta-Nehisi Coates, who introduced me to this horrifying subject a decade ago. His discussion remains unparalleled. Ta-Nehisi Coates, "The Case for Reparations," *Atlantic*, June 2014.

186   **Not only did Jones:** Williams, interview by Depue.

186   **In the decade after:** Lizabeth Cohen, *A Consumers' Republic: The Politics of Mass Consumption in Postwar America* (New York: Vintage Books, 2004), 171; Louis Lee Woods II, "Almost 'No Negro Veteran . . . Could Get a Loan': African Americans, the GI Bill, and the NAACP Campaign Against Residential Segregation, 1917–1960," *Journal of African American History* 98, no. 3 (2013): 392–417.

186 **One veteran in the Detroit:** World War II Veteran, "The Voice of the People: Negro Veteran," *Detroit Free Press*, Sept. 7, 1946, 6.

186 **"Our market in Flint":** "Building Code Change Urged," *Flint Journal*, March 18, 1948.

187 **"Typically, dwelling units":** "Housing Conditions," in *Comprehensive Master Plan for Flint Michigan and Its Environs* (Flint Planning Commission, 1969), 2–3.

187 **Black residents of Flint:** Charles J. Wartman, "Better Housing, Jobs Are Key Problems to Negroes in Flint," *Detroit Chronicle*, Jan. 3, 1959, 1.

187 **On January 10, 1855:** This deed restriction has frequently, and mistakenly, been attributed to the Lindens development in 1843, and even blamed on the nativism of Thomas Aspinwall Davis, who developed that land. That it was instead Lawrence, noted champion of the antislavery cause, who introduced the first racial restriction, is perhaps surprising, but not inconsistent with the subsequent political history of Brookline, a staunchly progressive community that remains only 3 percent Black. "233-1, 233-2, 233-3," Norfolk Registry of Deeds, Jan. 10, 1855; Ronald Dale Karr, "The Evolution of an Elite Suburb: Community Structure and Control in Brookline, Massachusetts, 1770–1900" (PhD diss., Boston University, 1981), 265.

188 **Nuisance covenants were already:** "Two New and Substantially Built Houses and a Cottage at Longwood, in Brookline," *Boston Evening Transcript*, June 26, 1857.

188 **In 1886, Alex Gandolfo:** Yda Addis Storke, *A Memorial and Biographical History of the Counties of Santa Barbara, San Luis Obispo, and Ventura, California* (Chicago: Lewis, 1891), 365–66; *Gandolfo v. Hartman*, 49 F. 181 (9th Cir. 1892); Michael Jones-Correa, "The Origins and Diffusion of Racial Restrictive Covenants," *Political Science Quarterly* 115, no. 4 (2000): 541–68.

189 **Steward wrote his racially restrictive deeds:** "Our Letter Bag—a Law Question," *Real Estate Record and Builder's Guide*, Sept. 13, 1890, 336; William Austen Carney, *Real Estate Business Self-Taught* (Los Angeles: W. A. Carney, 1906), 63.

189 **As time went on:** Karen Tumulty and Alice Crites, "LBJ Fought a Quiet Battle to Desegregate Housing—His Own," *Washington Post*, Jan. 5, 2015.

191 **These covenants might best:** Cass R. Sunstein, "Law's Expressive Function," *Good Society* 9, no. 2 (1999): 55–61.

191 **Hailing it as a "progressive step":** "Tilts on West Measure," *Baltimore Sun*, Sept. 27, 1910, 16.

191 **Twenty-six criminal cases:** Roger L. Rice, "Residential Segregation by Law, 1910–1917," *Journal of Southern History* 34, no. 2 (1968): 179–99; Gretchen Boger, "The Meaning of Neighborhood in the Modern City: Baltimore's Residential Segregation Ordinances, 1910–1913," *Journal of Urban History* 35, no. 2 (2009): 236–58; Emily Lieb, "The 'Baltimore Idea' and the Cities It Built," *Southern Cultures* 25, no. 2 (2019): 104–19; Garrett Power, "Apartheid Baltimore Style: The Residential Segregation Ordinances of 1910–1913," *Maryland Law Review* 42, no. 2 (1983): 303.

192 **The newly formed NAACP:** Power, "Apartheid Baltimore Style," 311–13.

193 **One Black buyer was told:** "Equal Housing Opportunities in Flint" (Civil Rights Commission, 1966), box 9, folder 13, Beasley Papers.

193 **Fair housing laws, a New Yorker:** Earl Brown, "The People Write," *Amsterdam News*, July 6, 1957, 8.

193 **Orville Hubbard, the mayor of Dearborn:** David M. P. Freund, "Making It Home: Race, Development, and the Politics of Place in Suburban Detroit, 1940–1967" (PhD diss., University of Michigan, 1999), 432.

193 **A Chicago man complained:** John A. Prestro, "'White Backlash' Bloc Appears Sizeable in Poll of a Chicago District," *Wall Street Journal,* Oct. 30, 1964, 1.

193 **But the clearest articulation:** "Let's Have Freedom of Choice!" (California Freedom of Choice Committee, 1952).

194 **The America Plus article:** Charlotte Brooks, "Sing Sheng vs. Southwood: Residential Integration in Cold War California," *Pacific Historical Review* 73, no. 3 (2004): 463–94.

194 **Progress toward formal legal equality:** Martha Biondi, *To Stand and Fight: The Struggle for Civil Rights in Postwar New York City* (Cambridge, Mass.: Harvard University Press, 2006), 286–87.

194 **In 1968, after a long:** Highsmith, *Demolition Means Progress,* 164–74.

195 **Flint's urban renewal program:** "Urban Renewal Development Plan, St. John Street Renewal Area" (Department of Community Development, n.d.), 19, box 1, folder 24, Flint Department of Community Development Collection, Genesee Historical Collections Center.

196 **Flint would manage to annex:** Highsmith, *Demolition Means Progress,* 114–44; William Orville Winter, "Annexation as a Solution to the Fringe Problem: An Analysis of Past and Potential Annexations of Suburban Areas to the City of Flint, Michigan" (PhD diss., University of Michigan, 1949), 12–14.

196 **In the 1970s, three justices:** Roger A. Cunningham, "Reflections on Stare Decisis in Michigan: The Rise and Fall of the 'Rezoning as Administrative Act' Doctrine," *Michigan Law Review* 75, no. 5–6 (1977); *Nickola v. Grand Blanc Township,* 209 N.W. 2d 803, 47 Mich. App. 684 (1973).

197 **Through the 1970s, Flint continued:** "Comprehensive Plan of Policies for Development for the City of Flint—Michigan" (City of Flint, 1981), 15, box 21, folder 32, Beasley Papers.

199 **The Harvard researcher Raj Chetty's:** Raj Chetty, "Tract 26049002000, Flint, MI," Opportunity Atlas, 2022, www.opportunityatlas.org.

200 **He doesn't tell me:** Eric Woodyard, "Single Flint Dad Raises Cancer-Surviving Son to Be Strong Athlete," *Flint Journal,* June 17, 2016.

201 **Almost half the kids:** Raj Chetty, "Tract 26049003100, Flint, MI," Opportunity Atlas, 2022, www.opportunityatlas.org.

CHAPTER NINE: A PLAGUE OF LOCALISTS

202 **On the final day of 1939:** "Camp Preacher Considers Fight Against Charges Under 'Indigent' Law," *Appeal-Democrat,* Feb. 10, 1940, 1.

203 **Frank Duncan moved off:** S. Boyd Hilton, "High Court Rule Frees Fred Edwards to Business of Home and Family," *Appeal-Democrat,* Nov. 25, 1941, 5.

203 **A federal circuit court:** Matthew Longo, "Right of Way? Defining Freedom of Movement Within Democratic Societies," in *Democratic Citizenship and the Free Movement of People,* ed. Willem Maas (Leiden: Martinus Nijhoff, 2013), 34–42.

204 **Justice Robert Jackson concurred:** *Edwards v. California,* 314 U.S. 160 (1941).

204 **Upholding the law:** "Anti-migrant Law Held Unconstitutional by U.S. Supreme Court," *Visalia Times-Delta,* Nov. 24, 1941, 1.

204 **"The early California pioneers":** Warren B. Francis, "Anti-Okie Law Ruled Invalid," *Los Angeles Times,* Nov. 25, 1941, 2.

205 **"There has been more movement":** "Interstate Migration and Other Population Changes: 1940 to 1943," P-44, U.S. Bureau of the Census, Aug. 28, 1944.

205 **"No doubt, war and war industries":** "Americans Moving," *Rochester Democrat and Chronicle,* April 23, 1944, 18.

206 **Between 1940 and 1945:** Robert D. Putnam, *Bowling Alone: The Collapse and Revival of American Community* (New York: Simon & Schuster, 2000), 55.

206 **Despite becoming sharply more likely:** Ibid., 17.

206 **In the first fourteen months:** "Postwar Migration and Its Causes in the United States: August, 1945, to October, 1946," P-20, U.S. Bureau of the Census, Oct. 7, 1947.

206 **"Being strangers in the city":** "An Idea Which in Twenty Years Grew into an International Institution," *Commercial Appeal,* Nov. 7, 1948, sec. 1, 12.

207 **In 1943, the magazine *The Link*:** "'What I Am Fighting For,'" *Daily Missoulian,* Oct. 23, 1943, 4; Clark Porteous, "Soldier-Son, in Germany, Wins Fight to Keep Home," *Memphis Press-Scimitar,* Aug. 8, 1946, 11; "Third of People in This Nation Desire to Move," *Asheville Citizen-Times,* March 31, 1946, 10A.

208 **All those people on the move:** The same 1946 survey that reported many Americans wanted to move also showed that a fifth of households were living doubled up in a space meant for just one family, and that as many expected to rent a new place as to buy a home. Kenneth T. Jackson, *Crabgrass Frontier: The Suburbanization of the United States* (New York: Oxford University Press, 1987), 232–33; Daniel K. Fetter, "The Home Front: Rent Control and the Rapid Wartime Increase in Home Ownership," *Journal of Economic History* 76, no. 4 (Dec. 2016): 1001–43; "Discarded Trolley Cars Converted into Home," *Gazette and Daily,* July 15, 1946, 8; "Bought House," *Plattsburg Leader,* Aug. 27, 1943, 4.

208 **Millions of Americans used FHA:** Jackson, *Crabgrass Frontier,* 233.

210 **By the beginning of the 1960s:** The works of Jacobs, Nader, Carson, Friedan, and other authors have frequently been linked. In 1994, for example, Howard Husock wrote that Jacobs "did to urban renewal what Rachel Carson did to DDT and Ralph Nader did to the Corvair." The point was later taken up by Anthony Flint, among others, but it finds its fullest and most fascinating expression in the work of Paul Sabin. Flint, *Wrestling with Moses,* 122; Howard Husock, "Urban Iconoclast: Jane Jacobs Revisited," *City Journal* (Winter 1994); Paul Sabin, *Public Citizens: The Attack on Big Government and the Remaking of American Liberalism* (New York: W. W. Norton, 2021).

211 **Carson detailed how the Department:** Sabin, *Public Citizens,* 17–23.

211 **Nader leveled a similar critique:** Ibid., 27–32.

211 **"Under such circumstances":** "Interagency Coordination in Environmental Hazards," Washington, D.C., June 4, 1963, 210.

212 **The students, dubbed "Nader's Raiders":** Edward Finch Cox, Robert C. Fellmeth, and John E. Schulz, *The Nader Report on the Federal Trade Commission* (New York: Richard W. Baron, 1969), vii.

212 **"You know, as a twenty-one-year-old":** Fellmeth, interview by author, Jan. 12, 2023.

212 **Nader wanted to use:** Harry Chatten Boyte, *The Backyard Revolution: Understanding the New Citizen Movement* (Philadelphia: Temple University Press, 1980), 40.

212 **One of Nader's Raiders:** Art Seidenbaum, "And Wait'll You Hear What Ralph Nader and His Boys Have to Say About California Land Development," *Los Angeles Times,* Oct. 4, 1970, 22.

212 **"California may keep right on":** "No Overpopulation Here," *Long Beach Press,* Aug. 30, 1921.

213 **The Nader group's finished report:** Robert C. Fellmeth, *Politics of Land: Ralph Nader's Study Group Report on Land Use in California* (New York: Grossman, 1973), xi.

214 **"Land policies play perhaps":** Ibid., 395.

214 **For more than a century:** "The only thing Nader's Raiders have accomplished with their sweeping generalizations and glaring omissions," the general counsel of the Western Developers Council wrote in response to the report, "is to fuel those reactionary forces in the state who, for selfish reasons, want to leave things exactly as they are at the cost of not solving our most pressing population-growth problems." "A Howl from Developers," *San Francisco Examiner*, Aug. 29, 1971, sec. Sunday Homes, A.

215 **At a California Assembly hearing:** Philip Fradkin, "New Approach to State Land Planning Urged," *Los Angeles Times*, Dec. 21, 1971, B8.

215 **In 1965, the ecologist Raymond Dasmann's:** A 1962 report from the non-profit California Tomorrow urged more intensive planning to accommodate the state's challenges, applying the classic progressive prescription of better bureaucracy and greater deference to expertise. The environmentalists would instead challenge bureaucratic decision making with their own expertise. Raymond F. Dasmann, *The Destruction of California* (New York: Macmillan, 1965), 207; Conor Dougherty, *Golden Gates: Fighting for Housing in America* (New York: Penguin Press, 2020), 72–86; Samuel E. Wood and Alfred E. Heller, *California Going, Going* (Sacramento, Calif.: California Tomorrow, 1962), 7–9; Ray Hebert, "L.A. Plan Rapped for Accepting Growth Instead of Inhibiting It," *Los Angeles Times*, April 17, 1970, B1; Greg Morrow, "The Homeowner Revolution: Democracy, Land Use, and the Los Angeles Slow-Growth Movement, 1965–1992" (PhD diss., University of California, Los Angeles, 2013), 333.

216 **"I happen to have a philosophical view":** Fellmeth, interview by author.

216 **Governor Jerry Brown, delivering his:** Most lawsuits under CEQA have been filed to oppose the construction of housing, overwhelmingly multifamily developments in built-up areas. It has been used much less frequently to protect open land—where there are fewer neighbors to object. Jennifer Hernandez, "California Getting in Its Own Way" (Center for Demographics & Policy, Chapman University, 2019).

217 **Two years after CEQA:** *Friends of Mammoth v. Board of Supervisors of Mono County*, 8 Cal. 3d 247 (1972).

217 **In 2008, a developer won approval:** Hernandez, "California Getting in Its Own Way"; Ryan Fonseca, "Dear LAist: What's Happening with the Sunset Gordon Tower and Public Park in Hollywood?," *LAist*, Oct. 16, 2018; *LA Mirada Avenue Neighborhood Association of Hollywood v. City of Los Angeles*, No. B259672 (Cal. Ct. App. Sept. 9, 2015).

218 **CEQA delays are used by:** Hernandez, "California Getting in Its Own Way"; Fonseca, "Dear LAist"; *LA Mirada Avenue Neighborhood Association of Hollywood v. City of Los Angeles*, No. B259672 (Cal. Ct. App. Sept. 9, 2015).

218 **Local agencies take an average:** Mac Taylor, "Considering Changes to Streamline Local Housing Approvals," Sacramento Legislative Analyst's Office, May 18, 2016, 8.

219 **The money that purchased:** Noah Goldberg, "A Single San Francisco Parking Space Is Selling for $90,000," *Los Angeles Times*, Sept. 13, 2022.

219 **Over the last half century:** Hans Johnson, "Who's Leaving California—and

Who's Moving In?," *Public Policy Institute of California* (blog), March 28, 2022, www.ppic.org/blog/whos-leaving-california-and-whos-moving-in/.

219 **Fifty years after the Nader report:** Fellmeth, interview by author.

220 **The same shift took hold:** Courts increasingly recognized that litigants could act to defend the public interest, even when they had suffered no personal financial loss, and some laws explicitly empowered them to do so. Sabin, *Public Citizens*, 94–99.

220 **In Los Angeles:** Morrow, "Homeowner Revolution," 223.

220 **Out of every ten buildings:** Quoctrung Bui, Matt A. V. Chaban, and Jeremy White, "40 Percent of the Buildings in Manhattan Could Not Be Built Today," *New York Times*, May 20, 2016.

221 **In San Francisco, a third:** Vadim Graboys, "54% of San Francisco Homes Are in Buildings That Would Be Illegal to Build Today," *Deap Thoughts* (blog), n.d., sfzoning.deapthoughts.com/illegal_homes.html.

221 **The quarter of eligible voters:** Phil Kiesling, "What's the Biggest Factor in Determining Who Votes in Local Elections? Age—Nothing Else Comes Close," *Who Votes for Mayor?* (blog), Oct. 27, 2016, medium.com/@whovotesformayor/whats-the-biggest-factor-in-determining-who-votes-in-local-elections-a9d809c31b93.

222 **But as unrepresentative as municipal:** Katherine Levine Einstein, David M. Glick, and Maxwell Palmer, *Neighborhood Defenders: Participatory Politics and America's Housing Crisis* (New York: Cambridge University Press, 2019), 101–9; Jerusalem Demsas, "Community Input Is Bad, Actually," *Atlantic*, April 22, 2022.

CHAPTER TEN: BUILDING A WAY OUT

226 **It has become a suburb:** Henry Allen, "My Strange Takoma Home," *Washington Post*, April 23, 1989; Kay Dellinger, "Sammie Abbott, a Passionate Fighter for Justice," *Takoma Voice*, Feb. 1991; Terence Mulligan, "Sammie Leaves Living Legacy for Takoma Park," *Takoma Voice*, Feb. 1991.

228 **Research by the economists:** Peter Ganong and Daniel Shoag, "Why Has Regional Income Divergence in the U.S. Declined?," *Journal of Urban Economics* 102 (Nov. 2017): 76–90.

229 **Choosing where to live:** Seth Stephens-Davidowitz, "The One Parenting Decision That Really Matters," *Atlantic*, May 7, 2022, www.theatlantic.com/ideas/archive/2022/05/parenting-decisions-dont-trust-your-gut-book-excerpt/629734/.

229 **But the biggest advantage:** Ran Abramitzky et al., "Intergenerational Mobility of Immigrants in the U.S. over Two Centuries," Working Paper 26408, NBER Working Paper Series, Oct. 2019, 24.

230 **Even those who headed back:** By one recent estimate, some thirty-two million immigrants arrived at ports in the United States between 1900 and 1920, and over the same twenty years some twenty-eight million foreign-born residents of the United States went back to their native lands. Those numbers surely include some who shuttled back and forth, returning to Europe during cyclical downturns or to visit family or to bring relatives back with them to America, and so are counted more than once. But that simply underlines the key point; immigration was less a directed flow than a continual churn as people leveraged mobility to improve their lot in life. Ran Abramitzky, Leah Boustan, and Katherine Eriksson, "To the New World and Back Again: Return Migrants in the Age of Mass Migration," *ILR Review* 72, no. 2 (2019): 300–322; Bandiera, Rasul, and Viarengo, "Making of Modern America."

230 **The prolific bank robber:** Sutton himself always denied having said this. And indeed, the earliest version of the quotation I've found dates from 1923, long before Sutton is supposed to have said it, and a bank robber named Robert Perritt. "Youths Admit Bank Holdups," *Detroit Free Press*, Dec. 19, 1923, 13.

231 **Someone without a high school:** Ben Sprung-Keyser, Nathaniel Hendren, and Sonya Porter, "The Radius of Economic Opportunity: Evidence from Migration and Local Labor Markets," Center for Economic Studies, July 2022; David Card, Jesse Rothstein, and Moises Yi, "Location, Location, Location," Center for Economic Studies, U.S. Census Bureau, Oct. 2021; Rebecca Diamond and Enrico Moretti, "Where Is Standard of Living the Highest? Local Prices and the Geography of Consumption," Working Paper 29533, NBER Working Paper Series, Dec. 2021.

231 **Americans, for example, still move:** Canada, Australia, and New Zealand have reported levels of geographic mobility that rival the United States in recent decades, although those numbers are surely influenced by the fact that the percentage of foreign-born residents in these countries in any given year has generally been at least twice as high as in the United States; data that would allow direct comparisons with the eras of peak mobility in the United States have not yet been developed, although narrative accounts of travelers point to the distinctiveness of the U.S. experience. Some Scandinavian countries have also shown rates of mobility in recent years that are roughly comparable to the contemporary United States. Michael J. Greenwood, "Internal Migration in Developed Countries," in *Handbook of Population and Family Economics*, ed. Mark R. Rosenzweig and Oded Stark (Amsterdam: Elsevier, 1997), 1:651–55; Larry Long, *Migration and Residential Mobility in the United States* (New York: Russell Sage Foundation, 1988), 252–82; Sanford M. Jacoby, "Labor Mobility in a Federal System: The United States in Comparative Perspective," *International Journal of Comparative Labour Law and Industrial Relations* 20, no. 3 (2004); Holger Bonin, Werner Eichhorst, and Christer Florman, "Geographic Mobility in the European Union: Optimising Its Economic and Social Benefits," Research Report No. 19, IZA Institute of Labor Economics, July 2008.

231 **A pair of economists:** The idea is that when people move to more productive places, they themselves become more productive, spurring economic growth. Chang-Tai Hsieh and Enrico Moretti, "Why Do Cities Matter? Local Growth and Aggregate Growth," SSRN Scholarly Paper, May 1, 2015; Chang-Tai Hsieh and Enrico Moretti, "Housing Constraints and Spatial Misallocation," *American Economic Journal: Macroeconomics* 11, no. 2 (2019): 1–39; Annie Lowrey, "The U.S. Needs More Housing Than Almost Anyone Can Imagine," *Atlantic*, Nov. 21, 2022.

232 **Between 1880 and 1980:** Jac C. Heckelman, "Income Convergence Among U.S. States: Cross-Sectional and Time Series Evidence," *Canadian Journal of Economics / Revue Canadienne d'Economique* 46, no. 3 (2013): 1085–109; Ganong and Shoag, "Why Has Regional Income Divergence in the U.S. Declined?"

232 **And over the last two decades:** Rati Ram, "Income Convergence Across the U.S. States: Further Evidence from New Recent Data," *Journal of Economics and Finance* 45, no. 2 (2021): 372–80.

232 **One study looked at thousands:** Patrick Sharkey, "Geographic Migration of Black and White Families over Four Generations," *Demography* 52, no. 1 (2015): 209–31.

232 **Another team of researchers:** Sprung-Keyser, Hendren, and Porter, "Radius of Economic Opportunity," 15.

233 **So, the land-use restrictions:** Daniel Shoag and Lauren Russell, "Land Use Regulations and Fertility Rates," in *One Hundred Years of Zoning and the Future of Cities,* ed. Amnon Lehavi (Cham, Switzerland: Springer, 2018), 139–49.

233 **In 1853, Ann Pamela Cunningham:** Whitney Martinko, *Historic Real Estate: Market Morality and the Politics of Preservation in the Early United States* (Philadelphia: University of Pennsylvania Press, 2020), 197–202.

234 **"If it suits them":** Grace to William Watts Ball, May 9, 1929, box 18, William Watts Ball Papers, David M. Rubenstein Rare Book & Manuscript Library, Duke University, quoted in Stephanie E. Yuhl, *A Golden Haze of Memory: The Making of Historic Charleston* (Chapel Hill: University of North Carolina Press, 2006), 42.

234 **Then, in 1931, Charleston adopted:** "The Zoning Ordinance," *Charleston Evening Post,* June 9, 1931.

235 **The Board of Architectural:** Yuhl, *Golden Haze of Memory,* 45–51.

235 **"The United States is a nation":** U.S. Conference of Mayors, Special Committee on Historic Preservation, *With Heritage So Rich* (New York: Random House, 1966), 207.

237 **Once again, the sovereign village:** Elizabeth Kastor, "The Panic in Cleveland Park," *Washington Post,* April 23, 1986, B1; Wendy Swallow, "Group Seeks to Save Park and Shop," *Washington Post,* Nov. 9, 1985, F1.

237 **In 1999, the City of Cambridge:** Sally Zimmerman, "White Tower Restaurant, 25 Central Square, Landmark Designation Report," Cambridge Historical Commission, May 10, 1999.

238 **In Manhattan, 27 percent:** Ingrid Gould Ellen, Brian J. McCabe, and Eric Edward Stern, "Fifty Years of Historic Preservation in New York City," NYU Furman Center, March 7, 2016, 4.

238 **Nearly 19 percent of Washington:** Luke Wake and Ilya Shapiro, "Brief for the Cato Institute and the National Federation of Independent Business Small Business Legal Center as Amici Curiae Supporting Petitioner, Stahl York Avenue Co. v. City of New York," July 6, 2016.

238 **But where landmarking has become:** Vicki Been et al., "Preserving History or Hindering Growth? The Heterogeneous Effects of Historic Districts on Local Housing Markets in New York City," Working Paper 20446, NBER Working Paper Series, Sept. 2014, doi.org/10.3386/w20446.

239 **Together with the "strict enforcement":** Zorita Wise Mikva, "The Neighborhood Improvement Association: A Counter Force to the Expansion of Chicago's Negro Population" (master's thesis, University of Chicago, 1951); Evan McKenzie, *Privatopia: Homeowner Associations and the Rise of Residential Private Government* (New Haven, Conn.: Yale University Press, 1994).

239 **If you're buying a new home:** "Community Association Fact Book 2021" (Falls Church, Va.: Foundation for Community Association Research, 2021).

241 **The crisis of housing affordability:** M. Nolan Gray, *Arbitrary Lines: How Zoning Broke the American City and How to Fix It* (Washington, D.C.: Island Press, 2022); Henry Grabar, *Paved Paradise: How Parking Explains the World* (New York: Penguin Press, 2023); Daniel G. Parolek, *Missing Middle Housing: Thinking Big and Building Small to Respond to Today's Housing Crisis* (Washington, D.C.: Island Press, 2020); Daniel Aldana Cohen and Mark Paul, "The Case for Social Housing," Data for Progress & the Justice Collaborative Institute, Nov. 2020; Jenny Schuetz, *Fixer-Upper: How to Repair America's Broken Housing Systems* (Washington, D.C.: Brookings Institution Press, 2022); Shane Phillips, *The Affordable City: Strategies for Putting Housing Within Reach* (Washington, D.C.: Island Press, 2020).

242   **To approach a community:** Jacobs, *Death and Life of Great American Cities,* 373.

243   **In colonial New England:** Joseph S. Wood, *The New England Village* (Baltimore: Johns Hopkins University Press, 2002), 114–34.

243   **"A village, with its":** Nathan Henry Chamberlain, *A Paper on New-England Architecture* (Boston: Crosby, Nichols, 1858), 12, quoted in Wood, *New England Village,* 133.

244   **Homelessness, as the scholars:** Gregg Colburn and Clayton Page Aldern, *Homelessness Is a Housing Problem: How Structural Factors Explain U.S. Patterns* (Berkeley: University of California Press, 2022); Jerusalem Demsas, "The Obvious Answer to Homelessness," *Atlantic,* Feb. 2023.

246   **In 1961, New York City:** Harrison Ballard & Allen, "Plan for Rezoning the City of New York," New York City Planning Commission, Oct. 1950, 15; Voorhees Walker Smith & Smith, "Zoning New York City," New York City Planning Commission, Aug. 1958, 5; Dennis Duggan, "Zoning Critics See City Becoming a Ghost Town," *New York Herald Tribune,* May 17, 1959, C1.

247   **In 1958, on the other side:** André Sorensen, Junichiro Okata, and Sayaka Fujii, "Urban Renaissance as Intensification: Building Regulation and the Rescaling of Place Governance in Tokyo's High-Rise Manshon Boom," *Urban Studies* 47, no. 3 (2009): 556–83; André Sorensen, "Evolving Property Rights in Japan: Patterns and Logics of Change," *Urban Studies* 48, no. 3 (2011): 471–91; Gray, *Arbitrary Lines,* 122–24; Robin Harding, "Why Tokyo Is the Land of Rising Home Construction but Not Prices," *Financial Times,* Aug. 3, 2016; James Gleeson, "How Tokyo Built Its Way to Abundant Housing," *James Gleeson* (blog), Feb. 19, 2018, jamesjgleeson .wordpress.com/2018/02/19/how-tokyo-built-its-way-to-abundant-housing/.

248   **Japan's small number of straightforward:** Binyamin Appelbaum, "Tokyo, the Big City Where Housing Isn't Crazy Expensive," *New York Times,* Sept. 16, 2023, sec. A.

249   **Since World War II:** Andreas Mense, Claus Michelsen, and Konstantin A. Kholodilin, "The Effects of Second-Generation Rent Control on Land Values," *AEA Papers and Proceedings* 109 (May 2019): 385–88.

250   **One recent study traced that chain:** Evan Mast, "JUE Insight: The Effect of New Market-Rate Housing Construction on the Low-Income Housing Market," *Journal of Urban Economics* 133 (Jan. 2023).

250   **Another study found:** Andreas Mense, "The Impact of New Housing Supply on the Distribution of Rents" (German Economic Association, 2020).

251   **As things stand, roughly 20:** Lowrey, "U.S. Needs More Housing Than Almost Anyone Can Imagine"; Hsieh and Moretti, "Why Do Cities Matter?"

254   **A journeyman could do well:** *Preliminary Report of the Factory Investigating Commission* (Albany, N.Y.: Argus, 1912), 2:373; *Official Report and Proceedings of the Convention of the Bakery and Confectionery Workers' International Union of America* (Chicago: John C. Burmeister, 1917), 65.

INDEX

Page numbers in *italics* indicate illustrations.

A

Abbott, Sammie, 225
ACLU, 202, 240
Adams, John Quincy, 84
affordable housing crisis
    homelessness and, 219, 244
    as mobility crisis, 6–7, 242
affordable housing crisis solutions,
        241–42
    cash transfer to Americans living
        below poverty line, 244
    clarity of rules and, 246–48
    consistency in application of rules
        needed to solve, 245–46
    housing in right places, 248–51
    number of new units needed, 251
    tolerance of imperfection, 242–44
age and mobility, 11–12
agency
    choosing communities and, 19
    geographic mobility and, 19, 242
    Moving Day as assertion of, 75
Aldern, Clayton Page, 244
Ambler Realty Company, 148, 149–54
American character
    ability to choose community, 7,
        9, 78
    association mania as part of, 77–78

closure of frontier and, 67
geographic mobility as defining
    feature of, 7–8, 60–62, 65, 71,
    204–5
racism's role in, 83
xenophobia's role in, 83
America Plus, 194
Andrews, Josiah Bishop, 70–71
apartment houses
    as "bane" of owners of single-family
        homes, 104
    FHA financed, 183
    limits of developable land and, 102
    micro-apartments, 245
    negative effect on life of, 127
    rents, 134–35
    restrictive covenants separating
        single- and two-family homes
        from, 182
    zoning ordinances and, 103
associations
    American mania for, 77–78
    ethnic, 82–83, 256
    federations of local, 79
    geographic mobility and
        membership in, 80–81
    for historic preservation, 234
    of home owners, 238–39

associations (cont'd):
  individualism and, 78
  individual's sense of identity and, 81
  migrants as members of, 79, 272n79
  neighborhood improvement,
    238–39
  post-World War II membership in,
    206
  as providing instant
    communities, 79
  religion as matter of choice and not
    inheritance, 78
  voluntary nature of, 79–80, 84
The Atlantic, 21
automobile industry, 158, 171–72,
  173–74, 175, 184, 210, 211

B
Baker, Newton, 148
Baldwin, James, 210
Baltimore, 139, 191, 238
Barbier v. Connolly (1885), 95
Bartholomew, Harland, 139
Bassett, Edward Murray
  apartment buildings as bane of New
    York City, 119–20
  appearance of, 119
  background of, 117–18, 119, 244
  city planning as answer to
    development in New York City,
    120
  Commission on Building Districts
    and Restrictions, 124
  Commission on the Height, Size,
    and Arrangement of Buildings
    (Heights of Buildings
    Commission), 122, 123–24, 135,
    136
  on Euclid zoning ordinance, 151
  movement for national zoning,
    138–39
  political connections of, 148–49
  on "saving" Fifth Avenue, 138
  transit service as alleviating housing
    congestion, 119, 121
  zoning proposal of, 126–27
Bassett, George, 117–18
Bay Colony. See entries beginning with
  Massachusetts

Bean, Ivory, 188
Becker, Carl, 9
Berkeley, California, 101, 102–4, 105,
  106–8, 109, 110–12
Berkeley, George, 62
Bettman, Alfred, 151–52
Biondi, Martha, 194
Bishop, Bill, 16
Black Americans
  absence of, in suburbs, 159–60
  in Cleveland, 145
  decrease in mobility of, 232
  economic mobility of, in post-Civil
    War South, 166
  enslavement of, 50, 51, 160–63
  in Flint, 156–58, 159–60, 170,
    172–74, 176, 178, 184–87, 193,
    195
  geographic mobility and, 21, 57,
    165n21
  "land contracts" and, 185–86
  restrictive covenants and, 21, 185,
    187–88, 189, 284n187
  twentieth century migrations of,
    145, 158, 159, 167, 168, 170,
    184–85
  in Union Army, 163
  urban renewal and, 195
  voting by free, in Ohio, 57
  in World War I, 167
  zoning ordinances and, 109–10, 175
  See also race/racism
Blackburn, George E., 168
Black Codes, 163–65
Bokovoy, Phil, 111
Boston, 68, 69
The Boston Globe, 81
Brady, Maureen, 102–3
Brandeis, Louis, 152
Bressler, Bendyt and family, 253–55, 256
Britain, 39, 63
Brooklyn, New York, 93–94
Brown, Jerry, 216–17, 287n216
Brown, Rodney, 200–201
Bryce, James, 77–78
Buchanan v. Warley (1917), 192
building codes
  clarity of, 246–48
  consistency in application of, 245–46

lack of enforcement of, 176
management of growth by, 12
to restrict immigrants, 107, 128–29
Burns, Anthony, 162
businesses started (1985-2014), 13–14
Byrnes, James, 204

C

California
  building ordinance for tenements,
    104
  Commission of Immigration and
    Housing, 101, 108
  discovery of gold and settlement of,
    88–90
  environmentally unsustainable
    development in, 213, 215,
    287n215
  as in "era of limits," 216–17
  exclusion of indigent migrants,
    203–4
  homeless in, 219
  housing building boom, 213
  immigrants as percent of population
    (1920), 101
  Nader's Raiders report on, 213, 214,
    216, 287n214
  poverty concentrated by zoning
    ordinances, 214
  property tax cap, 221
  racism and zoning in, 87–88, 90–92,
    91, 93
  SB 9 and single-family zoning, 110,
    275n110
  scarcity of housing in, 219
  suggestions to lower population
    growth, 215–16
  Tenement Housing Act (1909), 108
  twentieth century migration to,
    212–13
  See also specific cities
California Environmental Quality Act
  (CEQA), 111–12, 216, 217–18,
  287n216
Cambridge, Massachusetts, 3, 4, 5–6,
  237–38
Caplan, Marvin, 21
Carson, Rachel, 210, 211–12, 286n210
Chamberlain, Nathan Henry, 243

Charleston, South Carolina, 234–35
Cheney, Charles H.
  appearance of, 105
  basic facts about, 101–2, 120, 139,
    214
  on Charleston's historic
    preservation zoning ordinance,
    235
  on reason for zoning, 137–38
  on regulations to extend restrictive
    covenants, 103
  single-family zoning and, 104–5,
    106–8
Chetty, Raj, 199
Chevalier, Michel, 7, 60
Child, Lydia Maria, 74
Chinese Exclusion Act (1882), 90
Chinese immigrants, 88, 89–95, 91,
  96–97, 100, 109–10, 188–89
Choy, Sam, 189
Christopher, David, 146, 147, 279n146
church membership, 14, 15
Cincinnati, 69
cities, 209, 233–35
  See also specific cities
Cleveland (city), 145
Cleveland, Grover, 117
Cohen, Daniel Aldana, 242
co-housing, 245
Colburn, Gregg, 244
Committee to Save the West Village,
  31–32, 35–36
communities
  ability of, to challenge decisions of
    government, 220, 288n220
  associations as providing instant, 79
  choice of, and American character,
    7, 9, 78
  common-law traditions for well-
    regulated, 92–93
  as corporate bodies, 40, 56
  exclusion of indigent individuals by,
    54, 55, 56, 203
  FHA and, 184
  growth as natural process of, 242,
    243
  homogenization of sedentary, 17
  local sovereignty's effects on, 36–37
  as members-only clubs, 54–55

communities (*cont'd*):
  mistaken attempt to impose order and rationality on, 242
  occupancy standards/conservation agreements, 238–39
  personal agency and choosing, 19
  preferences of Americans, 18
  public commenters at hearings, 222–23
  role of voluntary, in democracy, 82
  self-governing, selecting residents in colonial Massachusetts, 46–47
  urban renewal and, 32, 33
  zoning ordinances and ability of, to meet emergent needs, 243
  See also neighborhoods
commuting, 4, 35
conservation agreements, 238–39
Cornish, Frank, 104
corporate communities, 40, 56
Corrigan v. Buckley (1926), 192
"cultural pluralism," 82
Cunningham, Ann Pamela, 234
Curtice, Harlow, 172

D
The Daily Missoulian, 207
Daily Republican, 72
Dasmann, Raymond, 215, 287n215
Davis, Kingsley, 215
Davis, Thomas Aspinwall, 284n187
The Death and Life of Great American Cities (Jacobs), 29, 32, 210, 211, 286n210
Dedham, Massachusetts, 44–46
democracy
  geographic mobility as guarantor of, 9
  Jacobs's definition of, 32, 33
  loss of faith in, 219
  role of voluntary communities in, 82
  See also government
Democratic Party, areas of concentration of, 16
Demsas, Jerusalem, 221
The Destruction of California (Dasmann), 215
Dexter, Franklin G., 188
Dillingham Commission, 124–25, 131–32

discrimination. *See* race/racism
"disease of growth," 31
districting. *See* zoning ordinances
Doherty, Joseph, 5
Dort, J. Dallas, 175
Dotson, J. D., 168, 169–73, 197, 281n172
Dotson, Kennard, 168
Douglas, William O., 204
Droste, Lori, 110
Duncan, Fred, 202, 203

E
Earth Day, 216
economic mobility
  of Black Americans in post-Civil War South, 166
  decrease in, 14
  economic improvement of those not migrating, 63
  FHA and, 181, 182
  pre-Civil War, 162–63
  as result of geographic mobility, 9–10, 11, 43, 58–60, 75–76, 206, 230, 231–32, 245, 288n230, 289n231
  twentieth century migration of southerners and, 167
Edwards, Fred, 202, 240
election of 2016, 14–16
employment
  in auto industry, 171–72
  Black Codes in post-Civil War South, 164
  decrease in changing places of, 14
  discrimination against Jews, 133
  earnings decrease (1970-2000), 14
  of Jews in sweatshops, 24, 114, 120–22
  preferences of Americans, 18
England, 39, 63
entrepreneurship, 11, 14
environment
  Carson, 210, 211–12, 286n210
  CEQA, 111–12, 216, 217–18, 287n216
  Earth Day, 216
  effect of building on, 111–12
  government and pesticide use, 211

review process for new development
and, 216, 217–18
as tool to prevent change in
neighborhoods, 216–18
as tool to stop migrants, 216
Epictetus, 42
ethnicity, as mode of association,
82–83, 256
Euclid, Ohio, 145–54
Euclid v. Ambler (1926), 149–54
Europe
ghettos as form of zoning exclusion
of Jews, 138
impermeable barriers to new
residents, 84, 273n84
local sovereignty in communities
in, 37
Evans, W. A., 138
Everett, Edward, 64
"expressive function" of law, 191
EYA, 226, 240, 241

F
Fair Housing Act (1968), 194
fair housing laws, 193–94
Federal Housing Administration
(FHA), 180–82, 183, 184, 192, 208
Fellmeth, Robert, 212, 213, 214, 216,
219
Feminine Mystique (Friedan), 210
Ferrall, Simon Ansley, 61
Fire Next Time (Baldwin), 210
Flint (city)
Black Americans in, 156–58,
159–60, 170, 172–74, 176, 178,
184–87, 193, 195
condition of housing in, 197–98, 198
Genesee County Land Bank, 158–59
GM and, 158, 175
population loss, 200
suburbs of, 183–84, 195–97
zoning ordinances in, 174–77, 186
Flint, Anthony, 286n210
Ford, George B., 123, 139
Fourteenth Amendment, 94, 96, 150,
192, 202
franchise, 55–56, 57, 268n56
Franklin, John Hope, 162
fraternal orders, 79

Freund, Ernst, 153
Friedan, Betty, 210
frontier, 64–66, 67, 71
Fugitive Slave Act (1850), 162

G
Gandolfo, Alex, 188, 189
Gannett, Henry, 66
Ganong, Peter, 228
Geary, Blanche, 74
Genesee County Land Bank, 158
gentrification, 33
geographic mobility
absorption of immigrants, 81–83
age and, 11–12
agency and, 19, 242
association membership and, 80–81
Black workers in post-Civil War
South, 164
court decisions upholding right of,
203–4
decline in, 11, 12, 15, 228
as defining feature of American
character, 7–8, 60–62, 65, 71,
204–5
economic mobility as result of,
9–10, 11, 43, 58–60, 75–76, 206,
230, 231–32, 245, 288n230,
289n231
end of, as permanent, 252
as engine of American prosperity, 11
FHA and, 181
as flip side of exclusivity in colonial
Massachusetts, 46–47, 48–49
gap between races and, 232–33
as guarantor of democracy, 9
hereditary aristocracy and, 84
heydays of, 7, 11, 57
historic preservation and, 236
individualism and, 39–42, 43, 77
integration of American regional
cultures, 81
local sovereignty and, 31, 36–37
in Massachusetts (1880-1890), 68, 69
of middle class after Revolutionary
War, 62
Moving Day, 7, 71–75, 76–77,
271n73, 272n77
NIMBYism and, 22–23

geographic mobility (*cont'd*):
as philosophical right turned into national right, 42–43
pluralism and, 9, 10, 84
politics and, 16–18, 264n17
popular culture and, 205–6
pre-Civil War, 57, 162–63
as privilege of educated elite, 227, 231
Puritans and ideology of, 40–42
racism and, 84
rural to urban, 70–71
serial, 54, 69
since 1940, 205, 208, 286n208
slave system and, 161–62
social isolation and, 15
social mobility as result of, 9, 59–60
as threat to stability and public order, 33–34, 39
tolerance and, 242–43
in US compared to other developed countries, 231, 289n231
Veiller's reforms and, 134–35
of wealthy, 159
xenophobia and, 84
See also migrants/migration; restrictive covenants; zoning ordinances
George, Henry, 125–26
Gerholz, Robert, 186–87
GI Bill, 185, 186
GM and Flint, Michigan, 158, 175
government
bureaucrats in agencies, 211–12
communities' ability to challenge decisions of, 220, 288n220
complicit with big business, 213
environmental regulations and, 216, 217–18, 287n216
failure of, to defend public, 210
increase in powers of federal, after Civil War, 95–96
local, as basic building blocks of early U.S., 53
loss of faith in, 219
policies for mobility stasis, 252–53
Section 8 rentals, 249, 250
state-level control over use of land, 248

state-level limits on local zoning ordinances, 248
voters in local elections, 221–22
watch-dog groups and, 219–20
See also specific agencies; specific programs
Graber, Henry, 241
Grace, John Patrick, 234
Grand Blanc Township, Michigan, 196–97
Gray, M. Nolan, 241
Great Depression, 178–79
Great Migration of Puritans, 39–40, 41
Great Migrations of Black Americans, 145, 158, 159, 170, 184–85
Green, Sara, 224–25, 226, 227
Greenwich Village. *See* West Village
Greiss, Abe, 30–31
Grinnalds, Jefferson Cleveland, 139
Grotius, Hugo, 42

H

Halpert, Samuel, 24, 28
Harrington, Michael, 210
Hartman, Fridolin, 189
Hechler, Abe, 34
Hechler, Bertha, 25
Hechler, David, 34–35
Hechler, Louis, 25, 34
Hechler, Rudolph, 24–26, *25*
Hegemann, Werner, 120
Herscovici, Steven, 69
hierarchy/hierarchies
in colonial Massachusetts, 49
in colonial Virginia, 50, 51, 268n51
in England, 39
Highsmith, Andrew, 196
historic preservation
geographic mobility and desire for, 236
Greenwich Village, 29–31
growth of districts, 236
history of, 233–35
of neighborhoods, 224–25, 226, 234–35, 236–37
percent of lots in Washington, D.C. and Manhattan designated, 238
redevelopment plans and, 237–38
"History of Zoning" (Whitnall), 99

Holmes, George Kirby, 75–76
homecoming celebrations, 81
homelessness, 219, 244
home ownership
  associations and, 238–39
  disadvantages of, 143–44
  as economic asset, 209
  end of Moving Day and, 272n77
  FHA and, 182
  as hindering migration, 75
  increase in price of, 4, 36
  local elections and, 222
  percent of Americans (1950), 209
  public comments at community
    hearings, 222–23
  renting displaced by, 33
  segregation and value of, 195
  zoning ordinances and, 17, 21, 22
  See also single-family homes
Home Owners' Loan Corporation
  (HOLC), 179–80, 185
Homestead Act, 62
Hooker, Thomas, 41–42
Hoover, Herbert, 139–42, 144,
  278n139
housing
  access to schools and location of,
    233
  advocates of fair housing laws,
    193–94
  affluence of neighborhood and
    density of, 220, 221
  California building boom, 213
  California scarcity of, 219
  CEQA used to oppose construction
    of, 111–12, 217–18, 287n216
  as consumer item, 76
  crisis in Flint, 173–74, 175, 176–77
  experiments in affordable, 245
  GI Bill and, 185, 186
  governed by private, collective
    entity, 233
  government control over new,
    12–13
  homelessness as, problem, 219, 244
  importance of ability to choose
    where to live, 7
  increase in land use regulations and,
    228

  lack of adequate supply, 110
  migration and cost of, 198–99, 200,
    231
  mixed-income, 242
  mixed-use, 22–23
  need for multi-unit, 241–42
  New York City, shortage during
    World War I, 76–77
  post-World War II crisis, 185,
    186–87
  preferences of Americans, 18
  public, 182–83, 242, 249
  rehabilitation of derelict, 158
  Roosevelt's efforts to help, 178–84
  tenement-like conditions in single-
    family homes, 108
  tenements and slums associated
    with immigrants, 101
  transit service as alleviating,
    congestion in cities, 119, 121
  on western plains, 133
  zoning ordinances and cost of, 176,
    186, 228
  See also affordable housing crisis;
    apartment houses; home
    ownership; renters/renting;
    restrictive covenants; single-
    family homes; zoning ordinances
How the Other Half Lives (Riis), 131
Hubbard, Orville, 193
Hughes, Charles Evans, 117, 119
Husock, Howard, 286n210

I
immigrants/immigration
  building codes to restrict, 107,
    128–29
  California Commission of
    Immigration and Housing, 101
  California population of (1920), 101
  Chinese, 88, 89–95, 91, 96–97, 100,
    109–10, 188–89
  in Cleveland, 145
  economic advances made by sons of,
    compared to sons of native born,
    229–30
  1890 census map and, 65, 66,
    269nn65–66
  ethnic associations of, 82–83, 256

immigrants/immigration (*cont'd*):
geographic mobility and absorption of, 81–83
marital and family status of, 115
New York City population of (1910), 114
Porter's view of, 66
in post-Civil War South, 166
rate of return to native countries of, 115, 230, 276n115, 288n230
restrictionism movement and, 124–25
tenements and slums associated with, 101
in Union Army, 163
World War I and, 167
xenophobia as one defining American characteristic and, 83
zoning ordinances to restrict, 88, 107, 137, 138
See also Lower East Side
Immigration Restriction Act (1921), 125
improvement associations, 238–39
Indiana, land titles in, 58
individualism
associational life and, 78
geographic mobility and, 39–42, 43, 77
Industrial Revolution, in Britain compared to in U.S. (1850–1880), 63
innovation and geographic mobility, 11
In re Hange Kie, 97, 98
Italian immigrants, 66
Ives, Charles, 77

J
Jackson, Edmund, 55
Jackson, Robert, 204
Jacobs, Jane
on attempt to impose order and rationality on communities, 242
critique of urban planning by, 29, 211
democracy as defined by, 32, 33
importance of, 210, 211, 286n210
on increase in West Village house prices, 36
on influence of money in urban planning, 32
on landmark status, 30
mobility as threatening to stability and public order in neighborhoods, 33–34
stores in residential areas in cities and, 29
urban renewal and, 28, 29
West Village home of, 26–27, 27
Jacobs, Robert, 26, 31–32
Japan, 247–48
Jews
characteristics of Eastern European immigrant, 115–16
1890 census map and, 66, 67
employment discrimination and, 133
employment in sweatshops of, 24, 114, 120–22
ghettos as form of zoning, 138
"lodger evil" and, 130, 132–33
migration of, from Lower East Side, 131
restrictive covenants and, 21
Jones, Garland, 185–86
Jones, Robert, 15

K
Kallen, Horace, 82, 83
Kennedy, Albert, 5–6
Kentucky, 58
Khanenko-Friesen, Natalia, 83–84
Kie, Hang, 92, 95, 99, 100–101
Kildee, Dan, 158–59, 160
Knights of Pythias, 79, 80

L
labor
in colonial Massachusetts, 45
in colonial Virginia, 49–50
westward expansion and markets for, 63
See also employment
land
allocation rules under Northwest Ordinance, 53
availability of, and frontier as closed, 67, 270n67

California patterns of development of, 216, 287n216
government complicit with big business and, 213
headrights granted in colonial Virginia to, 50–51
housing and increase in regulation of use of, 228
labor and, in colonial Virginia, 49–50
legislation opening, for settlement, 62–63
as mark of success in colonial Virginia, 51–52, 268n51
need for open, 213–14
preserving, as means to stop development, 216
productivity as Puritan way of use of, 47–48
security of titles to, 58, 69
state-level control over use of, 248
tax on, proposed by George, 125–26
tenant farmers, 164–65, 169
use regulations in colonial Massachusetts, 48, 267n48
See also zoning ordinances
"land contracts," 185–86
landmark status
meaning of, 29–30
See also historic preservation
Landsmanschaften, 81
Lansing, Bert, 117
Lasker, Bruno, 137, 240
Lawrence, Amos A., 162, 187–88, 284n187
Lewis, John L., 172
Lewis, Nelson, 120
Lincoln, Abraham and family, 58–59, 78
The Link, 207
local control/sovereignty and geographic mobility, 31, 36–37
Long Beach Press, 212
Los Angeles, 97–98, 220
Lower East Side
American phobic fear of, 116–17
conditions in (early twentieth century), 113–15
infant mortality in, 132

migration of Jews from, 131
See also tenements
Lowrey, Annie, 111, 251

M

Marks, Marcus M., 123
Masons, 79
Massachusetts (colony)
company behind, 49
establishment of new towns in, 45
exclusivity as flip side of mobility in, 46–47, 48–49
government usurpation of royal prerogatives, 46
hierarchies in, 49
labor markets in, 45
land use regulations in, 48, 267n48
royal charter, 46
self-governing communities in, 47
towns as seats of power in, 44–45
typical settlers, 49
"warning out" of possible public charges in, 44–45
zoning ordinances in, 47
Massachusetts (state), geographic mobility in (1880-1890), 68, 69
Massachusetts Body of Liberties (1641), 42, 43
McAneny, George, 122–23
McDermott, Scott, 40
McDuffie, Duncan, 103–4
melting pot metaphor, 82
meritocracy, American discontent with, 60
Metzenbaum, James, 147–48, 151
micro-apartments, 245
middle class, geographic mobility after Revolutionary War by, 62
migrants/migration
of Americans to poorer regions, 231
of Black Americans, 145, 158, 159, 167, 168, 170, 184–85
in Britain compared to in U.S. (1850–1880), 63
to California in twentieth century, 212–13
characteristics of, 170
in cities, 68, 270n68, 272n74
in Cleveland, 145

migrants/migration (*cont'd*):
  costs of, 229
  economic improvement of those not
    migrating and, 63
  environment as tool to stop, 216
  exclusion of indigent, 54, 55, 56, 203
  as fulfillment of Christian duty,
    40–42
  during Great Depression, 178
  as habit in American West, 61, 62
  home ownership as hindering, 75
  housing costs and, 198–99, 200
  Jews from Lower East Side, 131
  legal residency and acceptance by
    existing residents, 54–55
  as members of associations, 79,
    272n79
  in nineteenth century, 69–71,
    271n69, 272n74
  into Northwest Territory, 54–55
  pre-Civil War, 162–63
  prosperity and futures of children
    of, 10
  rate of (1966), 235
  search for greater opportunity by,
    10, 11
  segregation and, 159–60
  serial, 54, 69
  from tenements, 132
  as threat to public order, 33–34, 39
  in twentieth century, 167–68,
    271n69, 272n74
  in U.S. compared to other developed
    countries currently, 231, 289n231
  of white southerners, 176–77
Miller v. Board of Public Works, 152–53
Mining Act, 62
Minneapolis, 105
Mitchel, John Purroy, 125, 126
mixed-use housing and zoning
  ordinances, 22–23
"mob," derivation of term, 39
mobility crisis, affordable housing
  crisis as really, 6–7, 242
Mobility Revolution, 52
Modesto, California, 87–88, 90–92, *91*,
  93, *95*, *97*, *99*, *100*, 100–101
Modesto Bee, 90, 91
Mortimer, George T., 135–36

Moses, Robert, 32
Mount Vernon Ladies' Association, 234
Moving Day, 7, 71–75, 76–77, 271n73,
  272n77
Mullen, Lincoln, 78
multifamily dwellings. *See* apartment
  houses
Mumford, Lewis, 31, 266n31
Murray, Henry Anthony, 61

N
NAACP, 192, 240
Nader, Ralph, 216
  Raiders report on California, 213,
    214, 216, 287n214
  Unsafe at Any Speed, 210, 211, 212,
    286n210
Napa, California, 96, 97
National Historic Preservation Act
  (1966), 236
National Housing Association, 128
nativism, 83, 84, 124–25
  See also immigrants/immigration
"neighborhoodism," 31
neighborhoods
  affluence of, and zoning ordinances,
    220, 221
  application of rules across all, in city,
    245–46
  blockbusting by realtors, 21, 165n21
  defining, 30
  efficacy of "expressive function" of
    law, 191
  environment as reason to prevent
    change, 216–18, 287n216
  FHA and mixed use, 181–82
  historic preservation of, 224–25,
    226, 234–35, 236–37
  HOLC redlined maps, 179–80, 185
  improvement associations, 238–39
  mobility as threat to stability and
    public order in, 33–34, 39
  urban renewal and Black-American,
    195
  See also communities
Neighbors Inc., 21, 22
Newburyport, Massachusetts, 68, 69,
  270n68
New Deal, 12–13, 178–84, 192, 208

Newsom, Gavin, 110
New York (state)
  Brooklyn, 93–94
  Commission on Building Districts
    and Restrictions, 123–24
New York City
  building ordinance for tenements,
    104
  Commission on the Height, Size and
    Arrangement of Buildings
    (Heights of Buildings
    Commission), 122–24, 135, 136
  Fifth Avenue, 120–23, 135, 138
  first- or second-generation
    immigrant population of, 114
  first zoning ordinance, 28
  land tax proposal, 125–26
  Lower East Side, 113–15, 116–17,
    131, 132
  Moving Day, 7, 71–75, 76–77,
    271n73
  percent of households renting
    (1890), 75
  percent of Manhattan lots receiving
    historic designation, 238
  population growth, 124
  West Village, 24–27, 25, 27, 29–31,
    33, 36
  World War I and housing in, 76–77
  Zoning Commission, 125–26
  zoning ordinance overhaul to limit
    housing units, 246–47
  zoning ordinances and existing
    buildings in Manhattan, 220
  zoning ordinances and population
    of Manhattan, 136
  See also West Village
The New Yorker, 36
Nichols, Bill, 101
NIMBYism, 22–23
Nixon, Richard, 216
Nolen, John, 173–75
Northwest Ordinance (1787), 53–55,
  58, 62
nuisance regulations, 188, 241

O
occupancy agreements, 238–39
occupational licensing, 12

Odd Fellows, 79
Ogden, William, 191
Ohio, 54–57, 69, 145–54, 268n56
Olmsted, Frederick Law, 162
Omaha, 272n74
Other America (Harrington), 210

P
Pacific Railroad Acts, 62
Pappas, Thomas N., 207
Parolek, Daniel, 241–42
participatory planning, 220, 221,
  222–23
Patterson, William B., 129
Paul, Mark, 242
Pease, Fred, 146–47, 279n146
Peck, John, 61
Phillips, Shane, 242
Pilgrims, 38–39
planter class
  cost of runaway slaves to, 162
  domination by, in colonial Virginia,
    50, 51, 268n51
  movement west of, 161
  in post-Civil War south, 164–65
pluralism and geographic mobility, 9,
  10, 84
police powers
  Black workers' mobility in post-Civil
    War South and, 164
  common law basis of, 92
  elasticity of, 105
  to enforce class distinctions, 153
  Euclid v. Ambler, 149–54
  exclusion of indigent migrants, 203
  Fifth Avenue raids, 121–22
  increase in powers of federal
    government and, 95–96
  uniform application of, 92–93
  zoning ordinances and exercise of,
    93, 95, 98, 120, 127
politics and geographic mobility,
  16–18, 264n17
Porter, Robert, 66
Port Huron Statement, 211
Portsmouth Daily Times, 55
Poverty and Progress (Thernstrom), 68
Price, L. V., 79
Price, Thelma, 156–57

productivity, of land, 47–48, 267n48
Progressive Era reformers, 127–32, 134, 240
public housing, 182–83, 242, 249
Public Religion Research Institute, 15
Puritans, 39–42, 47

Q

Quinn, McLean, 240–41

R

race/racism
  blockbusting by realtors and, 21, 165n21
  Charleston's historic preservation zoning ordinance, 235
  economic improvement and, 171, 177
  FHA and, 181, 182
  geographic mobility and, 84
  housing density and, 220
  maintenance of white supremacy in the South, 164–65
  mobility gap and, 232–33
  neighborhood improvement associations and, 238–39
  as one defining characteristic of U.S., 83
  in post-Civil War North, 165–66, 170–71
  redlining by HOLC maps, 179–80, 185
  renting and, 193
  restrictive covenants and, 102–3, 146–47, 185, 187–89, 284n187
  riots of 1919, 170
  zoning ordinances and, 21, 22, 87–88, 90–92, 91, 93, 95, 99, 101, 109–10, 137, 138, 149–54, 175
  zoning ordinances based on population, 191–92
Reagan, Ronald, 216
Reconstruction Amendments, 96
religion, 10, 78
"Removing Social Barriers by Zoning" (Cheney), 137–38
"rent burdened," 4
renters/renting
  advantages of, 144

displaced by homeowners, 33
effect of adding one market-rate unit on all rents, 250
FHA and, 182
increase in, 4
local elections and, 222
mobility of, 12
Moving Day, 7, 71–75, 76–77, 271n73, 272n77
national rent-control program, 208
percent of households (1890), 75
racism and, 193
Section 8, 249, 250
subsidized market-rate units, 242
zoning ordinances and, 17
See also apartment houses; tenements
restrictive covenants
  enforcing, 190–91
  GM housing in Flint, 175
  housing types and, 102–3, 104, 146–47
  limitations of, 103
  neighborhood improvement associations and, 238–39
  nuisance, 188
  origins of, 102
  racial/ethnic purposes of, 20–21, 146–47, 185, 187–89, 284n187
  separating single- and two-family homes from apartments or shops, 182
  Supreme Court decision on, 192–93, 238
Revolutionary War and westward expansion, 62
Riis, Jacob, 131
Rockefeller, John D., 145
Rollins, Frank, 81
Roosevelt, Franklin D., 178–84, 192
Roosevelt, Theodore, 82, 129
Rugg, Arthur, 117, 148

S

Sabin, Paul, 210, 286n210
salus populi, 92
San Francisco, 93, 94–95, 221
San Francisco Chronicle, 105
The Saturday Evening Post, 207

Sawyer, Lorenzo, 96–97
Schannon, Carolyn, 201
Schmidt, Benjamin, 269n65
Schuetz, Jenny, 242
Schweninger, Loren, 162
Second Great Migration, 184–85
segregation
    economic, 17, 21–22, 195, 209, 214,
        238–39, 249
    home values and, 195
    public housing, 249
    single-family homes zoning and, 17,
        22, 149–54
    slums and, 187
    spatial, and educational inequality,
        227, 231, 233
    in suburbs, 159–60
    zoning ordinances for class-based,
        137, 174–75, 238–39
    zoning ordinances for race-based,
        21, 22, 87–88, 90–92, 91, 93, 95,
        99, 101, 109–10, 137, 138, 149–54,
        175
    See also restrictive covenants
Shaker Heights, Ohio, 146–47
Shelley v. Kraemer (1948), 192–93, 238
Sheng, Sing and Grace, 194
Shepherd Park neighborhood
    (Washington, D.C.), 19–23
Shoag, Daniel, 228
Shoen, Leonard, 205
sic utere tuo, 92
Silent Spring (Carson), 210, 211,
    286n210
single-family homes
    advantages of, 143
    as American dream, 207
    apartment houses as "bane" of, 104
    disadvantages of, 143–44
    FHA financed, 183
    government loans to purchase, 208
    "land contracts" to finance, 185–86
    mortgages, 180–82, 185
    restrictive covenants for racial and
        ethnic purposes, 146–47
    restrictive covenants to separate,
        from apartments or shops, 182
    segregation and zoning for, 17, 22,
        149–54

shortage of, 208
subdivision of, into multiple units,
    108, 173
tiny houses, 245
virtues of, according to promoters
    of, 142–43
zoning and SB 9 in California, 110,
    275n10
zoning ordinances to protect, 17, 22,
    104–5, 106–8, 147–48, 149–54
slave system, 50, 51, 160–63
"snob zoning," 214
social housing, 242
socialism, 67
social isolation, 14, 15
social mobility
    decrease in, 14
    FHA and, 181
    identity as choice and, 10
    laws to prevent, in colonial
        Virginia, 50
    pre–Civil War, 162–63
    prevented by elite landholding
        families in colonial Virginia, 50,
        51, 268n51
    as result of geographic mobility, 9,
        59–60
    tenements as machine for, 134
South Carolina, 161
Spehar, Susan, 35, 36
Steward, 188–89
Stockton, California, 96–97
Students for a Democratic Society, 211
suburbs
    absence of Black Americans in,
        159–60
    commuting life of, 35
    development of, 196
    FHA and, 184
    of Flint, Michigan, 183–84, 195–97
    homeowners' association, 239
    middle-class flight to, 28
    in post–World War II popular
        culture, 206
    as white middle class enclaves, 207
    zoning ordinances in, 196–97
sumptuary laws, 50
Sutherland, George, 152, 153
Sutton, Willie, 230, 289n230

Swan, Herbert S., 123, 139
Sweeney, Margaret, 6
Sweeney, Thomas, 6

T

Takoma Metro Station (WMATA),
    224–26, 228, 238, 240, 241
Tenement House Act (1901), 128,
    130–31
tenements
    as agents of moral degradation, 114,
        129–30
    as agents of poverty and disease,
        128–29
    building codes for, 104, 107
    building of, with amenities, 133–34
    conditions in, 115, 131–32, 133
    fear of, and 1890 census, 66
    "lodger evil," 130, 132–33
    as machine for social mobility, 134
    migration from, 132
    phobic fear of, 116–17
    Progressive Era reformers and,
        127–32, 134
    reform laws and housing
        shortages, 76
    rents, 134–35
    residents in, 132
    restrictive covenants and, 103
    single-family homes as, 108
    updated, in Lower East Side, 254
    zoning ordinances to restrict
        immigrants and, 88, 107, 137,
        138
Thernstrom, Stephan, 67–68
Thomson, Mortimer, 72
three-decker buildings, 5
The Times-Democrat, 73
tobacco, 50
Tocqueville, Alexis de, 60, 77
Tokyo, 247–48
The Topeka Daily Capital, 72
towns/townships
    colonial Massachusetts, as self-
        governing communities selecting
        residents, 46–47
    establishment of new, in colonial
        Massachusetts, 45
    exclusion of indigent, 54, 55, 56

"warning out" of possible public
    charges in colonial Massachusetts,
    44–45
transit service and housing congestion
    in cities, 119, 121
Trillin, Calvin, 31, 35
Trollope, Frances, 271n73
Trowbridge, John Townsend, 163–64
Truly, Lawson, 168
Trump, Donald, 14–16
Turner, Frederick Jackson, 64–65, 66,
    67, 71, 265n65
two-earner households and geographic
    mobility, 12

U

United Auto Workers (UAW), 171–72,
    184
United States
    increase in inequality in areas of,
        232
    Industrial Revolution in
        (1850–1880), 63
    local governments as basic building
        blocks of early, 53
    migration in
        compared to Britain
            (1850–1880), 63
        compared to other developed
            countries currently, 231, 289n231
    population's identification by state
        not nation, 52
    See also American character
Unsafe at Any Speed (Nader), 210, 211,
    212, 286n210
"unslumming," 33
urban planning
    first comprehensive zoning
        ordinance and, 28
    goal of post–World War II, 27–28
    influence of money in, 32
    Jacobs' critique of, 29, 211
    proposal to replace zoning
        ordinances with comprehensive,
        241
    public participation in, 220, 221,
        222–23
    stores in residential areas and, 28–29
    See also zoning ordinances

urban renewal
    Black neighborhoods and, 195
    fight against, 32, 33
    Jacobs and, 28, 29

V
Veiller, Frank, 122
Veiller, Lawrence, 122, 127–31, 134–35, 142
Vennema, Carey, 32
Ventura, California, 188–89, *190*
Vermont, 81
Violette, Zachary, 135
Virginia (colony)
    company behind, 49
    domination by elite landholding
        families of, 50, 51, 268n51
    headrights to land granted in, 50–51
    land and labor in, 49–50
    land as mark of success in, 51–52
    as royal colony, 50
    typical settlers, 49
Virginia (state), 162–63
Vitoria, Francisco, 42
voting
    in corporate communities, 56
    by free Black Americans in Ohio, 57
    legal residence and, 55–56, 268n56

W
Wa-Chung Laundry, *100*
Wagner-Steagall Act (1937), 182–83
Warren, Earl, 204–5
Wartman, Charles J., 187
Washburn, Oliver Miles, 102
Washington, Booker T., 166
Washington, D.C.
    historic preservation in Cleveland
        Park neighborhood, 236–37
    percent of lots receiving historic
        designation in, 238
    Takoma Metro Station (WMATA),
        224–26, 228, 238, 240, 241
Washington, George, 49
Welcome Wagon, 206
Westenhaver, David, 150
West Village
    Greenwich Village landmark status
        and, 29–31

Hechlers in, 24–26, *25*
Jacobs move to, 26–27, *27*
loss of population, 33
as "zone of emergence," 26, 36
westward expansion
    1890 census map and, 65, 66,
        269nn65–66
    labor markets and, 63
    migration as habit and, 61, 62
    as one goal of independence from
        Britain, 62
    planter class and, 161
    Turner on frontier as closed, 64–65,
        265n65
White, Jessie, 6
Whitnall, G. Gordon, 99
Whitten, Robert H., 123, 139,
    149–50
Williams, Frank, 184–85
Wilson, Joseph, 20
Winkle, Kenneth, 55
Winthrop, John, 40–41, 42
Wo, Quong, 98, 99
Woolworth, Frank, 117
World War I
    Black Americans serving in, 167
    housing in New York City and,
        76–77
    immigration and, 167
Wright, Moe, 198–200

X
xenophobia, 83, 84, 124–25
    See also immigrants/immigration

Y
Yeats, Evan, 226
Yet, Fong, 189

Z
Zangwill, Israel, 82, 83
Zimmerman, Charles, 145–46, 147
"zones of emergence," 5–6, 26, 36
zoning ordinances
    affluence of neighborhood and, 220,
        221
    apartment houses and, 103
    basic principle of, 92
    Bassett's proposal, 126–27

zoning ordinances (*cont'd*):
civic amenities from developers and downzoning, 221
clarity of, 246–48
for class-based segregation, 137, 174–75, 238–39
communities' ability to meet emergent needs and, 243
as communities' attempts to impose order and rationality, 242
consistency in application of, 245–46
cost of housing and, 176, 186, 228
as cure for poverty, slums, and urban blight, 28
different classes or residential, 105
early, 28, 47, 87–88, 99
for economic segregation, 17, 21–22, 195, 209, 214, 238–39
exercise of police powers and, 93, 95, 98
for fire safety, 127–28
ghettos as form of, 138
inclusionary, 248–49
increase in value of existing buildings and, 136
management of growth by, 12
mixed-use housing and, 22–23
movement for adoption of national, 138–39
occupancy standards, 238–39
as population limiter, 109, 136, 246–47
poverty concentrated by, 214
Progressive Era reformers and class-based, 240
proliferation of designations and restrictions, 220–21
proposal to replace, with comprehensive planning and nuisance regulation, 241
protection of single-family homes by, 17, 22, 104–5, 106–8, 147–48, 149–54
for race-based segregation, 87–88, 90–92, 91, 93, 95, 99, 101, 109–10, 137, 138, 150–51, 175, 191–92
state-level limits on local, 248
in suburbs, 196–97
Supreme Court decisions on, 149–54, 192
use regulation by, 123–24
variances to, 242
See also historic preservation
Zwick, David R., 212

ABOUT THE AUTHOR

YONI APPELBAUM is a deputy executive editor at *The Atlantic*. He is a social and cultural historian of the United States. Before joining *The Atlantic,* he was a lecturer on history and literature at Harvard University. He previously taught at Babson College and at Brandeis University, where he received his PhD in American history.

ABOUT THE TYPE

This book was set in Albertina, a typeface created by Dutch calligrapher and designer Chris Brand (1921–98). Brand's original drawings, based on calligraphic principles, were modified considerably to conform to the technological limitations of typesetting in the early 1960s. The development of digital technology later allowed Frank E. Blokland (b. 1959) of the Dutch Type Library to restore the typeface to its creator's original intentions.